# The Mass Communicators

# THE
# MASS
# COMMUNICATORS

*Public Relations,*

*Public Opinion,*

*and Mass Media*

*by*

**Charles S. Steinberg, Ph.D.**

HARPER & BROTHERS
PUBLISHERS, NEW YORK

*To*

Hortense and Harriet

214480

THE MASS COMMUNICATORS: Public Relations, Public Opinion,
and Mass Media
*Copyright © 1958 by Charles S. Steinberg*
*Printed in the United States of America*

*Library of Congress catalog card number: 58–6139*

650
gte

# Contents

vii Preface

# Preface

This book is an attempt to define the relationship between public relations and public opinion as conveyed by the content of the mass media of communication. It also explores the semantic principles of communication and public relations content.

At the present time, colleges and universities throughout the country offer undergraduate and graduate study in public relations and the communication arts, in addition to adult education and professional school courses. While there are satisfactory individual studies available in the fields of public relations, publicity, public opinion, and propaganda, there does not appear to be any volume which relates the practice of public relations to the phenomenon of opinion formation by means of the mass media. In the experience of the author, public relations cannot be practiced in a vacuum; nor can it be reduced to publicity techniques. If public relations is to grow in stature as an ethical profession, its practitioners—as well as the press and the public —must invest it with professional recognition. This means that those who seek a genuine knowledge of the theory and practice of public relations will require an understanding of the principles of semantics, of the history and function of the mass media, and of the nature of public opinion, propaganda, and ethics.

The practice of public relations, involved as it is with public opinion and mass communication, is never free from criticism.

Healthy criticism is a constructive force. What is unfortunate, however, is the frequent tendency to view any attempt to inform and/or influence public opinion as a destructive force. The process of persuasion is not always negative or nefarious. Of course, public relations (like law, or medicine, or any other profession) can be destructive and even dangerous. On the other hand, public opinion formation which comes about through information and honest persuasion can make an affirmative contribution to democracy. In a democracy, there are multiple choices, many alternatives. In a free and competitive society public opinion, which always reacts to implicit controversy, is not shackled. The democratic way of life makes possible the art of persuasion from many quarters; and the fact that many interests practice the art of persuasion does, in a sense, serve the ends of democracy.

The author has attempted to describe public relations in terms of function; to explore public opinion research and each of the mass media as it relates to public relations; to indicate how public relations is practiced both in terms of policy and in terms of publicity, promotion, and advertising; and, finally, to explore the relationship between public relations and propaganda and to indicate at least some of the major ethical considerations inherent in the practice of public relations and the use of the mass media.

The author is Director of Press Information for CBS Radio and Lecturer in the Communication Arts at New York University. He was formerly Eastern Publicity Director for Warner Brothers Pictures, Inc. and Director of Education for the Book-of-the-Month Club. In addition to his years of teaching in communications and public relations, he is the author of several articles and a doctoral dissertation in the field.

*December, 1957* C. S. S.

## Acknowledgments

The author wishes to express his appreciation to the following for their invaluable critical comments and suggestions on the contents of this book: Professor Richard T. Baker, Graduate School of Journalism, Columbia University; Dr. Benjamin Fine, Education Editor of the New York *Times;* Louis Hausman, Vice-President, Advertising and Promotion, CBS Radio; George Horsley Smith, Professor of Psychology, Rutgers University; Leonard Spinrad, Publisher of *Day & Date Service* and the Spinrad Report; Professor Harvey Zorbaugh, Executive Officer, Communications Arts Group, New York University. The author wishes to express, in particular, his deep appreciation to Bess Sondel, Professorial Lecturer in Communication and Consultant in Communication to the Industrial Relations Center, the University of Chicago, for her suggestions relating to the material on semantics.

The coöperation of the following for the material on concepts and campaigns is gratefully acknowledged: E. Huber Ulrich, Vice-President and Director of Public Relations, The Curtis

Publishing Company; The New York Central Railroad Company; James M. Beall, Director, Public Information, American Gas Association; Dudley Martin, Director of Press Relations, Institute of Life Insurance; Roy K. Wilson, Director of the Division of Press and Radio Relations, National Education Association; James W. Armsey, Assistant to the President, The Ford Foundation; Miss Lillian Green, Supervisor of Publicity, Metropolitan Museum of Art; William A. Platt, Director of Public Information, Community Service Society of New York; Jacob Schwab, Publicity Director, The National Conference of Christians and Jews, Inc.; Miss Irene Clynes, Manager of Public Relations, National Better Business Bureau, Inc.

# Part I

# Mass Communication and Public Relations

*The twentieth century as an age of mass communication—Relationship between public relations and mass communication—Semantic principles which underlie public relations and communication content*

# CHAPTER 1

## *The Era of Mass Communication*

Historians appropriately have recorded the nineteenth century as the age of that remarkable political, economic, and social transformation known as the Industrial Revolution. Even more appropriately, the most significant development of the twentieth century—and the one likely to leave the most compelling impression on modern society—has been the trenchant growth of the mass media. The development of the communication arts and the consequent germination of public relations as a social technique have been unique phenomena of the present century. For this century has seen the perfecting of the art of mass communication, with a variety of intricate and highly refined media and techniques employed to convey information, entertainment, and education to a large, heterogeneous group known as the public.

In a sense, the era of mass communication is a result of the absorbing interest in social and technical proficiency that grew out of the industrial upheavals of the previous century. Such devices as the telephone and telegraph were early scientific instruments of direct communication that subsequently sparked the invention of the more indirect social agencies such as the press,

3

syndicate, radio, and television. But our concern here is not so much with the science of communication as with mass communications and public relations as an art and a burgeoning profession, with the development and use of the various mass media and their influence on public opinion formation in a democratic society.

It has become increasingly evident that the very values and judgments by which contemporary man lives are closely connected with, and influenced by, the communication media and opinion-influencing techniques. Mass media have become vital centers for the transmission of knowledge, the dissemination of facts, and the directing of various emotional appeals to influence public opinion. Television, as envisaged by many educators, has an unusual potential for the transmission of knowledge. The press and the radio news programs are virtually unlimited sources of information and facts. And the technique of propaganda frequently is employed to direct emotional appeals to the public in the hope of channeling opinion formation toward a preconceived end or in favor of a special interest.

It would have taken a personal harbinger, such as Paul Revere, years, if not a lifetime, to convey a message which can now reach about 170,000,000 persons in a matter of minutes. Mass media, such as the press syndicates, the radio, television, and motion pictures, have superseded the more direct person-to-person contact of the nineteenth century New England town meeting or the eighteenth century coffee house. These communication media are indirect, intricate, and involved in their function, and they are equally indirect in their impact on the individual and the group. Although certain of the media, such as television, give the illusion of one person speaking to another, the media *are* mass media because they operate as a transmission belt of one or more persons speaking to many.

## POTENTIAL AND LIMITATIONS OF MASS MEDIA

The perfection of communications and public relations techniques has, in a sense, greatly enlarged modern man's horizons by providing an infinite variety of constantly changing experiences. At their best, therefore, mass media have a tremendous potential for good. Television has been acclaimed by educators as the greatest educational tool since the invention of the printing press. The easy access to newspapers, books, and magazines provides the basic material for the increasing growth of literacy. Communications have become a significant aid in modern educational techniques and methods of learning.

Under restrictive forces, however, mass media may also have tremendous potential for evil. The press, radio, or television in the hands of a demagogue can distort reality in the interest of propagandizing a cause whose purposes are antisocial. There have been many instances of divisive propaganda, directed at minority groups through the modus operandi of direct-mail letters or pamphlets. Restrictions placed on a free and responsible press can distort the news picture. The dual problems of censorship and monopoly in the American press are of increasing concern to students of the social sciences and, indeed, to all public-spirited citizens.

In addition, the communication media, because of the rapidity of their stimuli, are not cohesive. Despite the fact that they reach many groups simultaneously, their effect is frequently evanescent. The rapid succession of stimuli, for example, may not leave as much time for reflective thinking as does reading the book. At the same time, the growth of international communications appears to have made more of a positive contribution to psychological warfare and to the "cold war" than to the development of a peaceful world. Paradoxically, it appears that the development of more perfect instruments of international communication has rent asunder more alliances than it has welded together.

Mass media, therefore, are not without their restrictions and their limitations. Indeed, their very speed and relentless efficiency are implicitly self-limiting. The rapidity with which the news is gathered and disseminated gives rise to a succession of stimuli which are dispersed before their probable consequences can be appraised. Television, for example, is just about the most technically perfect of the mass communication devices, yet widespread criticism is leveled by educators and critics at the alleged inferior estate of a considerable amount of TV programming. The perfection of the mass media, it is argued, has not resulted in a richness and diversity but rather in a flat standardization of all experience for all individuals.

## PUBLIC RELATIONS AND MASS MEDIA

Many critics place the blame for such standardization on the so-called "hucksters" who ply the dual trades of advertising and publicity. But here again the criticism is relative to the end in view. At its best, public relations employs the media of communication in a constructive way, and its practice is a legitimate function of the free enterprise system in a democratic society. If it is true, for example, that public relations and advertising men work hard to sell washing machines and automobiles, it is also true that the average American enjoys more goods and has the highest standard of living of any individual in any country in the world. A good deal depends upon the training, judgment, and professional ethics of the public relations practitioners, the end in view, and the means taken to achieve that end. In this respect, public relations uses the instrument of mass communication in much the same manner as the lawyer and doctor employ the instruments of their respective professions. Necessarily, advertising agencies and the public relations counsel plan in terms of the thousands or the millions—the so-called captive audience—rather than in terms of individuals. But this is not so much an inherent flaw in advertising techniques as it is a natural outgrowth of the sheer proficiency of the electronic communication media. In a world which is growing ever more complex, the entrepreneur cannot conceivably reach the individual directly. The public relations man, therefore, serves as a useful middleman or catalyst between management and the public, interpreting each to the other. The mass media are the avenues of this intercommunication.

Does the widespread use of the mass media imply the restriction of free discussion? It is relatively easy, as the recent history of Russia and the Iron Curtain satellite countries has shown, either to employ or restrict the devices of communication to achieve control over the thoughts and actions of millions of people. Here, however, there is no public opinion at work, for there is no opportunity for the opinion-forming process to operate. Public relations techniques, which are implicitly competitive, would be useless.

On the other hand, democracy survives and grows through the dissemination of truth which, in terms of public relations and the communication arts, means scrupulous regard for fact and impartial coverage of the news. Mass media must not control public opinion but must be controlled by it so as to serve a socially useful end. This may be accomplished by keeping the media as fully competitive as possible and, when necessary, by a minimum of federal and state regulation in the public interest. In this way, the mass media become the servants, not the masters, of democracy.

## LANGUAGE AS COMMUNICATION

Although public relations and the communication media are phenomena of the twentieth century, their roots are to be found in the very origin of language itself. For man learned to communicate, in a literal sense, before he became civilized, and the art of communication, therefore, predates civilization. The two essential factors in the development of modern communication were the invention and use of the alphabet to construct verbal symbols and the subsequent invention of the printing press to convey symbols to the social group. It is a curious paradox that communication has run a full circle over the centuries. Its first uses were in terms of direct contact, when man communicated directly with man. The rise of the printing press and the development of the newspaper brought more indirect contact. And now the perfection of the electronic media of radio and TV has given the illusion of direct contact again, of man speaking to man.

Since language, written or spoken, is the basic material which the communication media use, it follows that any attempt to understand the nature of mass media involves an understanding of the symbols they employ. A study of the *meaning* of these symbols is called semantics. The public relations man who deals with the writing and dissemination of top policy speeches or statements to the public would do well to understand the science of semantics in the communication process, for words loosely used can be open to many and varied interpretations—or misinterpretations. One has only to think of the comment of a very responsible public official about the habits of bird dogs and kennel dogs to realize the dynamite of language in the communication process. On the face of it, the statement is one of simple preference for the habits of the bird dog, who earns his supper by hunting, to those of the kennel dog, who, presumably, stays at home and earns nothing. But the implications, when exposed to the searchlight of the press and public opinion, were startling. Public relations representatives for both business and labor had a field day until the tempest subsided. Those who defended the statement did so stoutly, claiming that the meaning was simple and clear, with no malicious implications. Those who attacked it attempted to show that it implied a disregard and a contempt for a large segment of the public, namely the labor groups. Basically, the statement may have been innocuous, but by the time it reached the front pages it became magnified into a national scandal. Careful study of the semantic implications of the statement by a skilled public relations man might have avoided an altogether unpleasant situation.

The bird–kennel dog statement is a simple example of what happens in the process of communicating. Here, a statement was uttered verbally. This statement reached the receiving audience, or public, through the media of mass communication—press syndicates, radio, television, and newsreels. What happened from that point on could not have been accurately predicted, even with the help of the public opinion poll. A statement may be received with indifference or inertia and die ignominiously. It may interest segments of the public or those special interest groups most concerned with its meaning; or, it may have the shattering impact of an atomic bomb, galvanizing many groups to quick approval or disapproval. This much may be said: Almost all data that are disseminated to the public via media of communication will, to a greater or lesser degree, move the receiving audience to thought and action. If the data given out are for the purposes of influencing public opinion, the greater the resultant action, the more successful is the public relations involved. Almost never, however, is there complete inertia.

## THE MEDIA AND SOCIETY

Our chief concern is with the structure and function of the communication media, with their effect on the receiving audience or public, and with that particular technique of utilizing the various media known as public relations. The use of the media of communication is never a one-way street. Perhaps the viewer cannot reply immediately when he watches a televised political speech or a commercial. But he does reply by his reaction—either directly, through comment to the group, or indirectly, when he expresses his opinion in the voting booth or at the store counter. The American public has constructed for itself a system of value judgments, a series of criteria or ends which it looks upon as good or bad from the standpoint of the social group. The communications media, and the practice of public relations, operate within this framework by attempting to satisfy the public's concept of its economic, cultural, or social goals and needs. The process of communication, therefore, is more than a scientific phenomenon. It is both an art and a social technique. And public relations involves the skillful use of the art of communication in the interest of informing and influencing public opinion.

## IMPORTANT MILESTONES

Following is a brief chronology of significant dates in the history of the communication arts:

*1456:* Printing of the famous Gutenberg Bible; beginning of the rise of printing, including the Caxton and Aldus presses in England and Italy, respectively, in 1477 and 1490

*1640:* Printing of the first book in America, *The Bay Psalm Book*

*1665:* First English newspaper, the London *Gazette*

*1704:* First American newspaper, *The Boston News–Letter*

*1784:* First daily newspaper in America, the Pennsylvania *Packet and Daily Advertiser*

*1844:* First telegraph message by Morse

*1858:* Laying of the first transatlantic cable

*1867:* First typewriter

*1895:* First wireless transmission by Marconi

*1920:* First regular broadcasting, in Detroit and Pittsburgh

*1926:* Establishment of first book club

*1927:* Talking pictures a reality with the presentation of *The Jazz Singer*

*1941:* First commercial television

*1952:* FCC licenses "final TV table of assignments," for commercial and educational stations

*1953:* New developments in motion picture projection such as 3-D, Cinemascope, and Vistavision

*1956:* Experiments in closed circuit and educational TV

*1957:* FCC considers toll television; medical science uses TV in research

# CHAPTER 2

## Public Relations and Communication

A result of the rapid development of the communications media and the expanding economy of the twentieth century was the rise and acceptance of public relations as an established profession. The growth of public relations was not accidental. It was a logical and inevitable outcome of the complex society which resulted from the rise of technology. Its application and acceptance by industry also were the result and logical outgrowth of the growing power of public opinion, heightened by the fact that more people than ever before had access to speedy information through such agencies as the newspaper, the motion picture, the newsreel, and the broadcast media.

### NEED FOR PUBLIC RELATIONS

Both during and after World War II, in particular, public opinion made itself felt with an unprecedented vitality. Vast opinion-molding services, such as the Office of War Information, were set up. Social, economic, and political agencies manifested a sudden respect for public opinion. Techniques of surveying and influencing mass opinion multiplied. The private public relations counsel and the company publicity director became key factors in the determination of sound business policy. Both the little man and the big business interests became keenly aware of the power of public acceptance and interested in ways of achieving such acceptance. Today, practically every commercial, industrial, and educational agency has accepted the creed that the good will of the public is important for survival and growth. The media of communication are the basic fabric out of which public relations men devise their good will and informational campaigns. Literally, public relations could not function without the mass media, and it is doubtful how successfully the media would function without the coöperation of public relations and publicity practitioners.

Recognizing that employees, dealers, and customers are an important part of its public, business now seeks the advice of the public relations counsel on internal operating policies as well as on external publicity coverage to the so-called public at large. Religious institutions, civic clubs, and community organizations now have publicity or public relations directors. Public relations has become standard operating procedure in all forms of management activity. Even those who were once skeptical of public relations now employ it, because the fact is that any organization that has traffic with the public has public relations, whether it likes it or not.

Significantly, the most graphic illustration of the recent progress of public relations and communication is to be found in our institutions of higher education. Ten years ago, only a few colleges offered training in publicity. Today, more than one hundred institutions of higher learning teach communication techniques as well as the theory and practice of public opinion formation and public relations. Many more are setting up pro-

grams and centers of learning in the communication arts and
the mass media. Even the newspaper editor, hardened by years
of special pleading from the press agent, now respects the ethical public relations counsel and the able publicist as sources of
newsworthy facts and information. No social historian could
argue with the statement that mass communication and public
relations are two of the dominant social factors of the day. The
mass media have become vital centers for the transmission of
knowledge and for social, political, and economic action.

## DEVELOPMENT OF PUBLIC RELATIONS

But the contemporary emphasis on public relations is not
quite as new as it seems. Although it has been called the new-
est profession, public relations literally began when individuals
banded into groups to form a society or a community of interest.
It grew when groups began using communicative devices to
transmit data for the purpose of conveying information or of
influencing public opinion. The art of persuasion has under-
written every successive period of social and political history.
Leaders have either gained or held their authority by their per-
suasive influence or control over the people. Even absolute
military dictatorships have been conscious of the importance of
influencing (and controlling) opinion. The aspirations of Cae-
sar for control and survival, the politics of Machiavelli, and
the political philosophy of Plato are all examples of a "public
relations" attitude and an awareness of public opinion and its
potential power in action.

Certainly the struggles of the American colonists, inspired
by the manifestos of the founding fathers, rest squarely on a
case of aroused public opinion. The Declaration of Independence is one of the greatest public opinion documents of all
time, and its influence on the opinion-forming process has even

more vitality today than when it was first written. Truly, the Declaration molded a cohesive public opinion for democratic government in a free society.

But this historical background has the relationship to modern public relations that primitive healing has to modern medicine. Contemporary public relations is essentially a by-product of the growth of business and industry in the twentieth century and a direct result of the development of the mass media. The Industrial Revolution mounted toward a climax in the first quarter of this century, in the era which James Truslow Adams has called "the age of the dinosaurs." Modern public relations is the handmaiden of this widespread industrial growth.

The acceptance of public relations as a social technique came partly by choice, partly by necessity. The rise of industry in America, from the close of the Civil War to the turn of the century, was a magnificent free-for-all in which vast empires sprang up overnight. Eventually, however, the "public be damned" view of the "robber barons" collided head on with the muckraking activities of Lincoln Steffens, Ida Tarbell, and other social and political writers. A new awareness of the voice of the people developed. The flamboyant leaders of expanding business enterprises were constrained to regard public opinion as a force to be reckoned with, not ignored. And the stage was set for the emergence of the counsel on public relations. Commodore Vanderbilt's dictum "the public be damned" no longer was tenable. The creed became "the public be informed." The communication media became the signposts of a two-way street. They served to interpret public opinion to management and to convey the new creed of management to the public. One of the underlying reasons for the need for public relations was the pursuing of the philosophy of laissez faire to its inevitable conclusion. And laissez faire, pursued relentlessly, ended in an impasse; business became intolerant of the public and the public became suspicious of business. The American tycoon became a stereotype—calloused, inhuman, and indifferent to human relations. Thus was the stage set for public relations.

## THE FIRST PUBLICISTS

Public relations had its modern prophet in Ivy Lee, a newspaperman who went into the "publicity business." Lee has been called the father of modern public relations. For it was he who, in his pioneer work with Rockefeller and with the Pennsylvania Railroad, started the trend toward placing publicity techniques on a policy-making level. The attacks of Tarbell and the other social critics and reformers forced business to pay respectful attention to the power of public opinion. But it was Ivy Lee who showed the expanding industrialist the advantage to be gained by giving the public the facts. Now that industry had become a dominant force in American civilization, the public began to take a keen interest in the activities of industrial concerns and their leaders. Public opinion could no longer be ignored. Through the press and the other media of communication it became a force to be reckoned with. The management executive and the business tycoon became vulnerable individuals, not myths in a gilded mansion.

Ivy Lee convinced his early clients, among them the Pennsylvania Railroad, of the importance of making facts and information available to the press so that the press could make them available to the people. It was also the acumen of Lee which developed a constructive program to improve the relations of the Rockefeller interests with the public after Ida Tarbell had published her vitriolic critique of the Standard Oil Company. Rockefeller was hardly the most popular tycoon in America until Ivy Lee stressed the importance of public opinion and showed the way to reach it and influence it. Every available instrument of communication—press, newsreels, magazines—recounted the deeds of the fabulous old gentleman who gave shiny dimes to children, founded public philanthropies, played golf before the clicking of movie cameras, and appeared on the feature pages almost with clocklike regularity. Here, indeed, was a lesson in practical publicity—for the businessman as well as for the public! The humanization of an abstraction or stereotype was predicated on Lee's conviction, however, that a favorable public opinion was not something to be fabricated out of legerdemain and press agentry but out of an aura of good will, to be earned by such efforts in the public interest as the Rockefeller Foundation.

In every endeavor, there is usually one individual whose farseeing efforts mark a turning point. The advent of Lee marked the turning point where publicity for its own sake became an important, but subordinate, part of a broader concept which later practitioners were to term "public relations."

If Lee laid the groundwork, other practitioners followed brilliantly. George Creel inaugurated a monumental program of information and voluntary censorship in World War I. His work marked a new concept in government public relations and a new attitude toward the working press. By 1923, Edward L. Bernays had published his incisive book *Crystallizing Public Opinion*, and the new profession was called public relations. Today, public relations is a highly skilled and challenging art and profession, with a core of extremely able and ethical architects of policy and public opinion. Today, a democratic society is buttressed by the firm foundation of its basically free communication media. Undoubtedly the greatest impetus given to the development of public relations came from World War II, during which skilled students of public opinion used the communication media to weld opinion into an appreciation and support of a common goal. And, in the process of public opinion formation, there developed new techniques of public relations and a better understanding of how it operates to influence public opinion.

## WHY PUBLIC RELATIONS?

At least five major factors contributed to making public relations an important and specialized operation in our economic and social system. The first was the increasingly complex structure of industry and its growing remoteness from direct contact with the people. The second was the development of a vast and intricate network of mass communication media. The third was the rise of large business interests and the vitriolic criticisms of the muckrakers and reformers. The fourth was the rise of increasingly keen competition which forced a regard for public opinion and a need for public support. And the fifth, a result of the development of literacy and education, was the demand for more facts and more information on the part of the public.

Together, these factors combined to make mass communication and public relations an operating necessity for those agencies whose activities impinged on the public and depended upon the public for support. For, despite the growth of modern transportation and communication, the various business agencies that seek individual and group support are often removed from their constituents. There is a constant need for some means of interaction between the public and these agencies. The needs, objectives, and problems of industry and other agencies must be interpreted to the public; the opinion of the public is equally important to industry. Communication media serve the dual purposes of interpretation and information.

It was the development of trained public relations men and

the perfection of communication techniques which made such two-way interpretation possible. Every modern institution needs the understanding and support of the public. Public relations techniques, by helping to understand public opinion, help also to influence it. The public relations man is a specialist in the techniques of analyzing, interpreting, and influencing public opinion. He is, therefore, an important cog in the activities of business and industry, education, the arts, labor or any social, political, or economic agency that makes contact with the public. The large industrial institution and the small business both look upon public relations as an indispensable tool in creating and maintaining good will.

Why have public relations techniques become so important a function of modern business and industry? The answer is necessity. Industry, business, and labor realize that they cannot survive in a healthy state and meet their competitive problems without some means of achieving and maintaining the good will of the public. Public relations is essential for healthy management function, whether the management function be applied in business, education, science, art, or profession. It is no longer a tool of management. It is the very function of management itself. It is, implicitly, part of any and every policy decision arrived at and promulgated by management. For, whenever the businessman or professional man engages in any activity which impinges on the public and calls for its support, he is implicitly engaged in the public relations function.

Modern management seldom has direct contact with its public. There are few, if any, town meetings today at which the businessman can meet his public face to face. There is no community market place in which management conducts its affairs. Industry grows more remote from its various publics every day. Transportation facilities expand markets beyond comprehension.

Communication facilities allow far-flung enterprises to circle
the globe and still maintain teletype and telephone contact in a
matter of minutes. Management must not only understand public needs, aspirations, and attitudes, but it must also develop
successful techniques for informing and influencing them. And
in both of these spheres, the public relations man performs an
important management function.

Yet this background only partially explains the growth of
public relations. The key factor is the strength of public opinion
which is now more powerful than at any other time in American
history. Group opinions affect business, politics, the arts, religion, and education. The American public maintains a watchful
interest in business as part of its democratic rights and privi-
liges. And business, as well as government, now functions and
flourishes only with the consent of the governed (i.e., the
public). If industry did not accept this concept, there would
be no point in forming expensive trade associations "in the
public interest"; nor would many business agencies and some
of the labor unions develop programs "in the public service."
Enlightened business groups are partially responsible for constructive public relations. But an informed public opinion is
equally responsible. And mass media have helped to keep the
public informed.

Finally, there is competition. There is competition among
educational, cultural, political, and civic organizations. There is
competition among various special interest groups. In the international sphere, there is competition between the "haves" and
the "have nots," between the free world and the Iron Curtain.

Competition for what? Specifically, for the attention and the
active support of the public—or publics, for the public as we
shall see, is not one entity but many diverse social groups.

It is this healthy competition, more than any other single

factor, that forces a regard for public opinion. And once this concern for public opinion makes itself felt, the need for the development of ways and means of understanding and influencing opinion is inevitable. That is where public relations begins.

# CHAPTER 3

## The Act of Communication

Since both the technique of public relations and the act of communication are dynamic rather than static, they defy any hard and fast academic definition. Both are operational procedures best described by what they do rather than what they are.

The act of communicating, in a public relations sense, involves the relaying or transmitting of a sign or symbol—verbal, written, or pictorial—from a specific source to a specific audience or receiver by means of any one, or all, of several media that act as channels for the transmission of the symbols—newspapers, magazines, books, radio, television, motion pictures, or direct speech—for the express purpose of influencing the opinion and actions of the receiving individual or group, i.e., the public.

Our concern, therefore, is not with the purely technical or scientific aspect of the mass media but rather with their functional or operational characteristics. From this point of view, the phenomenon of communicating via the mass media reveals certain salient facets for public relations. In a functional definition, we see that a symbol is written or spoken by some person, that it is transmitted by one or more channels, that it is directed toward influencing the behavior or habit patterns of one or more persons. Thus a relatively simple act has exceedingly complex implications. The act becomes significant from a public relations standpoint when it is pragmatically tested and justified in the arena of public opinion. The criterion is implicit in the result of the act. What happens to public opinion and behavior, if anything? Is an opinion formed? Is tangible action taken? Is the message lost in audience or public inertia?

## A PROCESS OF INTERACTION

The communication process, from a *functional* viewpoint, illustrates one aspect of the philosophy of pragmatism. An act of communication, generated for reasons of influencing public opinion, is successful if it accomplishes the original public relations objective of motivating public opinion to some overt act. Actually, no act of communication ever results in complete inertia. There exists a constant state of interaction between the organism and its environment. The societal area—the area in which public opinion is formed—is not inert matter. It is a dynamic, human area in which potential group energies are translated into kinetic energies by public relations techniques, influencing public opinion through media of communication. Stimuli and responses interact in this dynamic environment. There are those, for example, who draw upon the group as a source of information. This information, in the form of symbols of the communication act, is transmitted by the catalyst of a mass medium. It is revised, or reëvaluated, and used again by the respondent as a stimulus to other individuals and groups. And, in some instances, it is sufficiently significant to arrest the interest of the critic or the scholar, and it becomes part of the historical or cultural tradition of the group.

The concept of interaction between organism and environment has been demonstrated in the animal world by the biologist and the psychologist. It exists on the biological level in the world of humans also; and, in the act of communication, the human organism has the ability to transmit *verbal symbols,* or language, which are intended to convey meaning. These meanings, as we shall see, may be either cognitive, emotive, or directive in nature—they may deal with concepts, emotional reactions, or categorical imperatives or commands.

The central nervous system plays a key role in human communication; and in the act of communicating the cerebral cortex and the autonomic system will be involved. The cry "Watch out," shouted at a pedestrian in the path of a fast-moving car is purely directive and stimulates a predominantly automatic response. The query "What is your opinion of educational television?" calls primarily for a cognitive reaction involving the higher centers of the brain. The statement "He is a murderer" will elicit a basically emotional reaction. In planning or evaluating a public relations campaign, an opinion measurement may be taken so that the soundings will indicate which response a given campaign stimulus is likely to evoke. Recent studies in motivational research have contributed significantly to this area.

The brain and nervous system, which are, of course, an organic continuum, coördinate to produce an act of communication and to receive it. A stimulus may be directed to any of the senses, or it may originate in the cortex. By a series of nerve-end connections, or synapses, the stimulus is relayed to the cortex and other areas of the brain. By a series of intricate relays among the many millions of nerve cells, the stimulus elicits a response in terms of either a predominantly emotional or cognitive reaction. And the reaction is overtly manifested by the interaction which occurs through responsive signs or symbols, i.e., words, gestures, pictures. Where the stimulus is conceptual, the cortex dominates to transmit the cognitive ideas or meanings to the individuals involved in a given act of communication. The interaction continues when the recipient is exposed to the word or gesture and, in turn, responds to it or passes it on to another. The message may be altered, as the pattern of interaction continues, because of the orientation which the respective recipients bring to it.

## COMPLEMENTARY ASPECT OF MEDIA

In terms of the symbols employed, there is virtually no such phenomenon as speech alone or sound alone. The multiplicity of media and the welter of experiences created have done much to break down any isolationism in the communications world. Sound "images" are accompanied by pictorial images, expressed or implied. Verbal statements may include gestures. Television employs sight and sound. Pure sound on radio may, by emphasis on wording and inflection, conjure up images of concomitant gestures. The communication process, in an age of mass media, involves more than speech alone. In a TV talk by a political candidate, *what* is said, i.e., content, is not sufficient as an opinion-influencing device. The setting (blue shirt), the background (American flag), the emotional aura (playing of the national anthem) are all involved in an act of communication designed to influence opinion. What is said, plus the selection of the setting in which it is said, is the role which public relations plays in the communication process. Many people criticized a recent national convention, for example, for defects in staging which made for dullness of presentation. It was feared that this would cost important votes and, indeed, many claimed that only the personal popularity of the candidate overcame the stagnation of the "production."

## INFLUENCE OF VALUE JUDGMENTS ON OPINION

Communication content, in an age of publicity, public relations, and mass media, is the basic texture by which public opinion is influenced, consolidated, or modified—depending on the public relations objective. But adjunct to the content, or the *what* of communications, is the *how*. The content of a speech may be emotively heightened by proper environmental props. To say that these are contrived or staged artificialities may be sophisticated and logical and true, but the pragmatic effect on the public, or audience, indicates that these peripheral trimmings are of tremendous importance. In all public relations involving the opinion-forming process, indeed in any effort to communicate a message to the public, the function of the organism, its reaction patterns, and its goals or objectives are important. Most persons or groups, living in a social environment, draw upon and, at the same time, affect that environment to satisfy both physiological and psychological needs. And man lives to mold his environment for more than the readily apparent goals. Man also sets up certain criteria which he considers "good." He sets up a system of *value judgments* which are important determinants in his daily existence and which are also significant to those who are engaged in influencing opinion. Knowing what these value judgments are is basic to public relations. Some of them are palpably evident.

*Money* as such and for what it will bring in goods, power, and prestige is a value. When the $64 question became the $64,000 question was the increase in audience due to the heightened intellectual content or to the impact of winning a huge sum of money?

*Prestige* within the group is a value. This is the reason for national advertising campaigns that feature "important people" doing something that the reader is urged to emulate.

*Tangible goods* or possessions are values. The home-of-your-own promotions, the advertisements for owning a "brand new" something or other are examples of the public regard for goods.

In the United States, the judgments of what is good or valuable for our psychological comfort and well-being are shaped by many agencies in the society—the home, the school, the church, the social or political club. They are also shaped by the mass media—press, radio, TV, motion pictures. The latter, for example, is a particularly powerful force in shaping and reflecting value judgments. Neither the media content nor the group judgments remain permanently stable. The values and goals exemplified in the Horatio Alger books have been replaced by other symbols of success, other goals and variations in content.

In any event, public relations activities, disseminated by mass media, both establish and perpetuate those symbols which represent *positive* values—beauty, love, pride, health, esteem, and others. They also, in certain circumstances and to attain certain campaign objectives, conjure up *negative* values—fear and anger. And this societal structure of values is the basis for a formidable part of our advertising, publicity, and promotional campaigns.

## FACTORS INTERFERING WITH COMMUNICATION

There are, however, a considerable number of reasons for the frequent unevenness and lack of effect of mass communication. Not all public relations techniques are successful, and the reason is not always lack of skill. The reason may be one of the considerable barriers which frustrate the attempt to accomplish effective communication. Language itself (and its limitations) is one barrier which must be reckoned with. Technical difficulties are another. The fact that many television channels reserved for educational institutions are in the ultra-high-frequency wave is a barrier because UHF stations cannot be tuned in on most of the current TV set models. And, of course, there are psychological, educational, and even public relations barriers. The censoring of a syndicated column in newspapers, a radio newscast, or a speech creates communication difficulties which are set up predominantly for public relations reasons.

Certain propaganda efforts interfere with communication, such as the deliberate effort to convey untruths or false symbols in an effort to preserve atavistic social institutions against the tide of necessary social progress. Indeed, the press itself is not free from culpability, although the public relations man is usually first to be scored for using the communication media to attain a predetermined end. Devices such as changes in emphasis in a news story, slanting of headlines, and position in the paper can all be employed to interfere with the act of communication.

One of the principle purposes of mass communication is to relay information to the public. But a public becomes a cohesive entity only when it ventures to express an opinion. And public opinion always forms around an idea which is implicitly, if not explicitly, controversial. Because of this phenomenon, it is possible to interfere with the integrity of the communication act. Certain barriers are already implicit in it.

Public opinion formation, in a democracy, is utterly dependent upon the issuing of facts and information. The success and depth with which these factual data are issued, in accordance with the ethics and values of a democratic society, depend upon the orientation and basic integrity of those who are responsible for the use of the mass media. In a democracy, the power of public opinion makes itself felt on the basis of available evidence. Free choice and the selection of alternatives must rely upon information which is channeled via the mass media. And therein lies the potential of public relations and mass communication for social evil or social good.

The basic objective of the mass media should be to transmit information and informed opinions to the public, freely and responsibly, for the purpose of encouraging the public to form free and responsible opinions in the interest of attaining true satisfaction of its needs and of maintaining a democratic and progressive society.

# CHAPTER 4

## *Semantics and Communication Content*

Many social scientists have termed this the age of the publicist, the public relations man, the communication expert. The circumstances have made this terminology quite accurate. There has never been a time in history when public opinion was as aware of the impact of publicity techniques and the content of mass media as it is today. Communication is at the heart of our contemporary social structure.

The science—and it is a social science and a growing one—of the meaning of communication content has been called semantics. It is concerned with the symbols used in the process of communicating, and it has, therefore, rather formidable significance for public relations. Practitioners of public relations may not *consciously* apply the academic principles of semantics in their daily work, but they are doing so nevertheless. Sociologists are concerned with the meaning of communication content because, among other reasons, they know that the application of semantics to the communication process can make the difference between a public opinion that is truly democratic and cohesive and opinion that acts as a dissident or even dangerous force. The problem, therefore, for students of public relations in its juxtaposition to the mass media is one of understanding, interpreting, and evaluating the symbols that comprise communication content. This is no easy achievement because of the nature of the organism itself. The semantics of mass communication cannot be studied in terms of scientific equations or mathematical integers. It concerns social phenomena that are mercurial, fortuitous, and frequently explosive. The content is as emotive in meaning as it is cognitive.

Semantics itself is the social science of communicating by means of symbols, either verbal or written. But the result of an act of communication is never entirely predictable. It may, under various circumstances, lead to action, inertia, or disunity. Obviously the optimum task for intelligent public relations is to apply communication content toward developing a rapport between the various groups that comprise a public, a society and, ultimately, a nation or a universe.

## MEANINGS IN COMMUNICATION CONTENT

Semanticists are able to distinguish at least three classes of meanings in communication content, all of which have profound significance for applied publicity and advertising. First, meanings may be *cognitive,* in that they may appeal to the realm of ideas, to "reason." They may suggest that the receiving audience "think about it and draw your own conclusions." Second, meanings may be *emotive* in that they may be based on evoking a feeling or visceral reaction, as a plea to drive safely because "the life you save may be your own." And third, meanings may be *directive* in that they may be expressed as a direct command, a shout or an order to "look out" or "go and buy a box at your grocer's tomorrow."

Frequently, these meanings intermingle in communication

content. An advertising message may combine two or all three categories. A television commercial may explain the need for every woman to be beautiful on both an emotional and cognitive basis and conclude by a direct request to buy a bar of beauty soap immediately at the nearest drug store.

## THE TOOL OF LANGUAGE

In each of these categories, and in all communication content, the basic tool is language. *All* of the content of public relations is made up of language, either written or spoken—publicity releases, direct-mail letters, advertisements, speeches, reports, newsletters, press conferences, and interviews. Indeed, the difficulty in studying public relations and communication content arises chiefly from the limitations of language itself. We do not have, even in theoretical semantics, a *truly* scientific language about language. But *all* communication takes place because of the miracle of the tool of language. The only difference between direct discourse and the press story is that the written presentation *represents* the verbal symbol by a more indirect route, but with virtually an identical purpose.

Even with our relatively limited knowledge of communication content and meaning, however, it is possible for public relations to use language and the mass media intelligently. In this way, certain areas of public relations can prove a constructive factor in developing forms of social rapport among social, economic, and political groups and among nations. The possibility of social rapport is at least implicit, and public relations can help instrumentally by its choice of symbols which are transmitted by the mass media. A faculty representative for a large university looked askance at the president of the institution when the latter stated publicly that he was opposed to a college of "creative arts and mass communication." The president had told him privately that he was *not* opposed to the college of communication but that he thought it ought not to include creative arts training. The college public relations director resolved the imminent crisis by pointing out that the two were not talking about the same thing. The president had not meant to say that he was opposed *both* to a college of creative arts and mass communication. He was opposed to linking creative arts training with training in communication. The president, in fact, *endorsed* a college of communication but thought that the creative arts such as painting and music ought to be taught in the liberal arts college, while courses in public relations, journalism, public opinion research, radio, television, and motion pictures ought to be included in a college of communication arts. The president, in a simple statement of rejection, had implied that he was opposed to a college of communication arts, which was not true. The difficulty arose from a confusion resulting, first, from the president's choice of words for his statement and, second, from a wrong inference by the recipient.

Those who deal professionally with communication content are under a very strong obligation and trust. For the achievements of man, as Alfred Korzybski has pointed out in his pioneer studies in semantics, are indebted largely to man's use of symbols. Words are symbols that stand for, or represent, things or ideas. They are the stuff out of which public relations and communication content is made. But words are *not* reality; they constitute an abstraction or representation of it. The term American flag, for example, is not the flag or object itself but a symbolic representation of the flag for the purposes of communicating about it. By common *agreement,* such terms as "flag" or "table" or "book" denote and connote objects that may be pointed out in the world of things. The sight of the flag, of course, implies further symbolic meanings, such as "democracy" or "freedom," that are not so easily pointed out in the world of things as is a table or a book.

## SYMBOLS: WORDS AND THINGS

Of fundamental importance in all communication content, and of particular importance to those who write "idea" or "think" pieces for purposes of public relations, is the fact that words stand for things. They are symbolic. Since much of our social environment is symbolic, it follows that, if communication content is to influence public opinion, those who devise it must know how to use symbolic language effectively. Human response to symbolism is warm and immediate. That is why publicity men devise special events, such as the awarding of citations or medals or awards. A motion picture star will acquiesce more readily to a personal appearance if the promise of some award is made. The award is a symbolic procedure that is acceptable by such media as the press for communication to the public. Mere attendance by the star is not as good a story, and certainly not as good a picture, for the press as the staging of an award procedure.

This phenomenon is common knowledge and common procedure in the field of public relations. For example, the multi-million-dollar sponsor of a coast-to-coast television program complained that the program was not receiving any unusual attention in the press. The public relations director for the broadcasting network was asked to look into the complaint and rectify it. He brought the sponsor an award and considerable publicity by arranging for one program to be devoted to a national cause that was held in great public esteem. As a *quid pro quo*, however, the national figures who headed the cause appeared on the show and gave the program an award for its "providing great entertainment for millions of Americans and its contribution to the furthering of a worthy cause." Advance stories announced the event, and subsequent pictures of the giving of the award were serviced to newspapers throughout the country. Because of the respect in which the cause was held and the prestige of the figures involved, the stories and pictures brought a huge scrapbook of clippings for the network to show to the mightily pleased sponsor.

This procedure might be called a contrivance, typical of public relations techniques. What should not be overlooked, however, is that the organization representing the worthy cause reported a substantial increase in interest and in tangible contributions as a result of the event.

The human predilection for dealing with and accepting symbolic phenomena is at the root of almost all public relations and of a considerable portion of what is called "institutional" advertising. Such phrases as "men of prestige" use such a product, "the right shirt for the right man," or "specializing in clothing for men on the way up" are common examples of prestige symbols. These copy lines are predicated on the conviction that people live in an environment where things stand for something of value or social importance. To be a man of distinction is to smoke a particular brand. To be "right" is to select a specific product. To be popular is to use a brand name accepted by the majority.

The *literal* meaning of this kind of communication content, which is used so widely in public relations techniques, is not very clear. We see a four-color photograph in a class magazine of a nattily dressed sportsman sailing on a beautiful yacht. The purpose of the photo, according to the copy attached, is to symbolize the fact that men of position, distinction, and quality —men who enjoy sailing on yachts—smoke and enjoy a particular cigarette. The relationship is logically meaningless, but it is emotionally or symbolically powerful.

Semantic analysis is important in studies of public relations and communication content primarily because it helps to discern the basic differential between the symbol and what it stands for, between the thing in itself and the verbal or pictorial symbolization of it, for they are not one and the same. An appreciation of this difference is as important to those who devise public relations concepts and put them into words as it is to those who analyze the content of releases, statements, and reports that are the result of public relations efforts. Those who apply public relations, publicity, advertising, and promotion techniques to mass media should be aware of the semantic implications and the significance of cognitive, emotive, and directive meanings. What, for example, does the phrase "miracle ingredient" mean in its literal application? And what does it *intend* to mean in its nonliteral acceptance by the recipient of the advertising message? Obviously, the two meanings are different. The use of the term "miracle" implies some sudden, amazing transformation. Literally and historically it has a linkage with medieval religious tradition and certainly has no relevance with modern science. Yet the copy writer employs the phrase "miracle ingredient" for its whole emotional meaning, although it might be more accurate to describe the ingredient as "efficient" or "lasting in effect."

## LANGUAGE IN PUBLIC RELATIONS

Public relations and publicity use language for a multiplicity of reasons and purposes—for information, as in stockholder reports, financial statements, schedules of coming events. While statements such as these, usually published as brochures, are presumably verifiable, their objective is really more than the providing of sheer information. Because they have emotive value as well, they are garnished in their presentation by attractive art, type, and format so as to indicate the prestige and solidity of the issuing organization. The closest approximation to sheer information, with *minimal* emotive or directive aspects, is the straight "spot news" publicity release, such as a statement of the opening date of a new motion picture or the issuing of a schedule of events from a radio or TV station. Even a release from a pharmaceutical company announcing a new biological has more than informational value, for the biological may hold great promise for the cure of some disease. It has, therefore, many meanings beyond the informational.

Behind most informational releases is more than the sheer presentation of facts. Almost all statements of fact say something, or allow the recipient to infer something, about the institution. That is why it has been stated so strongly that even the simplest publicity release has public relations and, therefore, public opinion implications. It may suggest inferential judgments about the company to be formed by the persons who read or hear it via the media of communication. And, while the statements may be verifiable, the inferences drawn from them are not so easily comprehended. A political statement such as "We shall not contribute to an arms race" may suggest many alternative inferences. In still another context, it "means" one thing for a newspaper to state that a senator voted "in favor of desegregation." It "means" another, in an emotional sense, to state that the senator "defied the Southern bloc."

Those who deal with words, in a public relations context, have opportunities to "load" meanings. Ostensibly factual statements may, when disseminated through mass media, have a far more emotive meaning than that which appears at first examination. In a labor-management dispute, a statement from management which says "We are not against the hard-working people of this community, we are against their labor leaders who are nothing but exploiters" is a reverse usage of the term "exploiter" which is conventionally applied to management and which, in any case, has emotionally explosive overtones. Similarly, a labor leader who states "We are not against business, we are against the selfish and monopolistic antiunion exploiters of labor who run this company" is again an apparent statement of fact which has emotional implications. Both statements have a residue of fact with a heavy overlay of opinion. Cognitive meanings are immersed with emotional ones. Both statements are normative or evaluative. They imply a judgment which the speaker hopes will elicit a like judgment in the area of public opinion. Both statements take unfair advantage of the tendency to stereotype or symbolize on the part of the public which has, a priori, formed a picture of what terms like "monopolistic element" or "exploiter" represent. The tendency to "load" words is illustrated by a political speaker who stated "I am sure my worthy opponent is politically clean, despite the fact that he is alleged to have attended a meeting of an organization whose membership included one or two shady characters on the roster!"

Of course, no public-relations-motivated statement is without bias. Publicity releases, speeches, press interviews, and reports are slanted or directed, consciously or otherwise, toward some public relations objective or goal. But there are safeguards. In a democratically governed society, the opposition has opportunity to reply. And beyond the power of rebuttal is the question implicit in all ethical public relations: What potential damage can an irresponsible statement cause? Another safety factor is the education and orientation of the public which is becoming increasingly informed about public relations and propaganda techniques. And there is, finally, the safety device of the press itself. Theoretically, the editor is bound only by the criterion of integrity. Practically, however, the press is implicitly biased in one direction or another by the limitation of its owners as human beings who function in a competitive society. The owners *must* favor one viewpoint over another, but within this frame of reference the press makes an effort to be equitable and impartial in its coverage of the news.

## STATEMENTS IN AND OUT OF CONTEXT

For the purpose of understanding how language may be applied in a public relations context, it is important to describe certain of the functions of language itself. In the last analysis, the grist of any public relations campaign is language—a speech, a press conference, a report, a release, a telephone conversation with an editor, and so forth. For example, publicity and advertising copy frequently states simply "Here are the facts," the implication being that the facts are true, final, and irrevocable. Actually, however, the connotative purpose of the language is not to achieve objective fact *as such* but to influence *opinion*. And opinions arise only when there is potential conflict, i.e., the possibility of alternatives or choices.

Statements have significance not in themselves, but in terms of the context in which they are used. Examine the following subject-verb combinations which are appraisive (opinion) statements:

I like . . .
I like Democrats. (matter of opinion)
I like you. (matter of fact)
I like the moon in June. (matter of rhetoric; poetry for music)

Even with an understanding of semantic principles, the language of public relations is far from infallible. What the public relations man *means* when he devises a statement may be a far cry from the meaning it will have when exposed to public opinion formation through mass media. The bird dog–kennel dog confusion is a recent classic example of a statement which had one meaning when uttered and another when interpreted by the receiving audience. Indeed, the media themselves, acting as transmission catalysts, can alter meaning in its journey from sender to receiver. It is *possible* for the press, for example, to change context to suit a point of view. A business executive may state, in the course of a press conference, "Anyone should be willing to admit that there are times when labor is a racket." The newspaper headline may be made to read "Jones Scores Labor as Racket." The impact of the statement on the opinion of the labor public is not hard to conjecture, although the statement is clearly used out of the context of its original meaning by the omission of the words "there are times."

On the other hand, publicity and promotion men can, and frequently do, alter the meaning of words used by the mass media. This is particularly true in endorsement advertising. The simplest example is the book reviewer or the play critic who writes "It falls far short of being a great work of art." Promotion writers, on occasion, have perverted this meaning to "A great work of art!"

Language as communication has meaning only within a given frame of reference or realm of discourse. The statement "She's a beauty" may refer to any of the following: (1) a dog, (2) a ship, (3) a car, (4) a woman. Similarly, the statement "What a statesman!" may be interpreted in two ways. It may mean "What a (great) statesman" or, conversely, "What a (bad) statesman." When uttered verbally, inflection may have much to do with the communication of meaning.

Written statements, however, are frequently not sufficient

to convey the full import of a public relations message. Nor are press conferences, speeches, or advertisements sufficient. In a recent political campaign, it was originally decided to restrict the candidate's campaign to the television medium. In time, however, the public relations experts determined that there must be some whistle stopping in the campaign. Why? The sound public relations explanation is the necessity for adding the important element of group cohesion that comes, fundamentally, from gregariousness, from bringing a social group together, with all of the attendant symbols—bands, pennants, crowds, campaign buttons, newsreel cameras, and so forth.

This kind of direct communication is a two-edged sword. It can be done to *avoid* exposing issues to public scrutiny and discussion by obscuring the issues in the trappings of a parade or a mass meeting. It is the reason why the national anthem is played and the flag set up at some rabble-rousing rallies which may be no more than demagoguery. In these instances, accepted symbols of faith and strength are used as means to ends which have neither moral justification nor basis in fact. These symbols, used for good or evil, are potent factors in binding a public together and in stressing the human herd instinct. They tend to set an atmosphere for the easier creation of group consent and group action. An innocuous example is the device of the cocktail party to introduce a new line of fashions or a new screen personality. The same amount of publicity *might* be achieved by pictures and publicity releases, but the device of the party and its attendant news value increases the possibility of press acceptance and, therefore, public impact.

## PUBLIC RELATIONS LANGUAGE

While these special events are important, the public relations practitioner cannot escape the need to use language as communication. The significant factor in public relations writing is to understand, insofar as understanding is possible, how the words in a release, a statement, a stockholders' report, a promotion mailing, or a speech might affect the recipient. Publicity writing seldom, if ever, uses words that repel or words that are morally objectionable—although there are public relations situations where the idea of "plain speaking" can be valuable in influencing public opinion, as in a cancer crusade or a message directed toward safer driving.

Frequently, individuals will use language without regard for its potential impact on public opinion. A management executive who was under severe criticism by an opposing group replied to this criticism without discussing the implications of the following statement with his public relations man: "I will have no truck with the liars and pigs who are out to ruin my reputation." This judgment may have been warranted, but its effect was to repel, instead of win, a favorable public opinion. Consider now the public relations man's suggestion for a more soberly worded statement: "I believe my record of honor and decency speaks for itself, and I will not dignify such unjustified and unverifiable accusations with a reply. Let my opponents do the mud-slinging. I can afford to rise above it."

Skillful wording of statements for dissemination through the mass media can load and distort meanings. For example: "I will not stoop to the despicable level of my opponent by resorting to name-calling. I will *not* say that he is an embezzler. But you, the public, can draw your own opinions and conclusions from the record." How easily an unwary public can be led to accept false conclusions, with no basis in fact, by the perversion of language!

Public relations, as a communication art, more frequently

uses language in a futuristic sense than in the present tense. It is concerned with the impact on public opinion, with arousing the public to dynamic acceptance of an individual, institution, product, or idea. In the arena of politics, public relations functions to predict the result of a future act: If so-and-so is elected, a rosy future will result for Everyman. In the area of fund raising, it functions to describe the social benefits from an act of contribution: What a beautiful asset a new community center will be to the town!

Indeed, virtually all of public relations is adumbrative in content and purpose. It implies a thrust toward future accomplishment. It functions to create a climate of opinion *as a result* of an announcement that points toward the future, although that future may be as close as the directive "Buy one tomorrow!" It is based on the conviction that most groups live for tomorrow's promise rather than for today's fact. Therefore, public relations meanings are directive as well as emotive because the purpose is not only to influence opinion and create consent but also to lead to some specific future action.

Just how the varying combinations of cognitive, emotive, directive meanings are interwoven depends upon the specific objectives of the public relations campaign—to create pity and fear in order to raise funds for an anticancer campaign, to create reverence and love in order to build a new religious edifice, to create envy out of the appeal to vanity in launching a new car model.

But, again, language has its limitations in the arena of public opinion formation. That is why the advertising and publicity message is accompanied frequently by graphic illustrations, such as pictures, cartoons, mats, and other pictorial materials. For a publicity release is not deemed sufficient to describe the glories of a new car. The story must be accompanied by pictures and captions. In the advertising, there are the inevitable graphic symbols to join the language symbols—the pretty model, the golf club or yacht club terrace in the background, the pedigreed dog. Public relations meanings can be quite complex in their apparent simplicity.

# CHAPTER 5

## *Public Relations and Communication Content*

Public relations involves applying the art of mass communication to influence public opinion so that some *positive action* is taken by the public involved. Beyond strategic planning of the public relations campaign, therefore, is the problem of *what* to communicate (the content of the message), *how* to communicate (by a publicity release, speech, press interview, or some other instrument), and *where* to communicate (by one or more of the media—press, radio, television, and others).

The communicative phase of public relations must rely upon the technical resources of the mass media. But the act of communicating and the *content*—or the *what*—of the communication act are not identical. A great deal of the publicity content which is communicated is utterly meaningless, in some cases by design, in others by failure to understand the meaning of the statement. Much publicity writing has been criticized because its content has no relationship to reality, either in terms of present or future events. One major company consistently releases an annual product announcement the content of which is: "Our plans for next year call for the most concentrated effort in our history, and we look forward confidently to the most prodigious effort we have ever undertaken." This statement has been used, with variations, year after year by the company management, despite the efforts of the public relations director to devise a more meaningful content.

## PUBLIC RELATIONS CONTENT

What is communicated, in much public relations content, is a series of emotionally or directively loaded words or phrases which have no relation to the world of events and things. They are words used in a vacuum. However, they do have emotive force with the receiving audience; hence, public relations writers frequently employ these vapid phrases for the express purpose of avoiding the facts. There are situations, of course, in which publicity techniques purposefully employ emotionally loaded words and phrases to elicit an audience response of fear, anger, sadness, elation, and other emotive reactions. Generally, such meaningless content is best avoided. The public relations director can achieve a more successful operation by basing his campaign on solid facts and achievements rather than on the vacuum of loaded content. This is not to imply that public relations techniques must be colorless. The public relations man who represents an institution with a record of solid achievement can feel free to utilize a variety of exploitation devices and can, on occasion, call upon the richness of choice and variety of words which the language affords. Even the baldest of facts or the most unromantic array of statistics can be enlivened by the ingenuity of the enterprising publicist. There are, for example, a number of ways in which the public relations message or content can be driven home effectively and its impact on public opinion formation enhanced. One way to increase content effectiveness is by repetition. The writer of speeches, in business, education, and politics, will recognize the effect on the audience of driving a point home by sheer verbal repetition, as in the following:

We cannot tolerate intolerance!
We cannot tolerate interference!
We cannot tolerate viciousness!
We cannot tolerate those who would destroy our basic institutions!

The logic basic to these repetitive declarations may never be specified, although the statements might be less rhetorical and more meaningful if they were documented by facts. Yet, "poetry" or rhetoric has its place in public relations content because the receiving audience has been conditioned to respond emotionally to repetitive phrasings. At some future time, public relations content may move audiences by a communication content which uses the language both with informative accuracy *and* emotional overtones, but for the present it must work within its limitations—and its possibilities. At any rate, the device of repetition is an accepted procedure for publicity and advertising techniques. In radio, in particular, the sales value of radio time purchases is based upon radio's ability to deliver repetitive impact and penetration with the listening audience.

Another way in which content can be driven home effectively is through the use of color words. Metaphorical and allegorical content frequently plays a major part in speech writing and in certain by-line feature stories. This content has, broadly, the same validity as it has in the novel, play, short story, or poem. It is used preponderantly in the world of the advertising agency, as in the following: "Don't be as big as a house! Try Dr. Jones' *new* one-a-day diet tablets."

The impact of public relations content can also be enhanced by the use of "exploitation" words or coined words. These are

employed particularly in the amusement and entertainment industries. Such words, which have no cognitive meaning, catch
the public fancy by sheer sound as well as by their suggestive
connotations. Descriptions of the "it" girl and the "oomph" girl
caught on and became household words in millions of homes.
The "sound" words, plus the lavish use of "cheese-cake" photographs popularized the phrases "it girl" and "oomph girl" by
identifying them with attractively seductive young women.

Again, the public relations message may benefit from literary
or biblical allusions. Here the content has audience receptivity,
even though the public may be ignorant of the source. The
statement "Come to Tahiti—tropical paradise" is understandable, although the reader may not know the literary origin and
meaning of "paradise" in Milton or in Dante. Similarly, "Don't
be a Simon Legree—treat your wife to dinner at Smith's" is
understood by the receiving audience, although its source in
*Uncle Tom's Cabin* may not be known to those who respond.

Finally, the effectiveness of the public relations message may
be increased by sheer statement of fact. This is, by far, the most
powerful aspect of public relations content. No fancy phrase,
for example, can describe a picture of an auto accident victim
better than the simple statement "He wasn't covered by accident
insurance!" This is far more intensive in its message because
the content needs no rhetorical furbelows.

## ABSTRACTING

In oral communication and, to a great extent, in written
statements emphasis or stress makes considerable difference in
the impact which content has on public opinion. The mean-
ingfulness of a statement varies with tonal emphasis and even
in terms of its sentence structure. To say "That is a man" is
a simple declarative statement, pointing out or denoting an

object—man. But to lay certain stress or emphasis as *"that* is a *man"* takes the expression out of the realm of the simple statement of fact and implies strongly that the man referred to is an *unusual* man.

The key term or root term is "man." And we know that it is possible to classify or group together the sum total of individuals with certain common attributes or characteristics and state that they are "man" or "woman." We can go one step further, in fact, and single out a particular individual as a member of the class:

| | |
|---|---|
| This is Joan. | This is John. |
| Joan is a woman. | John is a man. |

These sentences are specific in that they refer to a particular man and a particular woman. But we can go one step further from Joan and John as man and woman and say that they are both human beings, a less specific and more *abstract* category than man *or* woman, but one which embraces the attributes of both. And the farther we move from the specific to the abstract in our verbal classification, the farther we get from our immediate referents which were a particular man called John and a particular woman called Joan. We may, for example, accept a series of common attributes of Tom, Dick, and Harry and call them "men," but we must disregard some of their individual differences in order to do so. At the same time, however, we have discovered a convenient and shorthand method of understanding each other.

These are simple abstractions. But public relations very frequently becomes involved in terminology which has no basic referent in the real or observable world, which cannot ultimately be reduced to simple "fact." Take the following syllogism:

All capitalists are monopolistic and selfish.
Mr. A. is a capitalist.
Therefore, Mr. A. is monopolistic and selfish.

The danger inherent in this kind of communication is clear.
It suggests a very easy way for public opinion to come to wrong
conclusions about people and about many issues and problems
which have profound sociological significance. For example:

All labor leaders are venal.
All Englishmen are dull.
All Americans are rich.
All actors are immoral.
All stockbrokers are rich.
All professors are forgetful.

In such easy generalization lie a temptation and a challenge
for public relations writers. It has its advantages in that it feeds
upon the common tendency to accept easy stereotyping, but it
has its dangers as well. While it is a useful device in publicity
techniques, it is only useful to the extent that it does not foster
a public opinion formation which can lead to socially harmful
or destructive action on the part of the receiving audience.
Here, indeed, is an opportunity for those who employ communication media to correct many of these false premises and
conclusions by the kind of public relations which will show
that the basic premise behind such stereotyping is false and,
therefore, that the conclusions are equally false and potentially
harmful to the group.

Because many advertising and publicity statements are ambiguous in their meaning, it is often necessary to include pictorial illustration to clarify meanings. Take the phrase "a time
for leisure" which, viewed in isolation, is not clear as to
the time (day or night, summer or winter) or leisure (at the

beach, at a ski resort, in the mountains). Now, add to the statement the picture of a group of persons at a picnic with a popular beverage displayed most prominently, and the copy becomes clear. We know what particular meaning the writer meant to convey by the terms "time" and "leisure" and with what particular situation and beverage he sought to have the particular terms equated.

## FACT AND TRUTH

An inevitable device in public relations writing is the use of variations of the phrase "Let's look at the record." This is sometimes communicated as "Let's look at the facts." The "facts" relevant to the solution of the Middle East crisis were different to the respective countries involved. What would be the "facts" if, for example, two countries to an international dispute paid for respective advertisements in the same newspaper and, by chance, both parties stated, "Our aim is justice; the facts are plain for all to see." The term "justice" has unique meaning to each of the disputants in relation to a concrete situation as defined. The meaning of justice is different because the selection of facts in each case is different.

Nevertheless, such terminology has an important bearing on public opinion formation, although it may be logically without concrete meaning or foundation. The political public relations writer who states that a Democratic Secretary of State is a "great statesman" *because* he is a Democrat is issuing the same kind of nonsense as the Republican who states that a Republican Secretary of State is a "great statesman" *because* he is a Republican. Vantage points, points of reference, or points of view provide the key to determining the accuracy or spuriousness of abstract statements made on behalf of some public relations objective. An industrial organization may release a statement claiming it is engaged in a particular activity "to protect our employees from labor goons," while a union official may state that his local is acting "to protect our members against the selfish interests of the Company." To some, the Tidelands Oil controversy was a national disgrace; to others it was a constitutional guarantee of states' rights.

What, then, is the kernel of "truth" in the welter of publicity releases, promotional literature, and advertising? One step toward a discovery of the truth may be made by reducing the terms employed to their lowest common *specific* denominator. Opinions are not true or false. They are better or worse as evaluated by the supporting evidence. The kernel of truth is the facts that underlie opinions. To speak of "justice," for example, in terms of the desegregation problem is to speak *ultimately,* not of an abstract term, but of the concrete application of what we accept "justice" to mean to those who are accorded, or denied, certain specific rights and privileges. To debate the issue of desegregation on the basis of states' rights is meaningless, unless we agree by common consent on what is meant by states' rights and then apply this meaning to specific situations in specific states.

The writer of public relations material for the mass media can be aware of the fact that there is an interaction of meaning between the general and the specific. The generalized statement frequently is obscure or meaningless unless ultimately reducible to some particular. One of the most vivid public relations examples of the application of this principle is the approach of Ivy Lee to the problem of humanizing the popular abstraction of John D. Rockefeller as a wealthy monopolist. Lee "reduced" the abstraction or stereotype "Rockefeller" to the dimensions of a human being who fostered significant charitable and philanthropic projects and, in this way, achieved two important objectives. First, internally, he showed the client the need for constructive deeds in the public interest. Second, externally, he communicated these positive acts to the public through the media of communication.

In procedures of this kind, the best public relations men are not unlike the best fiction writers. They can portray a type or "genre" by reducing it to a common denominator of humanity. Furthermore, intelligent use of public relations analysis and techniques can cut away a great deal of the obscurantism that cloaks so many public statements. To say, derisively, "Oh, Senator X is a Republican" is to say a great deal but also to omit a great deal. What is omitted, however, is more vital and meaningful than what is included. Is Senator X, the Republican, white or colored, Christian or Jewish or Mohammedan, charitable or stingy? The blanket use of abstract terms and stereotypes is fraught with dangers, largely because it is perhaps too short-sighted a way of minimizing human effort. Stereotyped responses are not an adequate substitute for critical thinking. A gossip columnist, writing in the midst of a political campaign, may carry this item: "John Jones, candidate for State Senator, was seen dining out last night with glamorous movie queen Kay Gray." Now, the purpose of the dinner may have been merely to ask Miss Gray to sing a campaign song at a rally. But, in the hands of the opposition, the political propaganda possibilities are legion. Such inferences as these might be suggested: Mr. Jones is a married man. Mr. Jones is unfaithful. Mr. Jones is unfit for office. In a recent novel, the entire town forces a teacher to resign because of one act. The teacher did not attend a meeting sponsored by a local religious group. Gossip called her "atheist." Gossip finally resulted in the conclusion, "unfit to teach."

It is the obligation of public relations men (to the client as

well as to the public) to see that the client practices what the
publicity releases preach. How simple it is for a management
executive to say, piously, "I heartily approve of the right of
every employee to have the best working conditions possible."
But that pious utterance, publicly expressed, has no validity
if the executive who pronounced it issues a series of petty
restrictions for the employees who work in his plant. It is not
enough for the public relations man to render an *apologia pro
vita* management by explaining such paradoxes away. Public
opinion has an ineluctable and ultimate way of getting down
to particulars.

These differences in meaning between the abstract statement
and the concrete situation explain, in part, why international
misunderstandings exist despite the technical proficiency of the
media of communication. They exist because of the extreme
difficulty involved in communicating what we mean, because
we cannot point denotatively but must rely on the less precise
business of connotation. When two diplomats speak of the
"freedom of colonial peoples," each may be talking of "freedom" in so different a context that there is no basis even for
intercommunication, let alone understanding. Here, communication and public relations experts can be particularly helpful
in defining terms and delimiting areas of discourse. A Japanese
or a German treaty is a ghastly thing to people who simply
cannot abide Japs or Germans. All Japs and all Germans become omnibus objects of hate. There is no leeway for reorientation or reëducation. In international affairs, what is an "act of
aggression" by one state is an "act of defense" by another.
Only by common consent as to the meaning of "aggression"
and "defense" in terms of the concrete situation can there be
hope of resolution.

Public relations faces a particularly difficult problem in reaching certain areas of public opinion which have erected barriers through which communication content cannot penetrate. Paradoxically, however, these barriers often have been erected by public relations techniques. The message carried by communication media cannot budge the kind of thinking which views all persons, all problems, and all alternatives and values *only* in terms of black or white. There is no area for discussion, no room for change. The public relations or advertising agency that calls for an "ivy league type" to fill a position sets the phrase up, in and of itself, as the *only* mark of satisfaction, the *only* criterion for excellence in filling the job. But the phrase and the man who fills the job are not one and the same.

## THE OPINION AREA

Problems and alternatives which call for a formation and expression of public opinion are not black and white. They are not always as simple as an either/or choice. There is a vast gray area in which public opinion operates and in which choices are weighed before conclusions are reached. What is socially harmful about the black or white kind of thinking is that it obviates thinking altogether. It allows little or no room for the individual or the group to view a problem in terms of the Gestalt, or the whole experiential nexus. The public relations man, sometimes by accident and sometimes by design, falls into the easy habit of presenting his case in an either/or fashion. The choice, presumably, is made easy for the public by the subtle or blatant suggestion to follow the "either" or the "or." This is a prime purpose of propaganda when group opinion is directed toward a preconceived end. It is either the end suggested, or disaster.

In reality, however, public opinion does not coalesce arbitrarily around one polarity or the other. Public opinion, arrived at by a democratic process, is a series of gradations or discussions of issues, of analyses of data until a decision to act is reached. Social, economic, and political problems are not solved by a categorical "yes" or "no." They ply for a time in the uncertain sea of the "maybe" where there is opportunity to weigh possibilities before coming to conclusions. And even these conclusions are not irrevocable. Wrong diagnoses and decisions are not always irreversible in the democratic society. They can be ameliorated. Our values are pluralistic, not monistic. There are many choices.

There are times when the purpose of public relations is to offer alternatives of the either/or variety. But, public relations also has the opportunity to point out, by disseminating relevant information, the multiplicity of choices available and to let the facts speak for themselves. Public opinion, democratically arrived at, consists of discussion and analysis until some conclusion is reached. While public relations techniques tend to bias in favor of one particular choice, they also stimulate discussion of the various choices available.

The following two examples of advertising copy are simple illustrations of the technique which lays stress on choice:

> Compare all alternatives. Try *every* cigarette. Then *see* which is the smoothest. You're bound to choose _____.
> Do you want pleasure or irritation? Choose _____ and *enjoy* smoking!

## A CREED OF INTEGRITY

Obviously, the most forceful contribution which public relations can make toward clarifying the content of communication is to foster a respect for the facts; it can inspire and aid in an exchange of viewpoints until a clarification of issues results and a tenable conclusion is reached. In this way, the client and the public benefit alike. There are some editors, but fortunately not too many, who will assert categorically that "press agents are dishonest." Let the public relations man not begin a defense by a categorical denial that press agents are dishonest. Let him, rather, ask simply: "Can you prove, by sheer weight of evidence, that press agents are dishonest? If so, why are they dishonest? Are there *any* evidences of honesty among press agents? Have press agents *never* been of news service to your paper?"

Inevitably, the editor must find somewhere along the line of experience that he has met one or more honest press agents. And careful exploration will probably result in a conclusion that *some* public relations men or publicists or press agents are, indeed, dishonest—as are *some* doctors, lawyers, or businessmen. Careful examination may result in the conclusion that *most* press representatives are not only quite honest but often a considerable service to the harassed editors. The editor in question may ultimately reëxamine not only his conviction about press agents, but also the peculiar meaning which he applies to the terms "honest" or "dishonest." In public relations, as a technique which utilizes mass communication to influence public opinion, we must try, whenever and wherever possible, to relate the content of the media to specific referents or objects. This effort will not only help to clarify issues, but also to provide objective data around which, and from which, public opinion formation can take place.

# CHAPTER 6

## *Roadblocks to Opinion Formation*

In public relations writing that is disseminated through the mass media, it is frequently difficult to distinguish what is written *about* the fact from the fact itself. "My opposition is a goat," said the political aspirant to a group of reporters. Obviously, the statement is untrue literally. The candidate is palpably not a goat, and the statement is *not* the same as the thing spoken about. But "goat" in a public opinion context is a conveniently emotional term which calls forth an image designed to place the candidate in a socially and politically inferior light.

What the uncritical public—listener or reader—fails to note is that emotive statements made about a person, thing, or situation usually omit the point of reference phrase "to me" or "in my opinion." While our expressions take the form of written or verbal symbols, these are the end result of a visceral, muscular, or glandular syndrome. We "feel" anger in the presence of someone or upon hearing some statement. Our reaction is physiological, and the reaction is transmitted to our higher nervous centers and ultimately verbalized. Probably no verbal or written expression is totally cerebral, however. We react to something which has stimulated our sensorium but does not terminate in the senses; rather it terminates in the brain.

## THE NEED FOR ADEQUATE EXPRESSION

Public opinion becomes overtly evident when a stimulus-response pattern reaches the stage of verbalization, or symbolic expression, by means of language. Paradoxically, however, the more we know about the nature of language, the more complex a phenomenon it becomes. The case is similar with public opinion. Studies of public opinion clarify many things about it but also reveal areas of complexity. Neither language itself nor public opinion, which utilizes language to express a point of view, is static. Nor can one postulate hard and fast rules about either. What is expressed depends, in part, on the reservoir of words upon which the speaker or writer can draw; and this depends, in turn, upon educational processes and other orientative factors. The most effective communication, from a public relations objective, is that which is neither too simple nor too involved. Public relations, in both advertising and publicity, tries to find the elusive common denominator. In a constantly changing environment, however, and with our experiential world growing more and more complex, have we the words available in our reservoir to express adequately what we think and feel and what we would like to convey? One of the basic requirements of public relations techniques, as they apply to the influencing of public opinion, is a reservoir of adequate expressions.

One of the most difficult tasks for public relations, and for all of the mass media, is that of finding adequate words to express our thoughts and feelings about the stimuli which emanate from our environment. It is one thing to react emotionally. It is another to express a reaction in words. But assuming that our expression were adequate, have we any general yardstick to determine whether the receiving audience, or the public, is equipped to understand what we are trying to convey and to act upon it? The "bird dog–kennel dog" statement is a classic example of confusion in meaning as it passed from its source, through the media, to the public.

## MISUNDERSTANDING COMMUNICATION CONTENT

Public relations may be said to be effective when it influences the opinion of the public toward whom the message is directed and when, as a result of this influence, the public is moved to consent and to act. This successful outcome presupposes, however, that the recipient understands the content carried by the communication media. But such is not always the case. A statement, whether in the form of a press interview or a publicity release, does not always achieve the purpose of influencing opinion. Because communication lines frequently break down, the content may have an effect exactly opposite to that which was intended. The problem may be that the party of the second part simply does not understand the import of what the party of the first part wishes to convey; or, and equally dangerous, there is the possibility that the receiving audience will accept the message at its sheer face value, with no attempt either to understand or to evaluate.

Propaganda techniques play upon human failure to take individual differences into account, upon the tendency to "identify" a whole category in terms of one emotive particular. There is a not inconsiderable number who would not question such statements as *"All* business men are venal," *"All* Americans are rich," *"All* poets are geniuses." By blanketing *"all,"* the statement blankets every individual *"one."* By accepting uncritically the statement that *"All* Republicans are antilabor," one must logically accept the consequent statements that Mr. Jones, who is a registered Republican is, therefore, antilabor. Conceivably, however, Mr. Jones, Smith, or Blank may be both a Republican and decidedly prolabor.

This tendency to accept blanket statements uncritically as true of both groups and of the individuals who comprise them is important in attempts to manipulate public opinion. By selling a vague generalization to the group, the propagandist has seen to it that the individual does not stand by himself but is identified with the commonly accepted stereotype. It is important, therefore, that in communication content which is designed to influence public opinion along political or economic lines both the source and the receiving audience be aware not so much of what is included in the generalization as of what is omitted. The media themselves are frequently guilty of this confusion. A newspaper headline, an article, or an editorial may abstract superbly from a message or release, but it may also leave out a vital essential. Recently, a large segment of the press criticized a broadcasting station for censoring a commentator's talk which was critical of a government official. But the press itself applies censorship every day of the week when it selects the words for headlines or places emphasis on one particular aspect of a story.

Public opinion formation, based on data extracted from public relations and communication content, is a fallible phenomenon. When a public, i.e., a group of individuals interested in some common problem or objective, discusses an event or object, what actually is discussed or externalized is a combination of the event or object itself *and* the reaction of the group to it. Public relations and consequent public opinion formation are eminently successful when both the issuing agent and the receiving audience speak the same language, when both are in agreement with regard to the idea or thing under discussion. But public relations statements are frequently of the kind which do *not* call forth a prior agreement by both sender and receiver. "The farmer is in a real plight" is such a statement. The public relations writer would like to project the idea that the statement is objective fact and would, of course, like to see it proliferate among the group. Such opinions, without documentation or with false documentation, may be successful provided that they do not meet with resistance from the receiving audience.

Public relations techniques, however, frequently call for positive declarations. They do not hedge. Although public relations is most effective in the gray area in which opinions are malleable, the alternatives offered are positive black or positive white. Stereotyping and generalization are less arduous tasks than the application of judgment. A faculty member who protests against some decision of the administration need not be an agitator or a professional troublemaker. Unless the rest of the faculty recognizes this fact, however, the dissenting member may find himself in serious difficulty and may be branded for what he is not.

These so-called "roadblocks" to effective communication are not easily overcome, nor are they resolved by semantic detours. In the absence of a hard and fast rule or solution, however, there is always the possibility of a common agreement or understanding that roadblocks exist and that the line of communication is not always simple, clear, and direct but frequently rocky and indirect. The static which one hears over the airways is symbolic of the static that makes human communication and understanding an exceedingly difficult accomplishment.

## PUBLIC RELATIONS CONTRIBUTION TO EFFECTIVE COMMUNICATION

Effective and ethical public relations can go a long way toward setting up or breaking down roadblocks to intelligent public opinion formation. Ideally, what we strive for is some means of developing an intelligent, effective, and adequate communication link between one public and another. The difficulties that obstruct are not merely scientific or technical. The United States and the Iron Curtain countries can be united by wireless, cable and radiotelephone in a matter of minutes. The interferences are not technical, however, but moral, social, economic, and political. They are problems not of technique, but of content; not of electronics, but of social psychology. The limitation is the human equation. Man can construct the marvels of overseas communication, but he cannot eliminate the psychological interferences that clog the most effective relay system. The media make it possible for peoples to speak to peoples, but the psychological differences are still evident. In this area, perhaps public relations techniques can serve as an effective catalyst or bridge.

## LANGUAGE AND OPINION FORMATION

The instrument for transmitting content over the media that we have developed is language. All public relations and communication techniques must rely upon the efficacy of written or spoken symbols which are verbal in character. And, in communicating by means of the instrumentality of language, we are symbolizing or making the words we use represent, or stand for, reality. Since our public relations content, transmitted by means of mass media and referring to some idea, person, or thing is *not* the same as the idea, person, or thing itself, the task of communicating is, at best, not easy and may be either unrewarding or impossible. We can surmount some of the roadblocks to adequate communication by means of the use of symbols which represent or distill from reality, but our conquest is neither complete nor entirely accurate. For, reality cannot be adequately symbolized. It still remains to be proved that public relations and communication techniques can develop a science of language which will adequately describe the external referents. Until then, our task of reaching and influencing public opinion is subject to the vagaries, the inconsistencies, and the frustration of finding adequate linguistic symbols to cope with and represent the world of peoples, things, and even ideas.

Since language functions, among other things, to influence public opinion, an understanding of the function of language itself is of some importance in public relations techniques. Language is, basically, functional or operational. We use it to express a felt need which is either emotive or cognitive in origin. Language is, secondly, directive. It is employed to exercise some degree of control over the actions and needs of others in the group. Language is also sophistic. It can be employed not to objectify meanings, but to conceal, change, or obscure vital issues.

We have noted the use of "loaded" words and phrases. Since language is not reducible to mathematical equations, since we cannot ascribe meanings as we can arbitrarily add integers, language can be employed ambiguously to mean more than one thing to different persons in the receiving audience. One of the factors which allows propaganda to influence public opinion is inherent in our misuse of language; we do *not* use language with any specific effort toward coördinating it with the reality which it represents. The public does not think critically unless forced to do so by crisis or acute need. Only laziness or inertia allows us to accept such advertising phrases as "it's different" without inquiring "why" or "how." The individual is surrounded by so bewildering a welter of conflicting advertisements, ideologies, loyalties, promotional "gimmicks," and other devices that he has neither the time, the patience, nor the orientation to analyze these symbols in terms of their ultimate referents in objective reality. In this respect, the media are not invulnerable. The press and other media have given front page prominence to the statements and opinions of officials who, after a whirlwind air tour of our overseas army installations, offer generalizations which the public accepts as fact but which may, in reality, have no relevance to the actual or real situation.

Language, in addition to its intrinsic difficulties, has the problem of overcoming the roadblock of geographic and psychological differences between one public and another. Public relations techniques, however ethical and earnest in intent, cannot easily help solve the problem of desegregation. The divergent publics involved think and act from a nexus of experience involving differences in folkways, schooling, parental attitudes, economic interests, and political objectives. Part of the difficulty inheres in the nature of language itself. The *meanings* of verbal content are not the *same* meanings to the prosegregationist and the antisegregationist. In international affairs, "freedom" means two different things to a citizen of the United States and to a citizen of any of the Iron Curtain countries. To apply a popular expression, they don't speak the same language.

An awareness of the difficulties inherent in communicating is important to the practitioner of public relations. For one truly creative function of public relations is to construct a bridge of understanding between two mutually antagonistic elements by seeking out a common denominator which is comprehensible and acceptable to all concerned. This particular function of public relations is creative as well as educational and has genuine social significance. Public relations can resolve many issues by showing graphically how both disputants can share a real situation in a real and tangible world.

Language, in order to be effective communication, must be related to the recipient's realm of discourse. When this relationship is not present, the public draws uncritically upon experiences or stereotypes which are in the common tradition of the group. And these quick and easy short cuts can be extended to embrace situations which the public does not understand. It is easier to accept the familiar pattern than to challenge or analyze it. Thus, "All Americans are rich," "All Britons have no sense of humor," "All girls who use the new miracle perfume will marry millionaires."

The language of public relations is many faceted. It refers to persons, things, institutions, products, and ideas. But each category referred to does not exist in a vacuum. It has a real counterpart in the real world. But it is easy to confuse categories. For example, the Democratic or the Republican party becomes the object of public rejection, not certain of the individuals who comprise it. "Business" or "labor" is blamed in the press for a strike situation, whereas both "business" and "labor" are no more and no less than a group of specific people at loggerheads over a specific situation. Thus, the very limitations and ambiguities of the instrument of communication, language, make public relations both effective and self-limited in scope, entail both an opportunity and a challenge.

# Part II

## Public Opinion and Public Relations

*Why public opinion measurement is important in public relations techniques—What is public opinion?—How public opinion may be influenced by public relations techniques—Potential and limitations of opinion measurement.*

# CHAPTER 7

## One Public—Or Many?

In an institutional (or public relations) advertisement, the General Electric Company states simply:

Public Opinion—
Nothing is Stronger
. . . given the facts
Nothing is Wiser

A credo such as this is an undeniably firm foundation for all sound public relations. For public relations in a democracy is predicated upon a wholesome respect for the strength of public opinion. Its objective is to make the facts available because it has faith in the ultimate wisdom of public opinion to understand and evaluate facts in the light of democratic social action.

The raw material of all public relations activity is, therefore, public opinion. But whose opinions are *public* opinion? Is public opinion the consensus of one group or many groups, majority units or dissenting minorities? If we are to accept Dr. Samuel Johnson's characteristically dogmatic statement that "The majority of a society is a true definition of the public," then the sailing is deceptively easy. Public opinion becomes only the opinion of the majority. Therefore, in order to reach public opinion, the public relations counsel should present and restrict the facts to the majority only and win only their support; for public relations deals with the public, and the public is the majority.

But Dr. Johnson's concept of "public" is not that easily accepted. If it were, the practice of public relations and communications could be reduced to an absurdity. The delicate tipping of the public opinion scales, now toward the minority, again toward the majority, makes public relations and other informational services a socially important process. The public is neither exclusively the majority nor exclusively the minority, although common usage of the term "public" frequently applies it to one or the other or to both. What, then, is the public?

## THE PUBLIC (OR PUBLICS)

Webster's variety of definitions and multiplicity of uses of the term "public" indicate its popularity and its ambiguity in the American language. This deceptively simple concept pertains to "the people of a nation, state, or community—opposed to private." That which is "open to common use" or "open to all" is public. Again, public also means "open, notorious, common, social, national, exoteric, general, generally known." And still more specifically, the public is described both as "the general body" and as a specific "body of people under the direct influence of a particular individual—as, an author's public."

Public relations men use the phrase "the public" in a special professional sense which partakes of all of Webster's diverse definitions. The public may be one group, several groups, or all groups, depending upon the nature of the problem and the publics affected by it. This pluralistic concept defines still further the principle of psychological and geographic areas in working out a public relations problem. The term public, in a public relations sense, stands somewhere between the flamboyant "my public" concept of the actress, author, or politician and the whole, or general, population.

Obviously, public relations must be applied within a well-defined psychological and geographic area. The public cannot mean everybody, everywhere. It must mean some group or groups, somewhere. The press, for example, will print important national events uniformly. But individual newspapers will carry regional news not covered by other papers in other areas. Even stories which appear in all newspapers reveal important differences in location, captioning, and news emphasis. The nature of different publics and the character of public opinion in different geographic areas are responsible for these variations in emphasis. The opinions of a coal miners' union will be different from those of a group of bankers. There may be areas of agreement, but psychological, environmental, and geographic factors make the areas of disagreement far more striking.

## PUBLIC OPINION

There is a rather formidable group of social and political scientists who question whether there is a *specific* phenomenon such as public opinion, manifested either directly or indirectly. If, indeed, there be a public opinion, can it be verified experimentally?

Although public opinion as a social power phenomenon exists, its power must be inferred. It is difficult to demonstrate by any method available at the present time, for a valid scientific method of demonstration has yet to be found. The meaning of the respective verbal symbols "public" and "opinion," taken separately and together, poses manifold problems not only for the social scientist, but also for the public relations and communications expert; and the solution, if there is one, is of specific importance for the theory and practice of successful public relations.

The term "public" is ambiguous. There is no palpable entity in society called the public, but there appear to be specific or discrete *publics*. For public relations, there is the motion picture public, the golf public, the "white-collar" public, the professional public, the labor public, the management public. These publics do form opinions about social and political institutions, about individuals, about ideas. They are, therefore, implicitly amenable to techniques which will influence their opinions. But what is an opinion as expressed by a specific public? Is opinion merely a random expression, or is there a basis in fact underlying opinion formation and expression? Is *public* opinion a result of what people say or of what they do?

Each, of course, is valid and real. Sometimes what people say coincides with what they do, and sometimes it does not. The formidable problem for public relations practitioners and for students of public opinion is to find a way of relating what people say to what they do. For example, an expert in motivational research found that when shown several different types of opening on catsup bottles, housewives almost invariably said they *preferred* a wide top because "You can get a spoon in it." However, when these bottles were placed on grocery store shelves, housewives *did not* buy them but selected another bottle top altogether!

How valid, therefore, are devices which, on the basis of opinion measurement, indicate that people will vote a Democratic victory, only to find that these individuals vote Republican in the privacy of the polling booth—or vice versa? Further, can public opinion be expressed on any issue, or is it limited to certain problems only? And, finally, if, as we have indicated, there are many publics, but no clearly demarcated public, is it possible to merge the sum total of these discrete publics into a homogeneous entity called "public opinion"?

These problems, and the solution to them, if there is an ultimate solution, are fraught with possibility for the practitioner of public relations and, indeed, for all who use the media of communication for the purpose of influencing public opinion. If, for example, we conclude that what people *say* has no relevance whatever to what they *do,* our public relations effort will be directed toward influencing what people *do,* regardless of what they say. Or, we may conclude that what people say is of peripheral importance regardless of what they do because other individuals may respond to these verbalizations. Public relations practitioners do know that what people say is important even though these people may take no overt action. What they say conceivably may influence *others* to take overt action.

For the purpose of discussing the application and direction of public relations techniques to reach one or more publics by means of the mass media, public opinion must be viewed not as a static abstraction, but as a dynamic and constantly changing process. Public opinion, in formation and in action, involves the acceptance or the rejection on the part of a public of an individual, a product, an institution, or an idea. Public opinion is malleable and not invulnerable; it can be influenced by publicity and propaganda disseminated by means of any or all of the media of communication, or by direct verbal contact with the source or sources of influence. And public opinion may be promulgated by means of an overt activity directed toward the individual, institution, or idea involved in the focus of the communications act.

Now, in terms of a functional definition, we leave no doubt

of the potential for public relations techniques, applied by means of mass media, to operate within a given frame of reference. Publicity and promotion to the "public," suggesting or urging acceptance or rejection of a person, product, organization, or idea, is possible. To suggest any mode of action, however, implies a prior understanding by the public relations man of the status of public opinion. What, for example, is the tenor of opinion on the issue under consideration? How did it come to be what it is? What probability is there, on the basis of current evidence, that a public relations effort will succeed in changing or consolidating a prevailing opinion?

## TWO-DIRECTIONALITY OF PUBLIC OPINION

Public opinion, aroused, has the power to move mountains, but opinions which are solidly formed are not easy to change. The power of public opinion, in terms of its social efficacy, acts in two directions. First, the opinions of a group or public are formed and influenced to a large degree by those in authority who use their authority to maintain and solidify these opinions. The press and other mass media are voices of authority to which the publics pay heed. On the other hand, these so-called authorities are influenced in a democratic society by the power of public opinion. It is evident, therefore, that the utilization of mass media for the purpose of influencing public opinion is not unilateral but operates on a system of healthy checks and balances.

Public opinion is the collective expression of the opinions of many individuals bound into a group by common aims, aspirations, needs, and ideals. To determine the opinion of groups or publics, therefore, the measurement experts study a cross section of individual opinions. But this can be oversimplified. The opinions of individuals do not spring from a vacuum. They are, in turn, influenced by the total prevailing temper of group opinion. They are influenced, as members of the group, by psychological and geographic factors which affect our social institutions.

When the public relations counsel undertakes a campaign to influence "the public" to react favorably to the cause he represents, does he mean the entire population or a segment of it? Actually, his researches and activities are predicated on being able to elicit a favorable reaction from certain specific segments, or publics, of the entire population; although in a related sense the good opinion of the whole population may also be important. But he is primarily concerned with communicating with those publics directly affected by the problem and only secondly with the population at large. A public relations counsel for a political candidate will be interested directly in those who are eligible to vote for his client. He will be indirectly interested in other groups (such as students) who may not vote themselves but who may influence those who do vote.

## MANY PUBLICS FOR PUBLIC RELATIONS

The public is really many publics. In a total population of about 170,000,000 Americans, approximately 25 percent are children; about 40 percent fall into the 20–50 age group; about 5 percent are over 68 or 70. Numerous other classifications may be applied in addition to age groups. There are Catholics, Protestants, Jews, and other denominations in the religious "public." There are job groups and professional classifications, such as "white collar," "skilled labor," teachers, doctors, lawyers, ministers. There are political classifications, economic and income groupings, and a variety of special interest publics. A simple example of the last would be the golf players or the lovers of classical music. A more complex example would be the Veterans of Foreign Wars or the American Federation of Musicians.

Many public relations campaigns do attempt to reach the whole population, but the program in action is many faceted, not uniform. A public relations campaign designed to generate interest in textiles, nylons, motion pictures, or some other national consumer product would direct its emphasis differently among diverse publics such as:

1. *The school public:*  By distributing teaching aids, charts, brochures, scientific and educational materials on the nature of nylon, how it is fabricated, career opportunities, etc.
2. *The women's groups* (women's clubs and organizations):  By club discussion materials, speakers bureau representatives, fashion shows, special brochures, "platforms" (such as the discussion pamphlets distributed at one time by *Newsweek* magazine) and forums.
3. *The retail stores:*  By the promotion of nylon as fashionable and useful, dealer display materials, coöperative dealer advertising, and various merchandising devices.
4. *The press:*  By selecting the important facts and information about the product, developing newsworthy activities in the field, reporting new developments and processes, scientific devices, feature and picture stories, and special events.

Here are only four avenues of approach, each designed to accomplish the total objective of making the public nylon conscious. The basic public relations theme is to engender and perpetuate an interest in nylon products and a desire to use them. But the program in actual operation, by means of publicity and promotion techniques to different segments of the population, develops variations on the theme in its direction to diverse publics. To the school world nylon is given an educational emphasis. A teaching aid may describe the scientific process of manufacturing nylon. Similar variations are geared to other groups, each having a common purpose and leading toward a common end—the promotion of nylon.

There are two sides to the public opinion mirror. For the public relations man there is no single public; there are many publics. For the individual, however, there is frequently one and only one conviction or set of convictions. Public relations develops many avenues of approach. But each public approached has already developed its own convictions and opinions. An ardent labor leader cannot be sold on the policies of certain business enterprises, no matter how skillful the public relations. An official of the American Medical Association cannot easily be convinced of the "rightness" of the policies in a government health bill. A member of a prohibitionist society will not yield easily to the public relations techniques of the distillers industry.

Society is composed of numerous segments or publics, and the opinions of these groups are usually either of the pro or con variety. Public opinion is the articulate expression of the group. And group opinion is formed by the coalescence of the opinions of individuals who have sacrificed to a degree their own freedom to think for themselves. The individual's prerogatives become part of the group. The individual opinion becomes submerged in the group opinion.

In a stable society, group opinion is far more inert and stubborn than it is malleable. It will yield to change only after stiff resistance, particularly if the group is bound by a strong special interest. It is doubtful whether any degree of special pleading or skillful public relations will cause an ardent antivivisectionist to abandon his views and condone medical experiment on animals. And so it is with other groups. The desire of the group to stick by its opinions makes any new public relations problem a genuine challenge. The basic barrier is, as we shall see, lack of effective communication. But public opinion can change quickly under the impact of events and crisis; America moved quickly, for example, after Pearl Harbor. Public opinion changed overnight.

There is still, however, a vast middle area where opinions have not solidified, and this is the area that yields to cultivation and change by public relations techniques. A bill to make vivisection illegal would result in pretty much of a stalemate if only vivisectionists or antivivisectionists were involved. Both publics, therefore, will direct their public relations toward influencing the opinions of the middle area groups. An individual who falls into the "yes" or "no" group on prohibition may fall into a middle area on vivisection. His opinions on the subject are still flexible. The implication of change is present.

An important determining factor in public opinion change, therefore, is the nature of the issue involved. For public opinion is both constant and flexible, depending upon the nature of the problem and the nature of the publics involved. Public opinion does vary, because groups themselves are not constant. As one generation succeeds another, ideas and attitudes give way, too. Social institutions and folkways change, albeit slowly. The division of the population into many publics would result in stultifying inertia if some group change were not always implicit. It is this implicit sense of unity in diversity which makes it possible to influence public opinion by public relations techniques.

# CHAPTER 8

# *The Publics and Their Opinions*

One of the singularly potent facets of public opinion is that it is, in action, peculiarly democratic. Public opinion knows no fetters, and, while it can be influenced, it cannot be coerced permanently. That is why attempts to stifle public opinion are never certain of succeeding for any length of time. The "voice of the people" may be silenced temporarily by a totalitarian show of force, but even authoritarian regimes have discovered that the people are influenced less by military coercion than by the dissemination of political propaganda through the mass media. The control of these disseminating agencies, therefore, is a more powerful factor in the influencing of opinion than is force. And, in a democracy, these very agencies insure a healthy system of checks and balances, a two-way street between opinion formation and the media that influence it, with public relations techniques acting as a catalyst.

## MANY PUBLICS—MANY OPINIONS

In an age of mass communication where the media are all-pervading, the salient characteristic of a public is that it is not a homogeneous local group, such as existed prior to the advent of modern means of transportation and communication. The public is really a number of heterogeneous groups—or publics. And, for public relations purposes, each public can be sub-divided into various segments or groupings based upon age, sex, economic status, educational achievement, and other variables.

The very nature of the mass media, and of the social and economic environment in which public relations operates, makes direct contact with the public a remote possibility, if, indeed, it can be achieved at all. An eighteenth century town meeting could debate an issue by direct person-to-person communication; the present-day receiving audience, however, is so large and so diverse that *direct* debate on issues involving public opinion formation is precluded. Individuals in San Francisco may be exposed simultaneously to the same communication content as people in New York or in Chicago, but direct discussion is well-nigh impossible. The receiving audience for communication content is not only heterogeneous, but it has no true social organization or cohesion. While these geographically separated audience units can boast of common traditions and folkways, while they may belong to the same *public* (e.g., the Veterans of Foreign Wars), the possibility of direct communication for the purposes of discussing an issue is not immediately feasible. Telephones, telegrams, letters, and even conventions are not the same crucible for opinion formation as a New England town meeting. This situation is one of the basic reasons for plant-city operations and for the tendency to decentralize large industries. It is sound public relations.

Within the organizational framework, however, reciprocal interaction is possible; and partly through representatives of organized groups, public opinion formation is achieved. An issue confronting a national labor union or a national businessmen's organization does allow for resolution in terms of public opinion formation and expression. Local response may cohere into a national pattern; or the national pattern, which is set by the executive group, may be used as a guide for local chapters. An address by Walter Reuther, no matter where it is delivered, does allow for some degree of effective interaction to take place between the various component chapters of the United Automobile Workers and, therefore, between the general membership and the speaker.

When we speak of "the public" as making a decision on an issue, therefore, the implication frequently is that the decision was arrived at as the result of a collection of individuals engaged in individual cerebration at a given time and place. Actually, an expression of public opinion is the collective opinion of the group, plus any subsequent action which may be taken by the group on the issue at hand. When a group of persons express an opinion on an issue, that group may be termed a public. But the opinion expressed is rarely final or categorical. The issue itself which generated opinion formation is almost always implicitly controversial, and the opinion expressed is almost always amenable to modification. It is this characteristic of public opinion formation which makes it possible for public relations to influence opinion through the channels of communication.

## INFLUENCING PUBLIC OPINION

People are influenced by what they read, see, and hear through the mass media. They are influenced also by what they say to each other. Even in an age of unparalleled electronic wonders, world statesmen still find direct exchange of views, on a person-to-person basis, more satisfactory than indirect transmission. There is still an implicit awareness, on the part of the leaders, that the act of direct human communication, of peo-

ples speaking to peoples, has within its framework greater possibility of world understanding than the semantics of the diplomatic note or the indirect address via the mass media. The
creation of consent, in a given crisis, may be invoked by martial
law or by military action. But even here some degree of persuasion, or "public relations," is necessary, because force cannot
be applied indefinitely without regard for public opinion. If the
democracies did not believe that this were true, there would be
no point in setting up such agencies as the Office of War Information or the Voice of America or Radio Free Europe. The existence of such agencies not only symbolizes the voice of a free
people, but these agencies also emphasize the point that opinions
*can* be influenced and that public opinion in action is a cumulatively powerful force.

The purpose of public relations techniques, applied through
the mass media, is to influence public opinion. Persuasion and
the creation of consent rest, at least to some degree, on the base
of leadership. The leadership may be individual, it may be a
symbol, or it may be an abstract idea. Beyond any peripheral
considerations of the respective candidates and the political issues involved, for example, it is generally admitted that the
leadership base for the Republican victory in 1956 was the symbol "Ike." Certainly the concept of leader as a symbol of persuasion and consent applied also to Franklin D. Roosevelt and, to
a lesser extent, to the second term election of Harry S. Truman.

Symbols create consent and are powerful public relations
forces. Abstract symbols such as the Red Cross, the American
flag, and "The Star-Spangled Banner" help rally public opinion
around an idea, but they can be used both as a divisive *or* a cohesive force, e.g., a bond rally or a soapbox speech denouncing
the American system of government. Much depends upon who
is doing the public relations and for what purpose and, impor-

tantly, upon the integrity and awareness of those who administrate the media of mass communications.

How do the mass media create consent among the receiving publics? Chiefly by the process of interaction between the media and the publics involved, between the organism and the environment. Persuasion and consent are created not by the media's coursing through a one-way street, but by the media's interacting with an audience which is implicitly receptive. Public relations can utilize mass media to influence public opinion, because the particular public involved is receptive to, and potentially interested in, having its opinions influenced. At the same time, however, the omnipresence of the means and methods of persuasion has induced a guardedness on the part of the public which has not restricted public relations efforts but has stimulated the development of public relations as an art and science of opinion persuasion. The result has been the development of sampling techniques, pretesting and the eventual wrapping of publicity and promotion techniques in more elaborate packages.

Public opinion, as a two-way process, germinates and coheres into a pattern when there is some issue at stake which is implicitly controversial. That is why the methods of persuasion —public relations and propaganda—must, implicitly or explicitly, commend one course of action and condemn another. Both issues must be, of course, within the same frame of reference. For example, automobile advertising may commend one car as better and more economical to operate than its competitors; but the choice resides between two cars. The frame of reference within which public relations operates is the choice of cars.

The efficacy of public relations and mass communication, however, is not simply that they operate within a delimited group or public, as important as that may be. Successful public relations not only persuades a given group, but also supplies that group with the tools or ammunition to persuade other groups to climb on the bandwagon. Beyond its potential power to create chain persuasion from group to group, public relations can also bridge the chasm which exists between two conflicting publics such as management and labor. By interpreting the objectives of one to the other, effective and intelligent public relations can bring about a rapport or intercommunication by setting up objectives which create a favorable climate of opinion for both sides.

Those who deal with the mass media for the purposes of influencing public opinion have several avenues of possible approach to the public. Thus the public may be approached by:

1. Cognitive reasoning, i.e., an impressive display of "logic" designed to show that the suggested course of action is the most beneficial one.
2. Emotive reasoning, i.e., an explicit appeal to sentiment or emotion, such as couching a message in terms of the flag, love of parents, or some similar appeal.
3. Directive reasoning, i.e., the command or categorical imperative in which the message directs the receiver to "Do it now!"
4. Stimulating and suggesting an exchange of opinion between an organized public, which has been persuaded to the desired point of view, and unorganized, unpersuaded groups.
5. Suggesting and providing the means of rapport or compromise between two opposing factions to the mutual satisfaction of both.

One other modus operandi can be utilized, and that is the method of sheer, autocratic coercion. But public relations techniques are not amenable to this method because the action is based on the assumption that no persuasion is necessary. Force always obviates, at least temporarily, the need for public relations as well as for the use of mass media as channels of persuasion. In any social situation where force is not invoked, however, the very complexity of our society generates a need for public relations to be practiced as an art of applied persuasion. There are many masses or publics, each far removed from the other by the growing size and remoteness of large industries. There are striking differentials in age publics, ethnic groups, white-collar groups, professional publics, economic strata, and so on. The economic and political structure grows more complex, and social groups become less cohesive.

## PUBLIC RELATIONS AND MASS MEDIA AS CATALYSTS

Public relations, therefore, is an important catalyst. Practiced wisely, its techniques need not apply the mass media merely for the purpose of creating consent, but also for the dissemination of information. And the dissemination of information may lead (but not necessarily) to the reconciliation of conflicting interests. It can enable diverse groups to understand, adapt, and cohere their views with the views of other publics. Only by such intercommunication can the great issues in areas of social conflict evolve toward an intelligent, logical, and peaceful solution. And the instrumentalities through which this rapport between conflicting opinions can be effected are the media of mass communication. We must *assume* that information will create a common meeting ground if public relations and mass communication are to be successful.

Despite the fact that certain aspects of the mass media may appear to be monopolistic, they are also basically democratic, but not only because they are *mass* media. The communications media direct their content to the masses, but the direction is not unilateral. There is interaction between the public and the press, radio and television. The publics influence the media and are, in turn, influenced by them. It is true, however, that some of the media may be tempted rather too frequently to give the public what they *think* the public wants or ought to have. The concept that motion pictures *must* be geared to the so-called twelve-year-old mentality is, of course, a spurious one. The conviction that the public wants only "entertainment" and not "education" not only sets up an arbitrary dichotomy between education and entertainment, but also rests upon a premise which has not been proved valid.

The mass media are the keystone of our social structure. They have become indispensable ingredients in our way of life. An understanding of the way they operate is important, therefore, to those who are concerned with problems of group action and social control and persuasion. Potentially, the mass media have the unique ability to disseminate knowledge. The degree of success with which they achieve this end depends partly on how the media themselves are employed and partly on the efforts to increase public education in other areas, such as the school. Educational television programming, for example, may be so far out of line with the educational orientation and receptivity of the listener as to have no effect at all.

Although public relations is not an educational force in a literal or academic sense, and although it is obviously prejudiced in favor of a client or cause, it does have the potential power to inform the public and to create a climate of opinion based upon an intelligent presentation of facts. Given the facts, says the General Electric institutional advertisement, nothing is wiser than public opinion. This statement not only epitomizes the contemporary attitude of public relations men toward public opinion; it also implies that public relations functions to give the public the facts because the facts help to influence public opinion.

True, there are opinions about public relations which imply that it is a conspiracy to dupe the public and to keep the facts from it. But the facts about public relations are otherwise. One of the most significant facets of contemporary American society is the vitality and the articulateness of public opinion. There is a desire for an informed public opinion because the communication media, which are essential to public relations, have created this need. And conversely, it is significant that public relations techniques reach the public almost exclusively by means of these very media of communication. A free press and responsible public relations have both contributed toward making public opinion the most powerful force in our democratic society. Public opinion and the media of communication interact on one another.

Public opinion, which is the articulate and collective opinion of a number of individuals welded into a group, cannot, therefore, be static. Opinions do not emerge from a vacuum but from the interplay and interaction of individuals and groups. And the flexibility of public opinion, its diversity and its unity, makes the practice of public relations possible and generates opinion change.

There are some issues, such as prohibition or vivisection, on which the opinions of the group are patently of the "yes" or "no" variety. There are other even more fundamental folkways in which opinions are fixed—if these fixed ideas can be called opinions. The inclination of some individuals toward communism, the creed of nazism in the Germany of the 1930's, the fanaticism of certain racial or religious groups yield to opinion change only after stress or catastrophe, when they yield at all. But most issues are amenable to opinion formation and change as part of the democratic process. This has been particularly true since the end of World War II. Not only are norms and values more volatile, but opinion itself is more flexible than it has ever been since the beginning of the twentieth century. Individual and group opinions are sought on a complexity and variety of problems. The compelling factor of competition for public support results in a variety of advertising and publicity appeals for consumer dollars, and an equal variety of pressure group appeals for consumer approbation. There is confusion, but the safety valve of democratic action makes the confusion a healthy one. There are many public relations appeals on behalf of many social, economic, and political institutions. But the alternatives are available by means of an appraisal of the issues as they are disseminated through media of communication.

Public opinion, as distinguished from belief, is never absolute or categorical. If it were not a relative concept, public relations could not be practiced with any purposeful objective. Because public opinion is implicitly controversial, because it is a result of the interaction of ideas between individual and group, it yields to modification and change. Only in matters of absolute belief, or statements of mathematical certitude, is there no room for opinion expression and no possibiliy of opinion change. There is no public relations issue, for example, on the scientific hypotheses that lie behind the H-bomb. But there *is* a dynamic public relations problem in the controversial issues that generate public opinion about the scientific uses and effects of the bomb. Public opinion, therefore, always concerns some issue, problem, or idea. The issue is always implicitly controversial. There is a "yes" and a "no" side to it. Public relations seeks to influence opinion, either toward the negative or toward the positive side of the issue.

What influences public opinion? Every day of the week, through the media of press, radio, television, magazines, newsreels, and other more indirect channels, the public is given alternative choices between products, institutions, and ideas. Advertising, publicity, and promotional appeals, subtle and unsubtle, present the facts of the case for the approbation of specific publics. Most of these appeals have specific public relations objectives—to build or maintain good will, to generate confidence in the product, and to elevate prestige of the company. And all of the successful public relations appeals are based upon an understanding of the psychological factors which motivate human behavior. Public relations men, in other words, must know what will influence public opinion.

## DRAMATIC PRESENTATION OF FACTS

Since public opinion is the result of the interaction and solidification of a number of individual opinions, what influences the individual will, with certain modifications, also influence the group. A public is a group of people bound together by certain common aspirations and interests. Opinions are elicited from the group when some implicitly controversial issue arises. The purpose of public relations is to influence these opinions along positive and affirmative channels. In its public relations campaign against the government monopoly action, a store chain sought to win public support and affirmation first by offering evidence that the action was not based on the facts and secondly by stressing the public service and good will of the company.

Even in the best public relations campaign, however, the facts alone are often not enough. The facts must be presented with sufficient dramatic human interest appeal to call the attention of the public to them. The appeal itself must have enough emotional quality to move the public to action. A public which is neutral is not an affirmative public, unless neutrality is the goal of the public relations campaign. And in such a case, the achievement of neutrality itself would be considered successful public relations! Successful public relations, in the pragmatic or publicity stage, is the presentation of the facts of the case in terms of sufficient dramatic or emotional appeal to influence public opinion affirmatively. For the pattern of group behavior is not always rational. It is essentially emotional. The individual becomes part of the group because his aspirations and ideals seem to find best expression there. This is a significant aspect of public opinion expression, but it is even more important in public opinion formation. The judgments and opinions of most individuals are based upon a number of psychological factors— what they read in the press and other media, their learning habits at school, the environmental influence of the home, and other social and cultural influences. It is important for the public relations man to understand that these influences make for certain inevitable patterns of inertia and dogmatism in group behavior. Successful public relations frequently consists in reorienting or reëducating a group (or public) away from one set of convictions toward another pattern.

## STEREOTYPING

Walter Lippmann developed a classic public opinion concept when he termed these patterns "stereotypes." Sterotyping is constantly evident in individual and group behavior and is a powerful force in molding public opinion. In fact, popular opinions are frequently formed in the light of this common tendency to personalize abstract concepts or ideas. The playing of "The Star-Spangled Banner" at theatre performances during the war years; the hurling of epithets by politicians; the use of the symbol of the Red Cross; the uncritical use of such terms as "capitalist" or "liberal" are common, everyday examples of this short-circuit thinking. More typical of stereotyping, however, is the tendency to hold a rigid opinion about all members of a group. For example, "all New Englanders are stingy"; "all southerners are lazy"; "all doctors are mercenary."

The tendency toward stereotyping frequently involves a complete pattern of opinions and beliefs around which public opinion formation revolves. Stereotyping is the basis for popular group reaction to much of the widespread publicity which appears in the form of news or information in the daily press and other media. Certain concepts tend to become popular. Because everyone is reading a popular novel, everyone else in the group develops a determination to read it. Some of the most successful publicity and public relations campaigns have been based on this human tendency to join the popular bandwagon. Testimonial endorsement advertisements are another common example.

This tendency to develop concrete ideas from abstractions also involves an emotional factor. For public opinion formation in the group is strongly conditioned by an emotional response to such concepts as love, hate, fear, vanity and to various medical, sexual, and religious stimuli. A glance at most popular advertising and at many promotional appeals shows that the advertising people deem them important. But their ultimate effectiveness is tested, of course, by *sales*. Campaigns for deodorants, life insurance, health products, and various charities have all been based, in one way or another, on these emotionally generated symbols.

## CREATING CONSENT

An analysis of many promotional campaigns shows that they are predicated basically on the tendency to devise symbols which are common and acceptable to the interests of the group. A cancer fund drive or a campaign for general inoculation against smallpox is based partly on the emotion of fear, partly

on the desire for self-preservation. The motif might be the basis
for such a plea as "One hundred thousand people in this area
will develop cancer next year. Will one of them be Y O U?"
The use of the terms "Red Cross" and "Blue Cross" has special
significance, backed up by the universality of the symbols which
represent the organizations. The emphasis in beauty-aid campaigns is predicated upon the application of such concepts as
love, vanity, fear, and others.

The general nature of a public relations campaign, designed
to influence public opinion in favor of a particular objective, will
depend upon how accurately the public relations counsel has
gauged prevailing attitudes and opinions. The specific nature of
the public relations campaign depends upon those traditional
symbols to which the group has responded. Depending upon
the nature of the problem, the objective of public relations is to
make public opinion affirmatively articulate either by discred-
iting one set of stereotypes or by creating a new set for the
group to accept and follow. In special campaigns, for example,
the public relations counsel creates one or more ideas which,
when disseminated by various media of communications, make
news and influence public opinion. This flavor of "news interest" makes the idea travel and frequently catches on sufficiently
to develop into a uniformly successful campaign of public opinion formation. Public acceptance or "consent" to such a public
relations campaign will depend upon four important factors:

1. The campaign ideas must be based upon an analysis of the
   pattern or symbols to which the group responds, and upon a
   reorientation of public opinion by the formation of new authorities or symbols which will have group acceptance.
2. The campaign appeals must be based upon those emotional
   factors which will stimulate formation of new patterns.
3. The public relations appeal must be based upon one or more

symbols which inhere in the common tradition of the group. In other words, the public relations counsel must create some recognizable relationship between the *cause* he represents and those *symbols* common to the social pattern of the group toward which the campaign is directed.

4. Public relations must communicate these recognizable patterns to the group through the mass media of communication.

# CHAPTER 9

## *Measuring Public Opinion*

The basic job of a public relations counsel is twofold: to interpret public attitudes, opinions, and trends to his clients; and to devise ways to interpret the activities of his clients to the public through appropriate channels, or media, of communication.

It is those publics directly affected by the operations of the client (and all publics indirectly affected) which concern the counsel in mapping out a public relations campaign. Solid public support is essential to the success of the campaign because no single factor is as significant as the role of public opinion. The counsel who can develop, and retain, a favorable public opinion climate for his clients has accomplished a successful public relations program. There is a good quota of special pleading in a public relations campaign. And the nature of this special pleading, the communicative form which it will assume, is based on the knowledge the counsel can gather of the opinions of the publics with which his client is in contact. The public relations man for a railroad, for example, will be interested in

94

an opinion survey of the riders in communities served by the road.

## WHY SURVEY OPINION?

A private counsel or a public relations director who represents a major air line may need information as to the travel choices of the people in the areas served by the company—whether their preferences are plane, train, or bus and the *reasons* for these preferences. A counsel retained to discover why preference has changed from one product to another may find it necessary to ask questions of several publics—employees, dealers, consumers, and others. Public relations campaigns are almost always predicated on some tentative estimate or prediction of possible public reaction in the areas affected by the campaign. This estimate is part of the counsel's analysis of the problem. From the available data, an interpretation is made to management. New policies may be set up. Old policies may be revised. Finally, a program of active communication is carried out to the publics whose opinions were originally studied and estimated.

For example, an air line serving the New York to Washington area discovers that its traffic is declining. Analysis reveals that its clientele is shifting to train travel because the railroad serving the same area is convincing the public that, everything considered, the train trip is almost as short as the plane service, considering weather and other causes of delay. On the basis of these findings, the direction of public relations for the air line may revolve around a skillful campaign to show that air travel is actually quicker, *everything considered*, than any other means of travel. The railroad aspect may not be mentioned at all. By means of advertising, planting appropriately captioned publicity pictures, sales promotion, and news stories, the air line's public relations department may contrive to show that, in the long run, no other form of transportation has carried as many New York to Washington passengers as quickly and as safely as the plane.

Analysis of the reason for lack of public support of the air line may reveal other causes: poor explanation for accidents; employee grievances and strikes; or other factors. But, unless the cause is glaringly obvious, a careful *survey* or analysis can be infinitely helpful to the public relations counsel, both in his interpretation of the problem to the client and in selecting proper means of interpreting the client to the public. The survey of public attitudes and opinions helps ferret out the cause of management's problems, aids in laying out areas of public support and public rejection, helps to classify the publics involved in a specific promotional campaign, and frequently helps to determine the best mode or channel of access to the public. It is a valuable preliminary guide in preparing for any large-scale public relations campaign. The survey is equally important, incidentally, in measuring the success or failure of a campaign which is under way.

The public opinion survey, practiced by specialists, presents the same kind of diagnostic aid for the public relations counsel as the laboratory test does for the physician. The survey is a clinical method of estimating the force of public opinion. It is a barometric reading of the opinions of various publics and, as such, is actually a direction finder for the public relations counsel. Not only will an accurately designed and executed survey reveal the nature of public opinion in a given geographical area; it will also indicate whether the operations of the counsel are in tune with prevailing opinions. For, both the creation of the idea and the communication of it to the public may frequently develop out of a careful estimate of group opinions in the area affected by the public relations problem. Since business and industries seldom have opportunity for direct contact with the vast publics which are affected by their activities, public relations techniques must include the public opinion survey as an important diagnostic and prognostic instrument.

## THE SURVEY AS AN AID IN PUBLIC RELATIONS

The survey has been, from the beginning, a valuable aid in advertising and marketing procedures. It has now become equally valuable in the more intangible field of public relations. A few thousand interviews—sometimes even a few hundred—undertaken by specialists in sampling, will give a fairly adequate cross section of the opinions of many millions. For example, a company which has hired a public relations counsel to help it win public support against a government monopoly action may want to find out whether its campaign is winning or losing public support. A selective survey, proportioned properly, will reveal how the public is reacting, let us say, to an institutional advertising campaign. It will show areas of conflict and of public favor. Certainly it will aid the counsel in planning future moves because it tells what people think of the company and its campaign.

The field of public opinion measurement has moved rapidly since the end of World War II. The work of the pioneer "pollsters" has been supplemented by more modern experimental techniques such as motivational research, by the work of the Survey Research Center of the University of Michigan, and by the National Opinion Research Center in Chicago, among others.

Frequently, surveys reveal that prevailing opinions of many businesses are based not on facts, but on ignorance. A poll of public attitudes toward socialized medicine may show that most individuals have formed opinions which are not based on facts. Organized medicine has actually found this to be so in its concentrated campaign in favor of group and community health plans as opposed to government compulsory health bill. The public relations problem for the medical profession is to combat this bill not merely by pointing out that it will not achieve its purpose, but by a positive presentation of *facts* which will convince the public that organized medicine can serve its needs more efficiently and economically. In this instance, as in others, public opinion research is a signpost or direction finder. From the data of a survey, the public relations counsel can help the medical groups to plan constructive policies in the public interest. Should a survey show that people favor government medicine because they believe that it will provide better care for all, it is incumbent upon organized medicine to show by actual *facts* that it can actually do a better job and then set out to do it.

The public relations counsel may suggest changes in basic policy. The new policies may be communicated to the public by means of various informational media. And a second survey may be undertaken, after a time lapse, to test the effectiveness of the campaign.

It should be made clear that public opinion surveys assume a certain amount of canceling out. Opinions, based on traditional folkways and familiar stereotypes, are difficult to change. What testing accomplishes is largely tentative, but it does provide a valuable guide in finding out what people think about an issue and why they think as they do. It is an equally valuable guide in assaying the success or failure of a public relations campaign. A few hundred dollars (or a few thousand, depending upon the size of the survey) may actually save a company many additional thousands of dollars of money spent unwisely. Surveys give *information*. They do not, however, offer airtight opportunities for *prediction*. The best that they can offer is an estimate of probable action.

Public opinion, as interpreted by the survey to the public relations counsel, means those attitudes, convictions, beliefs, or prejudices which prevail among the publics being estimated. The basic concept behind the sample is simply that the group or public which is being interviewed must be selected to represent all the publics whose opinions are relevant to the problem. The actual device for measuring or sampling opinions is usually a questionnaire which is so constructed as to make the content as simple, brief, unemotional, and pointed as possible. The group selected for sampling is based on the total population, and the breakdown within the group is again based on a proportion of the total group being sampled. A survey to determine the attitude of the people of Chicago toward a government health plan could successfully be applied to a few thousand out of a total of three million persons *provided that* the sample selected for surveying was chosen on the basis of its proportion in terms of age, sex, income, education, etc., to the total population. The number of people over 40, for example, must be proportionate to the total number over 40 in the population.

### WHAT MEASUREMENT REVEALS

According to George Gallup, Director of the American Institute of Public Opinion, the public opinion poll actually aids in the preservation of the democratic way of life by making ascertainable the will of the people. This, of course, depends upon who does the survey and how the results are used. For example, the questions about the Taft-Hartley Act might be biased, consciously or unconsciously, in favor of either capital or labor. The goal of a survey, experts agree, is to determine prevailing opinions at all times and under all circumstances. Public opinion polls can discover the viewpoint of practically any group or segment of the population. The survey can show whether employees have genuine interest in the welfare of their company, whether they have specific work grievances, and what their attitude toward management and its policies is. Surveys show product preferences and frequently reveal why products sales fall off—or increase. As a public relations guide the survey is valuable because it reveals what the public is thinking and may indicate, therefore, how certain attitudes can be reoriented through public relations techniques.

The important aspect of any survey, if it is to give accurate information, is not its size but its appropriate representation of the whole population. Basic population figures are obtained from the Census Bureau, Treasury Department, Commerce Department, and other agencies. Surveys may be undertaken to determine opinions in various specific segments. The entire population, or the entire *voting* population may be polled. Basic to any sample, however, is the appropriate selection of that sample to represent the entire population in all relevant characteristics. The survey questions are constructed by trained experts in opinion measurement. Before a final survey is undertaken, pretests or pilot tests may be made on limited groups to determine the quality of the questionnaire. Indeed, the final survey itself may be presented in various forms. Some questions call for a categorical "yes" or "no," others offer multiple choices.

No sampling expert would claim that polls are completely accurate. A margin of error is, however, provided for. And errors do crop up. There may be, for example, an error in measuring, a statistical error, an error in predicting, or a human error, i.e., an error in the interview situation. Measurement does, however, constitute a valuable public relations guide to almost any situation which calls for careful study of public attitudes and opinions.

## SURVEYS AS SIGNPOSTS

Surveys tell the public relations counsel what the public is thinking. They tell him why certain groups think as they do. They indicate areas of public acceptance or rejection of the public relations counsel's project—be it a product, an individual, or an idea. The survey is part of the analysis of a public relations problem. On the basis of what the public relations counsel interprets from the data, company policies may be maintained, altered, or completely rejected. New policies may be modified. The function of the survey is to present data about public opinions. The public relations counsel must interpret these data, in the light of the economic, social, and cultural conditions of the time, and plan his course accordingly. Public opinion polls are not meant to solve public relations problems but simply to guide the counsel through the conflicting welter of opinions, attitudes, and convictions with which he must deal in the successful implementation of a campaign.

For the public relations man, a public opinion poll, or measurement, is not an end in itself. It is a means to an end, a signpost, a direction finder. Its findings are helpful to the public relations man in interpreting public opinion to management and in devising a program which is consistent with both management's objectives *and* the public interest. Public opinion measurement reveals areas of ignorance and of knowledge, of good will and ill will, of strength and of weakness. Unfortunately, too many companies do not undertake a measurement of opinion until critical needs make it a necessity. But frequent measurement, judiciously accomplished, can provide the important ounce of prevention. It can contribute to positive rather than negative public relations. For, the results of a poll delineate the black, white, and gray areas of opinion. They clarify the symbols and stereotypes to which the public responds—or which it rejects. Public opinion measurement may, or may not, stimulate creative publicity ideas. What measurement does, however, is to help delimit the areas in which those ideas can be applied. In recent years, motivational research, by showing *why* people select products, has provided new idea material for advertising agencies. As psychologists and sociologists continue to specialize in this area, the chances for more creativity in advertising appear brighter.

Management frequently looks upon the findings of a survey as the categorical answer to all of its problems. But the trained public relations man knows that a survey is simply a means of analysis and exploration. It must be interpreted. It must be implemented in specific directions. And, finally, action must be taken through legitimate avenues of mass communication. Surveys, as such, do not invariably change opinions or attitudes. They supply public relations with the information needed to devise—or revise—a campaign. They are the foundation for the ultimate engineering of consent. The changes in opinion or attitude take place—when they do—by a process of slow penetration. And these subtle changes ultimately may be expected to have pragmatic consequences at the store counter or in the voting booth. As a result of information gleaned from measurement devices, public relations may be expected to:

1. Undertake a new program of information for the purpose of eradicating misinformation about a person, institution, product, or idea.
2. Suggest the substitution of one stereotype for another, with a resultant change of opinion.

3. Bring about a situation (as between management and labor) where understanding of common problems and good will replaces misunderstanding and ill will.

Public opinion polls indicate desirable ends as well as the potential means for achieving those ends. They are of importance, therefore, in many areas of advertising, publicity, promotion, and general public relations because:

1. They reveal to management the opinions, wants, needs, and complaints of employees.
2. They indicate the attitudes of acceptance and rejection on the part of the consumer.
3. They reveal the attitude, pro or con, of the community toward a company or plant.
4. They are valuable in pretesting of advertising campaigns.
5. They offer a mode of testing of publicity copy, brochures, visual materials, and promotional ideas.

## SURVEY ACCOMPLISHMENTS

How is opinion measured? As we have seen, the survey may be objective or subjective. Although the experts have argued earnestly for the objective method as more scientific and accurate, the shorthand or informal or casual method does have a kind of "pilot" significance in public relations. Informal measurement means, simply, stopping to ask questions of the butcher, the baker, and the candlestick maker. Even a handful of answers is frequently of significance in a given area and on a specific problem.

On the other hand, the objective method is, of course, more scientific and more accurate, but it must be accomplished under the auspices of a trained organization. This method carefully selects the group to be queried and the questions to be asked in

terms of the desired information. The medium is the questionnaire (which is more or less structured) and the purpose is
fourfold: to discover what the respondent knows, what he does
not know, what his opinions are, and, in some cases, why he
holds these opinions. Here the basic problem is, once again,
the limitations of language. Words symbolize or represent
things, but people may respond quite differently to the identical
question, put in two different phrasings, because they do not
understand the linguistics involved. The question "Are you in
favor of federal aid to education?" may mean the same as asking
"Are you in favor of having the government contribute to your
local school building program?" The answers to each question,
even from the same individual, may be different. An individual
may reply affirmatively to the first and negatively to the second,
or vice versa. People may say that they want better schools, but
at what cost? Do they confirm complete federal aid, partial aid,
or no aid at all? Do they favor federal aid, but with no strings
attached? In short, an entire group may unanimously favor
better schools, but there may be extremes of opinion on the
means to this end. The original question, on second thought,
is not as simple as it would appear. It is questionable whether it
can be dismissed with a simple "yes" or "no."

When one speaks of the sample or survey, he is speaking of
the various modes of discovering public opinion. The purpose
of measurement devices is to determine and analyze prevailing
opinion and to predict probable future behavior on the basis of
the criteria which are set up as standards of judgment. For, to
understand public opinion and to know how it may be influenced and with what results, one must try to determine what
people think about certain issues around which the tides of
opinion flow. In advertising and promotion in particular it is
claimed that opinion measurement is indispensable because if

content of one kind or another is to be relayed to the receiving audience via communications media, then we must determine what *kind* of message is likely to be most successful in molding opinions. We must know, through gathering evidence, how people are thinking and how they are likely to behave under a given set of circumstances. The basic aims of opinion measurement are twofold. First it aims to find a group of persons who will represent an *adequate* cross section of the larger public involved, a microcosm which represents the macrocosm. This group must be an adequate representation of the larger group in terms of age, sex, economic status, and other characteristics. Second, after the group has been selected by proper sampling techniques, the measurement device must be so constructed as to be as objective as possible, i.e., the question technique, the recording of the answers, and the evaluation procedures must give results which are not biased in the direction of either those who construct the questions or those who ask them. An aura of impersonality must be maintained.

Moreover, the answers to the question asked are more than factual statements to be accepted on their face value. They give important clues and indications as to how positively and how strongly the public feels about the problem at hand. This aspect can best be illustrated by noting two related questions, the second of which need not logically stem from the first:

1. Do you think that American intervention is important if Red China attacks the Nationalist army? (The answer to this question may be an unequivocal "yes.")
2. Would you personally enlist to fight in such an action? (The answer *may* be "yes," but with reservations. Or, it may be an unequivocal "no.")

At any rate, those who are experts in the business of opinion measurement claim that their procedures are not only worth while but that they are often highly accurate. Whether this is so has been the basis for considerable debate among psychologists, statisticians, and social scientists. But the poll does have a unique relevance for the activities involving public relations. The practitioner may not be trained in the intricacies of sampling techniques, but he is in a position to evaluate the results and to put them to use as a guide in planning the advertising and publicity campaign. Given a public relations problem, the measurement expert may be expected to take steps to:

1. Decide upon a set of questions and determine how they are to be worded—multiple choice, yes or no, etc.
2. Determine the measurement situation—by mail, by direct interview, by phone, or by some other procedure.
3. Weed out the weak spots by the use of preliminary or pretest questions.
4. Sample a selected group which represents a larger segment of the population.
5. Analyze, evaluate, and interpret results for presentation to the public relations man and to the management.
6. Predict possible action.

A simple problem in polling, for advertising purposes, will reveal basically how the pollster operates. A motion picture company's advertising agency wants to be able to tell the public relations director which one of four possible advertisements will be most likely to motivate people to see the picture at the theatre. By varying the ads ABCD-BADC-CBDA-DABC until all combinations of presentation are exhausted and by testing these combinations on equivalent samples of about 1500 people of movie-going age (15–50), it was found that most people who were exposed selected ad C regardless of the order of presentation. The director of public relations proceeded to use the C ad as the major campaign strategy.

This is, of course, a bland simplification. On major issues, such as capital versus labor, political issues and religious problems, the measurement devices are more complicated. Frequently, interview polls are not accepted as sufficient evidence and must be supplemented by direct mail and by analysis of press content as well as that of radio, television, and the magazines.

## THE QUESTIONNAIRE

Much of the controversy over the accuracy of opinion polling has whirled about the device of the questionnaire. Most experts agree that certain criticisms are valid. It is claimed, for example, that the people selected may have no knowledge at all about the issue; that various individuals bring different orientations and background to problems and interpret them differently; that some people know so much about the topic as to throw the entire questionnaire off balance; finally, that no real effort is made, beyond a yea or nay, to determine *why* the answer was affirmative or negative or to determine *how strongly* the individual feels about the issue.

Efforts have been made, of course, to devise questionnaires which rectify these criticisms, but intangibles will always be present in a situation involving the human equation. In opinion measurement on an issue of deep social importance, the superficial answer is not only insufficient; it is misleading as well unless the interviewer can obtain sufficient data to determine the direction of public opinion, the strength of its potential energy, and the likelihood of transformation into kinetic energy, i.e., overt action. The questions, therefore, must be selected with great care, for they determine and delimit the boundaries of the area to be measured. "Slanted" questions, for example, do not give information and are useless from the standpoint of public opinion research; but they may have propaganda value to special interest groups. It is not inconceivable that the objectives of a survey, from a public relations viewpoint, may be twofold—what is gleaned as information and what is utilized for public consumption. Such a procedure, of course, is lacking in integrity and the profession of public relations has had to withstand rather severe criticism because a few venal practitioners have resorted to slanting and perversion of information obtained from opinion measurement.

According to measurement experts, the material for the questions used in a survey is obtained from the best possible sources —editors of newspapers, congressional leaders, educators, and scholars. However, the sources of question content are not so important as the phrasing of the questions themselves. Unless, for example, the question elicits more than a mere "yes" or "no," unless it includes some recognition of related attitudes and intensity, it may prove ultimately to be misleading and inaccurate. Is it enough to ask "Do you favor desegregation?" Most answers to this query would not be a categorical "yes" or "no." The majority would be of the "yes, but . . ." or "no, but . . ." variety, and understandably so. Intense social issues are not usually resolved by complete rejection or complete acceptance.

The survey expert, of course, does not use one question form. Many variables are employed, each carefully designed and purposeful. What happens when the question is exposed to the respondent, however, is unpredictable in the chemistry involved. The answers may be confused or meaningless, for the questions may be exposed to persons who know little and care less about the problem. Let us note the two following questions:

1. Do you favor the policies of the present administration?
2. Do you favor the concept of "dynamic conservatism?"

Now, both of these questions may be equated, for the policies of the administration have been termed those of a "dynamic conservatism." Yet, it is entirely possible that those who answered positively to the first question would respond negatively to the second. The prestige of the president may add immeasurably to the affirmation of the first question. At the same time, many who supported the president may not understand the meaning of the phrase "dynamic conservatism."

The measurement experts are not unaware of these problems in the human equation. Certain preliminary steps are taken to make the question content and the survey situation as objective as possible, i.e.:

1. The pollster claims that the survey is not intended to find any absolutes. The measurement of opinion tries to show what will happen to people's behavior under certain conditions.
2. Certain issues do not require, and should not be subjected to, a survey situation because public opinion is obvious. All that a measurement will reveal is the extent of the feeling involved.
3. The measurement expert claims that the sampling of opinion in a small group, carefully selected, will predict accurately the opinions of all involved in the area of the subject measured.
4. Tests are conducted prior to the real survey. Questions are subjected to questioning.
5. More than one questionnaire is employed. Many parallel forms are used in order to increase chances of accuracy.

## AN INDICATION OF FEELING

What is of particular importance to the public relations man is that the survey does more than reveal the nature of public opinion on a given issue; the measurement device also acts as a barometer of feeling. The survey reveals how *deeply* people feel about the problem. This is of great importance because the deeper the feeling, the more difficult it is to change. Public relations campaigns must take depth and intensity as well as mere statement of opinion into consideration. For the results of measurement offer a direction finder. They indicate the strength or weakness of conviction. They delineate the depth of emotional involvement. And, finally, they indicate the possibility of overt action. Thus, the results of measurement draw a frame of reference in which public relations campaigns can be devised and promulgated.

Some public relations men object to the use of an interviewer-interviewee situation. They claim that the "chemistry" of interaction between the two may affect the survey situation and thereby affect the impersonal nature of the poll, for there is no way of knowing whether the interviewer has been able to be completely honest and objective. As a result, some public relations men prefer to use direct-mail questionnaires, but these also pose a problem in that usually they are answered only by those who are interested in the problem. This need not, however, alter the efficacy of the direct-mail method. The method is valuable, and the chances of higher return are increased if the poll includes a reply envelope and perhaps a personal touch, such as a promise to inform each respondent of the ultimate result.

In addition to the interviewer poll and the direct-mail questionnaire, public relations men rely also on the content of mass media for their information about public opinion. While the content of press, magazines, radio, and television is not as accurate as the more direct poll, it is nevertheless a useful guide to the opinions of a particular public. It is also of importance in determining the opinions of the so-called "opinion makers," such as newspaper publishers, radio and television broadcasters, and magazine editors.

## VALUE OF MEASUREMENT FOR PUBLIC RELATIONS

Some rather formidable problems crop up in attempting to evaluate the significance of opinion measurement as an aid in public relations techniques. Since public opinion is never stable but is always in flux, is it measurable? Even if one were to assume that opinion is measurable under certain optimum conditions, are not these conditions still in the future? In other words, do we now have a scientifically accurate device, capable of accurately measuring opinion and, on the basis of findings, *predicting behavior?* But, even if such a device were available, how is it possible to make predictions about behavior when we know, from psychological studies, that the opinions of individuals may *not* be predictive of their behavior.

The measurement expert, however, does not claim that opinion studies are absolute. He does not say that a given finding *necessarily* implies the promulgation of a given public relations campaign. For the fact is that opinion measurement is not absolute, but relative: it does not attempt to supply final answers or absolutes, but merely to point the way toward possible goals. Opinion measurement is important in public relations not only in revealing what people know, but also what they do *not* know. It is as revelatory of negative areas as it is of positive. Public opinion itself does not allow for final answers. It is a dynamic phenomenon, not a static one. And the results of opinion measurement are not categorical, but tentative. With these reservations in mind, the public relations man will find opinion measurement a useful device for indicating areas of knowledge and of ignorance, of weakness and of strength, and of predicting *probable* group behavior.

Honest measurement of opinion, apart from its significance as a road map for public relations, can contribute to the democratic way of life by revealing the opinions of minorities as well as of the majority. Honest polls can advance, by their integrity of purpose, the democratic philosophy by revealing social needs as well as areas of ignorance, bias, and misinformation. Certainly, public opinion polls can make minority opinions articulate. And, in rebuttal to those who claim that publicity men for special interest groups tend to "load" the poll situation, it can be claimed also that public opinion polls are capable of showing that certain special interest groups do *not* express the popular will—or the true public opinion.

It may be concluded, therefore, that public opinion studies and measurement devices act not only as a barometer, but also as a stimulus toward the formation of opinion. They help make obscure issues clear, and they indicate the need for public opinion and action on certain important issues. Of course, polls and their results have been misinterpreted by venal publicists, and they have been "loaded" by special interests in order to make the worst appear the better reason. But, with vigilance and a high sense of professional ethics and obligation, polls and those who use them can prove a healthy influence, particularly in revitalizing areas of "cultural lag," i.e., in instances where our institutions fail to adapt themselves to need for change. The future of opinion measurement, as a genuinely important tool in public relations, lies partly in the education of the public and partly in the professional ethics of the measurement expert who devises the survey and of the public relations man who interprets the findings and puts them to practical use. It should be pointed out, in conclusion, that one can measure with accuracy but fail in predicting. There is an unfathomable gap between opinion expression and overt behavior.

# Part III

# The Mass Media

Brief history of each of the
mass media—Their structure
and function—Their significance to modern society—
Relationship between communication content and opinion
formation

# CHAPTER 10

## The Impact of Mass Media

The study of public opinion is not unique to the twentieth century. The nature of public opinion, and of ways and means to influence it, occupied the thoughts and efforts of social and political philosophers in both the eighteenth and nineteenth centuries as well. But these studies were more theoretical than practical. Public opinion in the twentieth century is a trenchant and powerful phenomenon largely because of the growth of mass communication and of public relations. For the latter supplies the techniques, and the former the direct avenues, by which public opinion may be influenced.

### MASS MEDIA AND THE MASSES

In a literal sense, the masses can be reached by means of the mass media which convey public relations content, the major purpose of which is to influence public opinion. Techniques of advertising and selling, the sciences of marketing and merchandising, have taken on a new significance with the rise and influence of such media as radio and television which not only supplement, but in some ways overshadow, the influence of the press and the magazine.

Public relations techniques, and the mass media through which they are applied, are, however, not unilateral. They constitute one side of a two-way street. The mass media influence public opinion and are, in turn, influenced by public opinion. What has been glossed over frequently, however, is this influence of opinion on public relations and on the various media. Much has been written about the impact of press, radio, and television on the opinions, attitudes, and habits of the public. But the public exerts a very strong influence on the media. This interaction cannot be equated precisely, but it is nevertheless in constant operation.

The point has been made that the press, to some degree, gives the public what the public wants. The radio and television broadcasters explicitly recognized this same influence when they rebutted the demand for educational stations by asserting that they did not *emphasize* educational programming because the majority did not want it. The motion picture industry strives to find the common denominator in themes and symbols that will give the public what it wants or appears to need. Magazine writers slant their material for the respective readers —the "slicks," the pulps, the class books, and so forth. In short, public opinion exerts almost as strong an influence on media content as the media do on public opinion. All of the mass media make some effort to acquiesce to public demand, primarily because they would lose the public as readers or listeners if they ignored this demand. If, for example, the New York *Daily News* were to take on the journalistic attitudes of the New York *Times* and vice versa, both papers would lose their respective publics and, incidentally, their respective advertisers. There is an implicit community of interest between the mass media and their public environment.

## MEDIA AND THEIR PUBLICS

The basic media through which and within which public relations techniques operate are the press, radio, television, motion picture, magazine, and book. Related areas in which public relations techniques are applied include direct-mail promotion, brochures, posters, display cards, and other written and graphic presentations. Thus, public relations, as an umbrella title, embraces or covers the areas of advertising, publicity, promotion, and exploitation.

Breakdowns and statistical studies show that while there is overlapping among media publics, it is perfectly legitimate to speak of a book public, a newspaper reading public, a radio public, a TV public, and so forth. In other words, the receiving audience for the mass media can be categorized and stratified to some extent, and thereby the direction of public relations techniques is made more specific. A study might reveal, for example, that 25 percent of the "public" reads one book per month; that almost 100 percent reads one or more newspapers every day; that about 65 percent reads a magazine regularly; that about 45 percent goes to the motion picture theatre approximately every three weeks; and that almost 100 percent listens to radio or watches television daily. Further breakdowns would show the choice in book reading, the number of hours spent listening to radio (and the time of day or evening), and the kinds of magazine read.

On the basis of such studies, advertising campaigns and publicity techniques are devised. They reveal vital information about the receiving audience, and they serve as a guide to ways and means of influencing its opinions and habits. Audience surveys of the radio listener reveal why such programs as the symphony orchestra concerts go unsponsored. For, while the audience may be of high educational and even of high economic caliber, this total group is *not* the group which the advertiser considers a strong, potential buying public. The advertising man almost invariably—and the publicity man frequently —seeks out the common denominator of as many publics as can be encompassed within the framework of a campaign. The concentration of effort is upon those who will be overtly influenced (i.e., influenced to act) by exposure to mass media.

## BOOKS AND MAGAZINES

The basic concentration on the *mass* explains why books are not used as frequently as are other media for public relations purposes. There is a direct relationship between the steady habit of reading books and the degree of education of the individual. Because book reading demands habit formation and concentrated effort, as well as reading skill, the "book public" is relatively small. It is a hard-to-get, but challenging, target. Therefore, the public relations man who will utilize the book will usually represent a very large industrial institution. These organizations may subsidize company histories or similar themes which are frequently of considerable historical value, since several of them have been written by reputable authorities. Their basic public relations objective is to enhance industrial or company prestige.

But the "book public," unfortunately, is not large when compared to the public which reads newspapers and/or listens to radio or watches television. For example, the 500 book publishers in the United States issue about 12,500 titles in an average year, including new books *and* new editions. Many of these are bought in the relatively few bookstores around the country or borrowed from the 10,031 public libraries. But the total group reached is, by comparison, a minority one. Only for special occasions does the publication of a book carry genuine public relations impact—a company history in connection with an anniversary or similar milestone; a political biography in an election year; or a startling exposé which reaches the public through press reviews and by word of mouth.

On the other hand, certain magazines carry enormous influence. Such publications as *Life,* the *Saturday Evening Post, Look,* and a few other major magazines have a circulation and readership of millions upon millions. *Life,* for example, not only carries weight with its more than twenty million readers; it also has public relations impact on political, civic, educational, and religious leaders. It is a powerful opinion maker. Indeed, it is somewhat startling to consider the total impact if, for example, all of the book clubs plus all of the major magazines were to agree simultaneously to press some social, economic, or political objective. The system of healthy checks and balances would find it hard going to maintain a sense of democratic equilibrium.

Ayer's *Directory of Newspapers and Periodicals* for 1957 reported 7,907 periodicals published in the United States, including consumer, trade, technical, college, club, local, and so forth. A count of the magazines and groups in *Standard Rate and Data Consumer Magazine* section listed most recent circulation figures as follows:

| | No. of Magazines and Groups | Average Circulation per Issue |
|---|---|---|
| General magazines | 413 | 185,190,287 |
| Comic magazines | 11 | 36,598,566 |
| Farm magazines | 193 | 21,969,759 |

The Magazine Advertising Bureau's "Nationwide Magazine Audience Survey" indicates some interesting characteristics of U.S. magazine readers 15 years of age or over. For example, magazine readers represent:

82.5 percent of all U.S. families
68.9 percent of all individuals 15 years of age and over
63.6 percent of all men 15 years of age and over
73.5 percent of all women 15 years of age and over
83.7 percent of all urban families
78.3 percent of all rural nonfarm families
83.7 percent of all farm families

Magazine readers are younger than nonreaders. They have a median age of 36 years compared to 50 years for the nonreaders. Magazine readers are better educated than nonreaders. They have a median education of three years of high school (eleven years of schooling, compared to six years of grade school for the nonreaders).

Magazines are read by:

92 percent of college-educated individuals
85.3 percent of high school graduates
48 percent of those with less than a high school education

The magazine-reading family has more income than the nonreading family:

97.4 percent of the prosperous families read magazines
94.5 percent of the upper middle families read magazines
89.1 percent of the middle income families read magazines
64.5 percent of the lower income families read magazines

So far as national advertising is concerned, among the respective media, the most recent estimates prepared by *Printers' Ink* indicate the following comparative media statistics:

| | Millions |
|---|---|
| Newspapers: | |
| National | 825.0 |
| Radio: | |
| Network and | |
| Spot | 295.0 |
| TV: | |
| Network and | 1 billion |
| Spot | 15 million |
| Magazines: | |
| Total | 820.0 |
| Business Publications | 545.0 |
| Outdoor: | |
| National | 138.0 |

Every magazine has a promotion department, and virtually every one makes extensive use of direct mail to advertisers and agents. A number of large circulation magazines make extensive use of newspaper space and have campaigns in the advertising business papers. The larger publications almost invariably have their own publicity departments. The Magazine Advertising Bureau functions to promote the increased use of magazine advertising not by taking orders for space, but by selling "the concept, the idea of magazines and magazine advertising."

## MEDIA AND PENETRATION

To say that a public is "amenable" is to raise the question of how deep or how penetrating an influence the mass media exert on public opinion. Certainly all of the communication media have some influence some of the time. Public relations techniques also are successful in communicating their content by means of the media at least some of the time. But the degree of penetration and the durability or permanence of the content in influencing public opinion cannot be measured in any absolute manner. Nor can accurate predictions be made. Too many fortuitous or extraneous factors must be weighed into the situation—the immediate social, political, and economic climate; the kinds of publics involved; the psychological pattern of the publics and their geographical distribution; the issue at hand.

Television and radio, because they appear, among all of the media, to have the most direct line of communication to individuals are perhaps the most influential. At its best, the newspaper exerts a tremendously powerful influence. But it is less personalized than the broadcast media, and certainly less intimate in concept. The press, however, allows for privacy of thought, for only one person can read a speech in the newspaper, but several may watch and listen to it on television or radio. A televised speech is directed electronically to "you," the listener. The same speech, reprinted in the morning paper, is one step removed from immediacy and directness. Fund-raising telethons, based on the concept of direct plea, have earned more money for various causes than newspaper advertisements or editorials. The personality states the case visually and directly to the viewer or listener.

But even the broadcast media, paradoxically, are direct in an indirect way. An electronic tube is the transmission agent. And, even in an age in which all of the mass media are approaching their peak of perfection, and when public relations techniques are both an art and a science, the most powerful influence on public opinion formation still remains direct communication contact. The strategy of a recent political campaign originally was to omit all public or "whistle-stop" speeches and to rely upon a few televised appearances. At the height of the campaign, however, the strategy was altered. A few whistle-stop speeches were still found expedient, not only for their own sake, but also because this social situation, from a public relations point of view, framed a necessary setting and background for the publicity to be disseminated through the avenues of the mass media. Editorials, for example, were important to the strategy; but more important was the day-by-day news content. The campaign needed the stimulus of several personal appearances before the public to heighten its news significance.

Mass media, even at their optimum, are basically indirect. Because of their indirectness, it is difficult to gauge with any final accuracy the success or failure of a publicity campaign. The impact of the message may reach the entire audience, or part of the audience. The receiving audience may accept all, or part, of the message. And, in the acceptance of part of the message, it is important to know which part and *why* that particular element as opposed to others. In short, what has the individual selected for acceptance value, and, more importantly, what has he rejected?

Those who apply the mass media are helpful in answering these problems. Radio and television have extremely intricate and elaborate measurement devices. They can predict, for example (and with considerable accuracy), the nature and size of an audience for a given program at a given hour of the day or night. Magazines have done similar studies of circulation breakdown and readership, as have book clubs. These studies have a two-pronged significance for the public relations practitioner. Sampling methods can furnish him with salient information about the communication media and their relative strength and effectiveness; but sampling methods can also tell a great deal about the habits, attitudes, aspirations, and needs of the publics toward which the content is devised and directed.

## AUDIENCE AND MEDIA INTERACT

The receiving audience and the media are no longer two separate and distinct entities. They are no longer clearly distinguishable, one from the other. The communication media range so far and wide, are so ubiquitous, and have such widespread areas of potential audience acceptance that audiences and media merge into one another in a constant interaction. Television, radio, and newspapers are not casual phenomena to the American people. The receiving audience is daily exposed to all of them, not briefly, but cumulatively for several hours. The "average" person watches television about two and one-half to three hours daily—a huge swathe of his waking time. Prior to the advent of television, the "average" person went to the movies about once a week. Movie attendance is now more sporadic, and the individual choice more selective, with consequent implication for those who are concerned with motion picture advertising and publicity. The "average" individual will report that he has *not* read a book for at least thirty days; but more than 50 percent of the population will have read "some magazine" at some period of the month. Almost 100 percent will have read one newspaper every day.

The mass communication habits of the receiving audience

are an important direction finder for public relations techniques. They affirm, for example, that the media are vigorously competitive, the competition centering around both the advertising allocation and the attention of the public. A serious center of competition developed for the motion picture industry with the successful advent of television, and the solution for the movies is still being explored. In general, however, the mass media tend to be competitive, but complementary, in their impact on the public.

Both radio and television have enormous impact on the public, but it must be pointed out, too, that public opinion has considerable influence on all of the mass media. From an advertising viewpoint it is widely felt that no campaign is fully rounded out or complete without including both radio and television in the budget allocation. Indeed, it might be said that the communications circle is not complete without due regard to all of the relevant avenues. From a publicity viewpoint, both radio and television offer frequent opportunities, both on sponsored and public service programs, for the dissemination of content in terms of the news broadcast as well as through the "tie-in" or "plug" on the entertainment shows.

For specialized audiences, both books and the "class" magazines are appropriate public relations outlets. Those public relations campaigns which include the book, however, are usually long range and institutional; and their impact, in terms of public opinion penetration, is directed toward the literate public which has had the benefit of a higher education. The popular book has a more practical value in day-by-day publicity when it can be related to a motion picture or a television program. It is widely believed, although not proved, that reading a book from which a motion picture has been adapted increases audience attendance at the motion picture theatre. Those who have worked in this area of book-movie promotion, however, do not hold with this point of view. What happens more often is that motion pictures stimulate reading of books. The motion picture of *War and Peace* proved a tremendous buying stimulus for the novel and created a new audience for the classic. The growth of the paper-back reprints, particularly from novels which have become movies, offers an important new promotional area for the book business.

An important factor for public relations techniques, as applied to the mass media, is accessibility. Exposure, and the consequent influencing of public opinion, is in direct proportion to the accessibility of the medium. The audience for mass communication is not homogeneous, and it varies in size and in interest, depending upon easy or difficult access to the medium. The younger group probably will make more effort to go out to the motion picture theatre than any other segment of the public. Those with benefit of higher education will make an effort to buy a book. But of all the media—even including the press—radio and television appear to be the most readily accessible. And radio becomes more powerful daily as more sets are sold. This easy accessibility is the reason why radio and television have revolutionized publicity and advertising techniques. Radio and television truly have added "mass" to communication.

## RESULTS OF EXPOSURE TO MASS MEDIA

The critical question for all practitioners of public relations and, indeed, for all who are concerned with techniques of influencing public opinion, is what results can be anticipated when people are exposed to the content of the mass media? For, in order to devise successful modes of operation in public relations, one must have some prior knowledge of why, and how, individuals and groups react to the communication media. How, for example, do the media attract audience attention? Does exposure to mass media lead to an increase of knowledge? If so, through what particular function? How does exposure to mass media lead to overt action? And, most important, how can the techniques of influencing opinion by the employment of the mass media bear results which are socially beneficial, i.e., which lead to social cohesion rather than to lack of harmony or disintegration?

The individual is literally immersed in a sea of communications. The group, of which individuals are component parts, is influenced by its communication environment and, in turn, it tends to influence this environment. Within the framework of the communication universe, the media also interact upon each other. Indeed, it is no longer tenable to consider any one medium as purely competitive with another so far as public relations techniques are concerned. The communication arts have grown to such a degree of intricacy that they are related almost as are the isotopes of a chemical element. Few, if any, public relations campaigns, involving both publicity *and* advertising, can be launched in one medium without considering all media. Radio has survived and prospered, despite the growth of television, because the networks have shown the advertiser and sponsor that his dollar does not reach a complete public unless *both* media are employed. The national advertiser, therefore, will allocate his public relations spending among all of the major media—press, radio, television, and magazines.

## SYMBOLS AND THINGS

Does the content differ with the medium used? Basically, it does not, although the presentation trimmings may vary to suit the peculiar demands, possibilities, and limitations of the respective channels. The content must still be framed within the semantic limitations of the language, as well as within the range of receptivity and understanding of the receiving audience. The audience does not, with few exceptions, relate words to the world of external reality, except through the necessary process of identification, in which an idea or concept of reality is made coördinate with reality itself. The receiving audience tends to see the world in terms of black or white and not in tones of gray. The dedicated Republican paper sees all Democratic politics as evil and vice versa. The multitudinous problems besetting the world are identified only with specific political figures, with no regard for the many other contributing factors. An official's signature on a Middle East resolution was viewed as a solution in itself, despite the fact that Egypt reëntered the Gaza strip almost at the moment of signing.

The average individual, therefore, thinks and conducts his daily business in terms of symbols of things, not in terms of the things symbolized. This symbolic behavior, based on the failure to distinguish reality from a representation of it, is at the base of most of our reactions to communication content, and it must serve as a basis for public relations techniques if they are to be successful in influencing public opinion. Only during a great moment of crisis is group behavior truly cohesive. Once the crisis is passed, alternatives are again in evidence. Conflicts of interests and ideals arise. And public opinion formation and change are possible.

Symbolic behavior is linked significantly to the art and the science of communication. The average individual, faced by many conflicting issues, tends to concentrate his attention or focus upon one basically simple idea or personality. This tendency to localize the area of concentration explains why publicity techniques also tend to focus the content or message around a concrete idea or personality wherever possible. The American flag, or some other appropriate symbolic setting, is an example of the simple technique of concentrating attention upon a simple, comprehensible, and emotionally acceptable symbol.

Even on so seemingly direct a medium as television, the receiving audience does not enter *directly* into an experience. Events are experienced vicariously by a process of mental abstraction. The audience does not act *directly* upon, or react *directly* to, the external environment. It acts in an intermediate area. It accepts this psychological buffer state by a "willing suspension of disbelief," but its *acts* nevertheless do influence the external environment. Skillful public relations techniques, for example, may "sell" a political figure to the public, partly because of the skill used and partly because the public has tacitly agreed to be influenced. The symbolic figure represented may be entirely out of kilter to that figure as he behaves in the "real" or external world. But an overt act of voting on the part of the public may put the figure in office.

The receiving audience behaves not on the basis of its own careful research, but on the basis of its own abstractions, or on the basis of graphic information which is presented to it as infallible truth. What public relations techniques strive to accomplish is to maintain or alter these images of reality. Frequently, public relations strives to substitute one image for another. Public opinion studies are difficult because it is difficult to pierce through the buffer state in which one finds symbols of reality instead of reality itself. The mere use of the term "opinion" and not "fact," for example, indicates the nature of the problem but does not indicate a solution. Man constructs his own image of the real world. When a group of individuals *accepts* this image, a public and an opinion come into being.

Public relations content is aimed at these group formations. Purposefully, public relations strives to influence group opinion and group action. But no prediction can be made with regard to the success of public relations techniques because of the unpredictable behavior of the individuals who make up the group. Man absorbs and responds to content stimuli in terms of his own unique individual and group orientation. He comes to the content not with a *tabula rasa,* but with a whole set of ideas of his own. And he assimilates content in terms of his own peculiar interests, desires, and goals. The media do not *organize* opinion. There must be some opinion already organized in order for public relations techniques and communication content to function. When issues which are implicitly controversial arise, opinion formation occurs. Public relations operates within this framework.

# CHAPTER 11

## *The Newspaper*

A scholar in the field of journalism stated categorically, "It might be the most creative thing that ever happened to newspapers if public relations men would quit trying to fit their hands into the newspaper glove."

The point expressed was that public relations men ought to tend to their knitting and let the journalists run the newspaper. But that is only part of the story, although there is some truth to it when publicists try to tell an editor how to handle a story. The real point is that public relations men have daily business with the press, and the press must contend with the ministrations of public relations men. What is more practical, therefore, than some knowledge of the history and function of the press on the part of the publicist, and some understanding of the function of the publicist on the part of the newspaper editor? Far too many publicists have far too little understanding and orientation of the history, function, and purposes of a newspaper. No one requires, for example, that the publicist have an encyclopedic knowledge of the development of the newspaper in America. But a working knowledge of the structure of the paper and of its development is an important tool in the pragmatic business of knowing what is news and how to place it. An understanding of the place of the newspaper, too, offers a clue to the attitudes of certain newspapers and their editors—why, for example, some newspapers are more amenable to publicity than others; why the newspaper opened its pages to publicity news in the first place; why newspapers accept some stories and reject others. Many industries, in fact, insist that the public relations director be a former newspaperman, presumably because his training in journalism and his experience on the paper offer better equipment for practical publicity. This is a moot point, but there is no doubt, among experienced publicists, that a knowledge of the working of the newspaper offers valuable equipment for those who deal with reporters and editors.

One of the reasons for this is that journalism is a proud profession. More frequently than any of the other mass media, the press is referred to as an institution. This concept is not without foundation. The press is the oldest, the most traditional, and the most revered of the mass media. Despite the fact that today's newspaper is old newsprint tomorrow, there is still an aura of permanence about what is printed in the press. The newspaper stands for a sense of stability and truth. Despite the tremendous inroads of such media as the radio in the areas of information and news, the newspaper is still viewed as indispensable in most quarters.

The press has come to mean more than the newspaper. When publicity men speak of "press coverage," the term is used in an omnibus sense to embrace the newspapers as well as other media which have reportorial functions, such as radio and television. To invite the press to a function frequently implies inviting all of the representative media which are relevant to the occasion. A businessman's press conference may include the editors and reporters of local newspapers along with wire services; reporters and researchers of such magazines as *Time, Newsweek, Forbes, Business Week* and others; selected radio and TV commentators; and other specialists and analysts of the news. The press, in publicity parlance, may mean only the newspapers, but it may mean other reportorial and informational agencies as well.

## A BRIEF HISTORY

Prior to the growth of wire services and of radio and television as news-gathering and news-disseminating media, the press meant simply the newspaper. Not until the latter part of the nineteenth century did the newspaper become a medium of information, advertising, opinion, and entertainment. The early newspapers bore only a remote resemblance to the paper of today. They were, in reality, newsletters or pamphlets, and their essential function was the dissemination of news, but not as news is defined in this day of mass communication and public relations. Their function was different. The Colonial American newsletter was a derivation in form and content of the eighteenth century English newsletter. Newsletters began circulating in England in the seventeenth century. Their appearance grew out of historical necessity. Special publics, rather than the general public, needed certain information about the recurrent wars, the price of silver, the crops, and other sundry but important matters. The same impulse sparked the first newspapers in America. They were not only organs of social news, but purveyors of news from Europe which was important for diplomatic and commercial reasons.

The first newsletter appeared in the last decade of the seventeenth century with the publication, in 1690, of *Publick Oc-*

currences *Both Foreign and Domestic.* Fourteen years later, *The Boston News-Letter* made its appearance. *Publick Occurrences* appeared only once. *The Boston News-Letter* was published weekly. The first daily letter was brought out in 1784 as *The Pennsylvania Packet and Daily Advertiser.* None of these were newspapers in the contemporary sense of the term. Their audience was not popular, but select. These pamphlets were, however, important precursors of what was to become one of the most powerful and proficient communication avenues in the world.

The newspaper which was to fashion its content for the so-called general public did not come into being until 1833 with the establishment by Benjamin Day of *The Sun,* a famous masthead which ultimately became one of the country's most important newspapers until it closed its doors in a merger with the New York *World-Telegram* a few years ago. *The Sun* was a paper for the people. It was scaled to sell at one cent per copy, and it devised its news content for the "average" reader.

Two years later, in 1835, James Gordon Bennett brought out the *Morning Herald.* Like its predecessor, the *Herald* was a popular newspaper. It sold at one cent and grasped the importance of headlining significant news events. More significantly, however, was the fact that the Bennett newspaper provided the first competitive influence. Its publication, following the appearance of *The Sun,* foreshadowed the rise of the newspaper to an estate of tremendous influence and power. Ten years later, Horace Greeley published the *Tribune,* a paper more devoted to moral and spiritual values than its more flamboyant competitors. And, still one decade later, in 1851, began the distinguished career of the greatest newspaper in the history of American journalism and the most influential print organ in the world, the New York *Times.*

These newspapers laid the foundation of American journalism. But the press was to become truly a popular medium with the advent of Joseph Pulitzer and William Randolph Hearst and their publication, respectively, of the New York *World* and the New York *Journal*. In these papers appeared, for the first time, a sense of uncanny timing and understanding of the basic drives, goals, and interests of the reader as a human being. Truly popular journalism began with Pulitzer and Hearst, and these brilliant journalistic ventures sparked the appearance of the human interest story, the cartoon, and the news picture. In a sense, these developments also opened the door to the early antics of the press agent, although in recent years a great deal of dignified news has come from publicity men as a result of the new concept of public relations which has been accepted by business and other institutions.

Circulation of these papers increased as the population grew, for there were no other competing media. The inevitable use of newspaper space for advertising came to pass and gave rise to furious battles for higher circulation and a consequent effort to devise angles and features which would increase circulation. The result, again, was inevitable. Stories, pictures, and arresting headlines were devised to attract reader attention. And, finally, the increasing importance of the press caught the attention of pressure groups which sought not only to control what was printed, but also to find a medium for the expression of their own propaganda.

But the American press, by its own canons, by its own system of checks and balances, and through the power of public opinion, also developed a sense of responsibility despite its heavy reliance upon advertising and circulation. Competing media, such as radio and television, heightened that sense of responsibility. The character of the modern newspaper changed with changing institutions, with competition, with the development of wireless communications, with cheaper methods of printing, and, most significantly, with the increasing growth of literacy on the part of the receiving audience. The growth of the American press (and, indeed, of the press agents) reflects the growth of our social institutions and the importance of public opinion. The newspaper and the publicist are outgrowths of our social institutions, and, at the same time, they are forces in shaping our institutions.

## THE NEWSPAPER TODAY

At the present time, there are about 1,750 daily newspapers published in the United States and about 10,000 weekly newspapers. The daily circulation varies from a few thousand to more than a million. Weeklies command a circulation ranging from several hundred to several thousand. One or two weeklies run much higher. Since almost 100 percent of the population reads the newspaper with some degree of regularity, the influence of the press is obviously a significant one. The press is particularly important to the publicist because it reaches *people*. It grew out of social, political, and economic necessity, and, at the same time, it fulfills an important social, political, and economic function.

The great newspapers of today are a skillful amalgam of many ingredients, some concrete and some abstract. The compounding of copy on newsprint, which is put together into a basic format, circulated to the public, and read by the receiving audience, makes a newspaper come alive. It is a powerful agency in molding the opinions of its readers; and, by the same token, what it selects and prints as news and as editorial matter is influenced to some extent *by* the opinions of those same readers. For, as we have noted, the press must have an audience. It is static without it, dynamic with it. In order to achieve audience and readership, the newspaper faces the problem of building circulation, manifested in recent years by the fact that newspapers themselves have undertaken their own publicity and promotional campaigns. Even with huge readership the newspaper cannot exist in a competitive market without advertising which, in turn, depends upon circulation. Despite the holier-than-thou attitude which some newspapermen exhibit toward the press agent, the press, *as it is constituted today,* cannot function without the service it receives from public relations men, publicists, and press agents. Many of the important departments of the large metropolitan newspapers depend upon publicity sources for the major portion of their news. Certainly the popular columnists would be hard pressed for news if they were not serviced by press agents who feed innumerable items in return for a "plug" for the client.

The press, therefore, has two major sources of news: its own reporters and the public relations men. The press also has two related audience potentials: the number of readers in the receiving audience who form opinions based on the content in the newspaper and the number of persons in the receiving audience who are motivated to buy the products advertised in the newspaper.

Primarily because of advertising revenues, but also owing to its circulation, the newspaper is the cheapest form of reading available to the public and, in the last analysis, the most important from a temporal point of view. The press does not offer the immediacy of radio, but it offers the opportunity to reflect upon what is read. Some captious critics have ascribed implicit moral commitments and obligations upon the press which it does not, and cannot, undertake. The press, as all responsible publicists must learn, tries to live up to standards or canons of journalism. It is a public institution, but it is also a business enterprise and is subject to the laws of supply and demand and the exigencies of profit and loss as are other enterprises. But a responsible press will carry, along with its legitimate business objectives, a need and desire to live up to its obligation as a public servant. The best newspapers honor this obligation. Because, however, the press has had to juxtapose its public service obligations with its business interests, its obligation and function have never been clearly defined. Its structure and function, as a social institution, are still undergoing change and analysis.

## NEWSPAPER CONTENT

The newspaper, as it is published today, combines both news and an editorial viewpoint. From a circulation standpoint, and therefore from an advertising one, the *news* is the paramount factor. Since much of the news which appears in print is news which is serviced by publicists, either via news releases or other avenues such as interviews, press conferences, or special events, the crucial question for the publicist is to determine what the press means by news. By and large, the press considers news to be a two-faceted phenomenon. First, the news is something which attracts the attention of the reader. Second, the news is also something which, once having attracted the attention of one reader, will generate discussion and interest among other members of the social group.

Each newspaper takes the same news material and displays it according to its own format. A story or release may be displayed prominently in one paper and omitted or used casually in another not because it is unimportant, but because it simply does not fit in with the formula of presentation. The readers, to some extent, determine how news is displayed. A story which may be used on page one of our particular paper may be placed on the last page of another. In addition to the daily press, the weeklies have their own mode of presentation and this, too, is not uniform, although there will be a tendency to emphasize local and community news items.

The New York *Times* is a great newspaper because, among other reasons, it offers the most complete and accurate coverage of the news. But other great papers have flourished for other reasons. They have not only reported the news, but they have editorialized trenchantly, have found a creed to expound and a cause to espouse. They have seized upon controversial issues for coverage in the news columns and comment in their editorial pages.

The noteworthy feature of these papers was not sobriety, but a search for the startling, the new, the controversial. The common denominator was something called "human interest." And, as the press became aware of what human beings were interested in, there appeared the gossip column, the feature, the use of pictures, comic strips, sports, women's pages and, finally, the Sunday paper and supplement with its massive advertising and its regular feature and picture roundups. The extension of content and services meant, of course, a corresponding extension of the horizons and possibilities for publicity techniques.

The content of a newspaper is the material—pictorial or written—which is included in the news, editorial, and feature columns of the paper for reading by the public. The content sources are many—happenings or events that make news, stories and events set up by public relations men, press conferences and interviews, and other news-making devices.

A newspaper consists of a number of news columns, exclusive of advertising space. Almost everything in the columns of the paper which is not paid advertising may be classified as news—news which occurs spontaneously or publicity-inspired news. Many newspapers have pictorial material, many include comics, virtually all have editorial cartoons. Almost every newspaper has its news subdivisions—sports, society, women's pages, and so forth. What is included and what is omitted in certain newspapers depends upon format, advertising, and reader interest. The function of the newspaper, in large part, is to provide interesting data for the audience which reads it. Apart from the news coverage, the newspaper tends to print partly what the readers want and partly what the editor deems important material.

These aspects are significant from the viewpoint of publicity. Although many stories may be identically worded for all newspapers, special stories and features need special angles in order to meet the needs of the particular paper. For the newspaper, perhaps more accurately than any other medium, reflects the attitudes, moods, wants, satisfactions, and desires of its readers. The newspaper, is, from this human interest aspect, the most respected and the most acceptable of the mass media. And, for this reason, the strategy in most public relations campaigns is based primarily upon the newspaper and adapted to the other media. In addition, however, there is a more tangible reason for basing the campaign on the foundation of the newspaper. The newspaper is not as flexible a medium as are radio and television. It is not as amenable to quick and easy change. The press remains the bedrock of our web of communications from a public relations viewpoint. The press does not undergo the need for constant shifts in entertainment emphasis. Its reader interest is consistent, high, and durable. Radio and television, on the other hand, accomplish objectives which are beyond the ken of the newspaper. Electronic journalism has done a superb job of reporting.

The newspaper, of course, does change its content to meet changing conditions, and public relations men must be alert to these changes for they reflect social needs, demands, and upheavals. Since World War II, for example, there has been a greater emphasis on foreign affairs, on places and people heretofore unfamiliar to the American reader. Government news and business content have also increased, particularly since the growth of such symbols as the "New Deal," the "Fair Deal" and, more recently, the doctrine of "dynamic conservatism." Federal aid to education has given school news a more prominent place in the news context of the paper.

## FUNCTION OF THE PRESS

Journalism scholars have given considerable attention to the function of the newspaper. What, for example, should the press strive to accomplish in a democratic society? What is its basic obligation as a mass medium? Certainly, as a medium of communication, the press has certain ethical obligations. It is expected to print the "truth," to expose cant, to help preserve civil liberties. The function of a newspaper, according to the Canons of Journalism of the American Newspaper Publishers Association, is "to communicate to the human race what its members do, feel and think." A summary of the Canons of Journalism follows:

1. *Responsibility:* The press must be responsible for what it prints. It must be concerned with the public welfare.
2. *Freedom of the press:* The press must be free to discuss and print the news without undue restriction.
3. *Independence:* The press must be free of any ties, except the

public interest, i.e., it must not be obliged to promote private or selfish interests, nor must it print editorials that knowingly subvert the truth.

4. *Sincerity, truthfulness, accuracy:* The newspaper must print the facts and must be careful that the headline does not distort or convey a false impression of the story that follows.

5. *Impartiality:* With the exception of signed articles, the press must be free of bias or opinion.

6. *Fair play:* The press must not invade private rights or feelings. It must correct mistakes. It must not publish charges without the right of rebuttal from the accused.

7. *Decency:* The press must not publish lurid matter or material inimical to the general welfare.

The question arises Can the press fulfill these functions and obligations at all times and under all circumstances? Can it report, impartially, the *facts* about what people do, think, and feel? For this reportorial function is not identical with reporting the truth. What people think, do, and feel also may not be identical with truth. But the press proposes to report *truthfully* about the patterns of human behavior, not about truth itself. Indeed, it is questionable whether, in a literal sense, the press is obliged to function in terms of seeking and reporting fundamental truths. The *Times* does not say that it will print all the news that's true; it says it functions to present "all the news that's fit to print."

The question of truth versus news is one which embraces the particular area of public relations known as press relations. While ethical public relations should function to make facts and information available, are there not exploitation "gimmicks" or special events which do not concern themselves with any truths but which may make an interesting feature story for the paper while interpolating a favorable mention or plug for the client? Those who have criticized the press vis-à-vis public relations have pointed out that the press offers, because of circulation and advertising problems, open sesame to the gimmick story, the inconsequential, and the sensational. Advertising and public relations pressures, it is claimed, prevent the press from giving an impartial evaluation of business issues. And, finally, the press itself is not impartial because it is, in itself, controlled by a special interest group which, in turn, is controlled by the advertiser.

The press, therefore, has a public relations problem of its own as do all of the mass media. It is a problem which is of some concern to students of mass communication, for it raises the issue of a controlled press versus a free press. Business interests, represented through advertising and public relations, are not the basic issue. The issue is simply one in which the newspaper, in many areas of the United States, has an implicit monopoly over news and editorial matter *because* there is no growing competition. We have tended to become a nation of one-newspaper towns, except for large metropolitan areas—and even a city such as New York has seen giant newspapers merge their identity in the last decade. Even where there is more than one paper in a city, the chances are that both may be under the supervision of the same interested party. And, where there are chains of newspapers, it is anticipated that an editorial policy will assume an inevitable sameness for all individual papers in the chain.

In addition to the narrowing circumference of individual control, there are the press associations and wire services. These manifest both the positive and negative aspects of mass communication. Press associations are a boon to journalistic efficiency because they are fast, economical, and convenient. They render a tremendous public service by gathering and disseminating the news for, and to, blocks of newspapers. The three great associations, Associated Press, United Press, and International

News Service—plus the many smaller services—achieve a re-markable feat of immediacy and accuracy in reporting and distributing the news. But they also achieve an inevitable concentration which, in itself, is not unfavorable provided that those who operate the channels of communication do so with a sense of responsibility to the public. The era of such individual entrepreneur enterprises in American journalism as William Allen White's Emporia *Gazette* is disappearing, and the public is partly responsible. Mass communication techniques have developed a new kind of reader, and this reader now demands a new kind of news. The average small town cannot meet the demand for variegated content, and the newspaper must either join a large news service or become part of a larger chain in order to secure the services which the reader demands—syndicated columns, cartoons, and features which are now being sold on an across-the-board basis.

There are, of course, safeguards to the dangers of monopoly. We have mentioned the responsibility of the press itself. Public opinion is another safeguard. Competitive media, such as the radio, are also safeguards, although the tendency has grown for a newspaper owner to buy and operate the local broadcasting outlet as well. In the long run, competition is not the basic answer to the possibility of monopoly. The answer lies in the survival and healthy state of our democratic institutions, including the press, along with the degree of enlightenment and interest in public affairs manifested by the receiving audience. The school, the church, and the home are, therefore, as directly concerned with the preservation of a free and responsible press as are those who operate the newspapers.

Indeed, it must be questioned seriously whether competition *as such* between the press and other media is a healthy influence. For, competition may not lead to an improvement in service, but rather to an ever increasing and intensified effort to build circulation and attract new advertisers. The result may not be an improvement in services, but a pandering to sensationalism. And, at the same time, competition does not necessarily preclude monopoly, particularly if the competition is of the identical, or similar, coloration and motivation. In the last analysis the independence of the news and its integrity depend upon the independence and integrity of the editor, the ethics of the publicists who release the news grist, and the degree of culture and enlightenment of the community of readers which comprises a communication medium's public. The most reputable newspapers offer a public service by opening their letters-to-the-editor columns to the receiving audience. There, conflict of interest and disagreements with news or editorial policy can be stated openly.

## THE PUBLICIST

It has been estimated that a very large proportion of what is printed in the newspaper is the result of the efforts of press agents, publicity men, and public relations men. One editor stated that his desk received enough news releases and feature stories, *in one day,* to fill the pages of an average novel! What press release material is accepted and what rejected depend upon many variables—the pressure of news events, the policy of the paper, the inventiveness of the publicist. But it is certainly safe to say that what does get into the paper as a result of publicity must be predicated fairly accurately upon an understanding of what a newspaper is, of how it functions, of what it stands for to its readers.

The choice of newspaper content is, of course, of considerable importance for the publicist. The average newspaper seeks a least common denominator. It seeks to determine what its content should be for the "average" reader. The publicist seeks, in servicing the newspaper, to present release and feature material which coheres with the common denominator. The selection of content, over a long period of time, has varied with changing social and economic conditions, but certain subjects have become news staples primarily because they are thought to contain the basic human interest ingredients that cut across all publics to reach the average reader: children, animals, sex, crime, religion. The publicist's choice of picture material is, therefore, not capricious. It is based on the aforementioned newsworthy ingredients, i.e.:

1. A political anniversary picture may include, deliberately, the young *child* of a Senator helping to cut the birthday cake.
2. A figure seeking public support might be sure to include his *dog* in the photographs or, if feasible, on television. A vice-presidential candidate's reference to his dog in a famous pre-election television address aroused a storm of protest from the Democratic press which cried, "Republican public relations!"
3. The *cheese-cake* picture almost always has a good chance of breaking into the newspaper.
4. *Crime* has been almost traditionally front page news in most newspapers.
5. Stories and pictures which have a *religious* or spiritual aspect also have a better than average chance of breaking into the press.

There are exceptions, of course, but they prove rather than disprove the rule. Great newspapers have departed from these criteria, but not entirely. The creed of the New York *Times* is "all the news that's fit to print." But most newspapers do not enjoy either the advertising or the content values of the *Times,* which offers the greatest challenge to the integrity and ingenuity of public relations men because it will seldom print deliberate "plugs" or "puff" publicity. The publicity release must, in content and news value, conform to the *Times* criterion of what is fit to print.

The profession of journalism has been acutely aware of its obligations to the public. The public relations practitioner who understands these ethical concepts can operate more intelligently vis-à-vis the press—and perhaps more successfully—than the one who does not. For, while they are philosophical concepts rather than practical or procedural guides, they have succeeded in setting up a frame of reference for the behavior of the press in its relation to the public. A similar frame of reference also has been set up by practitioners of public relations through the establishment of such professional organizations as the Public Relations Society of America which is concerned, among other things, with the elevating of public relations to a solid and respectable status in the universe of mass communication.

# CHAPTER 12

## *The Broadcasting Media*

Radio and television—the broadcasting media—offer productive avenues for effective advertising, publicity, and promotion. These all-pervading media are profoundly capable of informing, educating, entertaining, and influencing the thoughts and habit patterns of their millions of listeners and viewers. They are important agencies for opinion formation and opinion change. Like all media, they are as capable of transmitting a new and progressive idea as they are of preserving moth-eaten and atavistic institutions. However, radio and TV represent a progressive idea in mass communication.

In evaluating the broadcasting media from a public relations viewpoint, two considerations should be noted. There is, first, the place of radio and television as communication media, and this consideration has public relations implications. And, secondly, there is the aspect of function, or the application of publicity techniques to each of the media. This second function— how the publicity man can secure mentions or "plugs" over the air—we reserve for a consideration of publicity areas. In this context, we are concerned with the broadcast media from the standpoint of their history and structure and with some of their problems from a public relations point of view. As in the case of the newspaper, no one expects the public relations man to command a scholarly grasp of the history of broadcasting. But, here again, the practitioner who knows the field, from the standpoint of its historical highlights as well as its structure, function, and problems, is in a position to work with greater confidence and with a knowledgeable grasp of his material.

Consider the staggering impact, actual and potential, of the broadcast media on public opinion. Consider their influence not only in terms of what people say, but in terms of what they do! Practically every home in the United States boasts at least one radio. In fact, the average is two or three, plus a car radio. Portable sets and transistors are contributing further to the approximately 13,000,000 radios sold per annum in recent years. Most recent estimates place the number of radios at about 150,000,000 and the number of television receivers at about 43,000,000. Independent stations as well as the networks and their affiliates literally blanket the country with news, information, and entertainment. The public can be reached through 3,024 AM radio stations and 540 FM operating stations; and through 477 commercial television stations and 23 educational stations—a total which will increase when the Federal Communications Commission decides what final disposition it will make of the remaining channels reserved for educational institutions and the ultra-high-frequency channels which are not as yet activated. About 40 percent of all AM radio stations, incidentally, are affiliated with networks.

With the exception of the area broadly termed "educational" programming, the commercial radio and television stations are supported by advertisers. As truly *mass* media, radio and television attract the largest audiences of all the communication media. Their product is programming—entertainment, informational, or public service, and they strive to present what is called a "balanced schedule" in the best interest of the listeners or viewers. The Federal Communications Commission, contrary to popular belief, does not regulate or control broadcasting, nor does it function to interfere with program content. As we shall see, it functions as a kind of traffic cop of the airways, seeing to it that appropriate allocations are made, that there is no spectrum space interference. It grants licenses to stations on the proviso that they function "in the public interest, convenience, and necessity" and may renew licenses, after three years, on the basis of how ably the station fulfills the broad stipulations of the grant.

The most arresting aspect of broadcasting is its tumultuous and rapid growth. In less than half a century, radio and television have paced all other media. They, more than any other, are responsible for our contemporary absorption in mass communication. They have, apart from their social, economic, and political significance, revolutionized the technique of advertising, and certainly they have broadened the base of the publicity and promotional operation. They have become a new branch of the press, functioning to report the news with incredible immediacy and accuracy.

## HISTORICAL HIGHLIGHTS

At the beginning of the twentieth century, the press was established as the most powerful medium of communication. The phrase "mass media" had little relevance to the term as it is used today. Publicity techniques were directed to the newspaper, occasionally to the magazine, almost never to the book. But the development of the wireless by Marconi in 1895 marked the true beginning of the era of mass communication. The impact of this invention and of what followed has yet to be fully appraised by social scientists. For the developments were not slow, once they gathered momentum. The revolution in social and cultural habits wrought by radio was followed by the equally great impact of television which, in about a decade, has provoked momentous changes in such areas as advertising and selling, in education, in reading and movie attendance, and, indeed, in the family living room. It has also made more subtle but no less significant changes in other media such as the newspaper, motion picture, book, and magazine. The broadcast media underscored the *mass* in the communication process.

Four years after the development of the first wireless signal, Marconi (in 1895) flashed a signal across the English Channel. Meanwhile, pioneer experiments were also taking place in the United States, culminating (in 1906) in the invention of the audion tube by Lee De Forest and in a broadcast, through De Forest radiophone, of Caruso singing at the Metropolitan Opera House in New York City in 1910. In 1912, the value of wireless in emergency was demonstrated during the S.S. *Titanic* disaster.

What was eventually to become radio, as we know it today, was being pursued relentlessly in the research laboratories of Westinghouse; and, in 1920, radio broadcasting began with the Westinghouse station KDKA in Pittsburgh sending out the Harding-Cox election returns. The result was, literally as well as figuratively, electrifying. By about 1922, more than five hundred stations were on the air. In 1923, the first telephone broadcast linked New York and Boston, and a multiple-station hookup by wire was established among stations WEAF, New York; WGY, Schenectady; KDKA, Pittsburgh; and KYW, Chicago. A major move was undertaken by the American Telephone and Telegraph when, in the fall of 1922, it agreed to accept *paid advertising* over its outlet, WEAF. The implications of this move are plain when viewed in historical perspective, although it is doubtful whether anyone could have predicted the consequences—multimillion-dollar radio and television programming and gigantic advertising and public relations expenditures.

But the growing importance of the medium created public relations problems. Even in its early stages of development, broadcasting was subjected to pressures.

However, public relations problems were paralleled by public relations opportunities. Vast listening audiences and, therefore, vast areas for informing public opinion became available with the development of line linkage between station and station and city and city. Independently operated stations became affiliated with WEAF, and within a few years the famous Red Network boasted a total of twenty-six stations from the East to the Middle West. These stations were owned by the American Telephone and Telegraph Company. Meanwhile, RCA had gathered several stations into its orbit. American Telephone and Telegraph, however, decided to give up its interest in broadcasting, and RCA, which had set up the National Broadcasting Company as a subsidiary, acquired WEAF and the Red Network. For several years, RCA held both the Red and Blue Networks until forced to divorce its dual holdings. In 1927, the Columbia Broadcasting System had gone on the air with a basic network of sixteen stations. Eventually, the emerging pattern of broadcasting saw the development of four major networks—the Columbia Broadcasting System, the National Broadcasting Company, the American Broadcasting Company, and the Mutual Broadcasting System.

The growth of broadcasting created technical as well as public relations problems, resulting in the establishment of the

Federal Radio Commission (later the Federal Communications Commission) in 1927. The Commission did more than clear channels. In 1932, after a six-month investigation of broadcasting practices, it concluded that any pressure "to eliminate the use of radio facilities for commercial advertising purposes will, if adopted, destroy the present system of broadcasting."

One of the major problems of broadcasting was access to syndicated news. In 1933, for example, the Associated Press membership voted against network broadcasts of AP news. Subsequently, the American Newspaper Publishers Association determined that radio logs were advertising and should be paid for—a far cry from the extensive radio and television schedules and the general publicity coverage accorded these media in the press of today. The Columbia Broadcasting System thereupon set about to organize a nationwide news staff to gather the news for network broadcasting. Eventually, however, the three major press syndicates (AP, UP, and INS) agreed to provide material for morning and evening broadcasts. Eventually, the press syndicates not only supplied news to the networks, but also sold news to sponsors—a significant decision because it established another regular avenue of news. Today probably no medium supersedes the immediacy and simultaneity of radio in the spot coverage of the news as it happens—one of the significant results of the establishment, in 1933, of its own news bureau by CBS.

The elimination of immediate areas of competition between press and the broadcast media proved a service not only to the public, but also to the public relations man. As newspapers established radio and television listings as well as columns, news features, and pictures, a vast new area was opened for publicity techniques. And, conversely, the press ultimately became amenable to publicity which emanated directly from the networks. While the media are still in competition for the advertising allocation, the competition is no longer mutually exclusive. To reach *all* of the publics, the advertiser cannot neglect any of the media. They have all become inextricable parts of a total communications framework. Their effect on public opinion is discrete, but it is also total and cumulative.

Although radio and the press were competitive media, publishers were alert to the economic possibilities of broadcasting. In 1935, Scripps-Howard decided to enter radio and applied for clearance to buy a station in Cincinnati as well as in other areas. Slowly, the newspaper publishers—and even some of the motion picture companies—acquired broadcasting facilities. In 1936, for example, Hearst radio acquired several stations in Texas and Oklahoma. The year 1936, incidentally, was a notable one for other reasons. It marked the first delineation of FM, a new "high fidelity" kind of broadcasting as well as the first demonstrated tests of television. By 1940, the first sponsored television program, a newscast, was transmitted, marking another milestone in the growth of broadcasting as a mass medium. In 1941, the FCC authorized full commercial operation of television.

Each forward step in the amazing growth of broadcasting was attended by problems in the arena of public opinion. Questions of obligation and responsibility continued to crop up. Finally, in 1946, the FCC issued its famous *Blue Book* on the "Public Service Responsibility of Broadcast Licensees" which marked out the criteria on which the FCC would give particular consideration for the renewal of station licenses. These included: carrying of sustaining programs, local live programs, and programs devoted to discussion or public issues. A significant criterion, also, was the elimination of advertising "excesses."

From 1948 onward, television literally entered the picture. Its growth has undoubtedly been more powerful and more all-pervading than any other single medium. For a time, as TV grew with boundless energy, radio faced a serious threat to its communication lifeline, but recently it has bounded back with renewed vitality as advertisers are finding that it can do many things which cannot be accomplished by television—and do them economically, efficiently, and frequently. But the motion picture industry has suffered from the competition of television, so much so that it has had to reorient its whole approach to the economics of production, distribution, and exhibition. Not only has television proved a major force in advertising; it has provided opportunities for educational, political, and cultural broadcasting as well. Television now offers unique coverage, along with the press and radio, of political conventions. It brought the Metropolitan Opera into the home with the telecast of *Othello* in full from the stage.

In 1948, the FCC had placed a "freeze" on TV station allocations, pending a survey of the entire spectrum. Finally, in 1952, the freeze was lifted, and the FCC revealed its final allocation plan, with 12 very-high-frequency channels; opening of the ultra-high-frequency band; and allocating 262 stations, in both VHF and UHF bands, for the exclusive use of colleges and other educational institutions. But this "final" Sixth Report and Order of the FCC was not to provide the ultimate in solutions. At the present time, the Commission still faces the formidable problems of what to do about the still unused and reserved channels for education, the ultra-high band, and the pros and cons of controversy which whirl about the problem of toll television.

## RADIO, TELEVISION, AND OTHER MEDIA

The broadcast media—radio and television—offer a productive avenue for effective advertising and publicity. They are profoundly capable of informing, entertaining, and influencing the thoughts and habits of millions of viewers and listeners. They are important agents of opinion formation and change and, therefore, of seminal importance to the public relations practitioner.

Of all the mass media of communication, the radio is still, despite the rapid growth of television, the most readily accessible to the public. Television has made enormous strides, and the development of movable and portable sets has increased the incidence of TV viewing in the home, but radio still sets a unique pace when compared with both television and other mass media. That television has changed the character and, perhaps, purpose of broadcasting, however, cannot be gainsaid. There are those who once claimed that, for publicity purposes, television has almost brought radio to total eclipse, for the public is where television can be seen. The radio network research experts, however, have ample proof to show that radio and television are not competitive, but complementary. Television does an effective but expensive job at certain times, but both network and local radio do an equally effective and less expensive job at times appropriate to radio listening.

Radio as a communication medium offers the phenomenon of pure sound. Television combines sight and sound. Obviously, the communications act differs in the case of radio from the communications act in the media of television, the newspaper, or motion pictures. Television, for example, adds sight to sound but loses the unique impact of sound alone because of the need to apply two of the senses instead of one. Both radio and television offer the undoubted advantages of immediacy. However, where the reader of the newspaper may reread and reflect, the broadcast media offer less pause for reflection. The impact is immediate, and it is followed immediately by additional sight or sound content. But radio programs are preserved by means of tape recording, and the kinescope lends permanence to the telecast. Video tape recording requires no processing and allows for immediate playback.

This phenomenon of immediacy offers advantages from a public relations viewpoint, but it also presents a publicity challenge. It behooves the publicity and advertising man, for example, to devise a strategy of repetition in the use of the broadcast media. A round-the-clock telethon may raise funds for a charitable cause because of the unusual nature of the program and the personalities involved. But the sale of an institution, product, or idea requires repetition based on careful selection of times and of the use of appropriate broadcast medium for the times selected. Radio is particularly important as a repetitive medium.

From a public relations viewpoint, it is important to bear in mind that fundamentally the broadcast media are part of the same social universe of discourse as are the other avenues of mass communication. They are, like the newspaper and motion pictures, products of our general institutional behavior. They are influenced by, and in turn influence, our "cultural lag." They reflect public opinions and needs, and they tend to create and change these opinions and needs. They are part of a total act of intercommunication or interaction between the human organism and his environment, but they contribute mightily to the molding of that environment.

The paradoxical aspect of the widespread use of radio and TV for advertising and promotion purposes is evident in the very history of broadcasting. For the fact is that the first sponsors did not discern that broadcast media had any appreciable impact on the public's buying habits; nor did they foresee that radio and television would become invaluable adjuncts to the public relations–advertising campaign. The employment of the media for advertising was tentative. Sponsors had no abiding faith in the ability of radio to sell products. And the reason for this inertia was simply the reason underlying all resistance to change. It meant adapting, against prevailing habit, new patterns of behavior, new stereotypes, new modes of action. The established institutions, the conventional communication media, were the newspaper and the magazine. No one could predict with certainty that, within twenty-five years, the broadcast media were to establish a new frame of reference, a new concept of advertising and publicity techniques.

Slowly, but surely, the growing profession of public relations recognized that the broadcast media offered vast and deep penetration. They offered a mass market, exposed totally and simultaneously, to the public relations message and to the advertising copy line. By careful measurement of the audience and its habits, by constant reiteration and repetition of the message, what heretofore uncultivated areas might be developed? When the electrifying possibilities became manifest, however, public relations and advertising took on a new dimension in the social and economic structure.

These developments, healthy from a business and entertainment viewpoint, nevertheless brought about strictures from pressure and special interest publics. The educators, for example, demanded channels for their own exclusive use, claiming that commercial broadcasting could not, under current economic conditions, service minority groups. But these representations were not based entirely on fact. For the fact remains that the broadcasting industry did develop programs of an educational, informational, and public service character. The networks made important contributions in the field of original drama, in stimulating an appreciation of music, and, particularly, in the area of social and political education. And, although programs were related to company and product, many of the larger sponsors relegated hard sell in favor of sponsoring institutional programs, such as concerts, opera, drama, and forums.

The program content of radio and television cannot be schematized precisely, but it does reveal certain characteristics of which those who would use the media for public relations purposes should be aware. Almost all content includes music, as part of the dramatic or comic continuity—or as such. Drama is also a formidable part of the communication content. Daytime serials consume several hours each day and are supplemented by many other half-hour and hour-long dramatic shows. News, talks, and other public service programs are daily phenomena. The commercial, of course, is the inevitable trademark of all sponsored programs, and it is devised by the advertising agency. But the publicity and promotional aspects of public relations are also very much in evidence. Giveaways, prizes, and contests are an amalgam of the efforts of the advertising man and the promotional expert. Publicity men also have developed a new and important area of talent representation. The networks themselves have now undertaken to publicize programs, both sponsored and unsponsored, as the result of the establishment of radio and television pages and listings in the newspapers. Radio and TV publicists are concerned as much with the exploitation of the program, the product, and the personality as they are with the public relations of the network. New areas of liaison or "tie-in" have been developed with motion picture studios and even with the press. From the standpoint of publicity, the broadcast media have magnificent scope.

It is not unusual that such media as radio and television should attract the attention of various special interest groups.

Educators, civic groups, and other social, economic, and political agencies have displayed, almost from the very beginning, an absorbing interest in the broadcasting media. The reason is, of course, the tremendous importance of broadcasting from a social, economic, and cultural point of view. Radio and television reach the eye and ear of millions upon millions with entertainment, information, and public service. From time to time, therefore, the Congress has investigated broadcasting practices through its various committees.

## NETWORK BROADCASTING

The place of network broadcasting—what it is, what it does, how it operates—has been described by Frank Stanton, president of the Columbia Broadcasting System, Inc., in a statement before the Senate Committee on Interstate and Foreign Commerce in June, 1956. Some excerpts follow:

One of its most essential functions is to provide *instantaneous national interconnection* day in, day out, between great cities and small towns throughout the length and breadth of America. It does so in more permutations and combinations than can be calculated. It does so for purposes ranging all the way from entertainment, through the presentation of unique-on-the-spot coverage of such essentials to our Government as the national political conventions and elections to be held this year—through this, I say, to the instantaneous alertment of the public in time of national crisis. No such facilities ever existed before the creation of the networks, nothing except networks can serve these functions, and nothing now imagined can take their essential place. . . .

The first, the absolutely primary, aspect of a network is its relationship to the public. A network renders its service to nothing else, and to nothing smaller, than the *national* American public. This service is its touchstone. . . .

Once you take your eye off the national American public you enter endless realms of conflict and confusion. . . .

## The Role of the Advertiser

The second aspect of a network is its relationship to advertising, and this rests upon its primary relationship to the national public.

A great deal of the criticism of networks springs from a lack of understanding of how network services are paid for. The support of all who contribute to the technical and creative aspects of network television comes, very simply, from the advertiser. Directly he supports programs of entertainment. Directly and indirectly he supports programs of information, news and public affairs.

Network television is in direct and strenuous competition with all other media for the advertising dollar. Advertisers use network television only when they are convinced that it is an economical and effective means of delivering messages to the people and thus stimulating product sales. The total effect of these dollar expenditures far transcends their specific effect in supporting the television networks' economy. Since our over-all economy is based upon efficient distribution of information about products, network television advertising represents an important factor in supporting the high level of our economy which relies on mass production and mass consumption.

But the advertiser is not required by law to spend his money with television—either nationally through a network or market by market directly through stations. If advertisers felt that network advertising had less value than spot advertising, they would use spot. If they felt other media were preferable they would never have come to television in the first place, or stayed with it very long. . . .

## The Role of the Networks

Without the networks' courage in taking enormous financial risks and investing vigorous energy, there would not have been the programs to stimulate the public to acquire sets at the rate it did. Without receivers in the homes, there would not have been the advertisers to invest in the medium and insure the continuation of the programming. . . .

*Networks serve the public:* Through network programming the American public—from coast-to-coast and border-to-border—receives a richness and diversity of entertainment and culture and information unavailable to even the wealthiest families living in major metropolitan centers a few short years ago. Today, through the networks and with the single requirement of a television set in working order, the entire nation can see programs as diverse as the Sadler's Wells Ballet, the World Series, *Peter Pan, The $64,000 Question, The Caine Mutiny Court-Martial,* a debate between Paul Butler and Leonard Hall, *Disneyland,* and a discussion by Joseph Welch on the Constitution —all of them free. . . .

Only networks can efficiently supply advertisers with nationwide television coverage. Through a single order advertisers are assured of the simultaneous exposure of their messages in all markets and as part of a rounded program schedule—in which each program reinforces and adds value to every other program in the schedule. Advertisers' increasing use of network television testifies to their endorsement of the network's function in providing these efficiencies in the marketing and distribution of their products.

## News and Public Affairs

One of the most vital of the network's functions is performed by the CBS News and Public Affairs Department. Through it the network fulfills its responsibility as a medium of mass communication by providing the public with news, science, religious, education and public affairs programs.

Only a network that is financially healthy could fully perform these functions. For the CBS News and Public Affairs operation represents a substantial loss. Few Public Affairs programs are sponsored. One program series, for example, *The Search* which reported the research projects of different colleges and universities, took 3½ years to produce. More than $750,000 was spent on it, without recovering any of this cost through sponsorship. The department, with an annual operating budget of $7 million, comprises 103 full-time employees and employs 600 contract and free-lance correspondents at 263 locations throughout the world.

Only a network could maintain a department to produce, and supply at no charge to stations, programs in the field of *education,* such as *The Search, Adventure,* which was produced in conjunction with the American Museum of Natural History; Report Card, a special five-program series devoted to schools and education; such weekly *religious* programs as *Look Up and Live, Lamp unto My Feet,* which, through long-standing CBS policy, are withheld from sale or sponsorship by any groups.

Similarly, only a network could produce and supply programs in the field of *public affairs*—by providing such series as *Face the Nation; Years of Crisis,* a live broadcast in which CBS News correspondents, flown to New York from their overseas posts, discussed the year's most significant events; *The U.N. in Action;* such science programs as the hour-and-a-half *Out of Darkness* which examined through case histories the problems of mental health.

Although this description concerns television, it is also applicable to network radio broadcasting.

## SIGNIFICANCE OF BROADCAST MEDIA

Obviously, the extent of network operations literally demands the term "mass" communication. For television and radio, along with the press and the motion picture, have made the force of communication the most important and powerful force in the contemporary world. Television and radio, through the electronic miracle of sight and sound, have set the frame of reference for greater social or group cohesiveness. They have enlarged experience from the circumscribed to the infinite. And, albeit from a vicarious point of view, they have brought about a sense of public participation in the event. There is a strong sense of participation in the Metropolitan Opera broadcasts, in the Kefauver crime hearings, in political conventions, sporting events, and other phenomena.

This sense of participation has great significance for public relations techniques. It develops a sense of potential energy in the receiving audience which is translatable into the kinetic. The public can be influenced to buy the product, to listen to a candidate, to evaluate a point of view. Participation occurs, of course, in other media as well. The motion picture viewer is a participant, but the experience is more remote. Radio and television offer a sense of the immediate. They are also gregarious influences—far more so than the newspaper or the film. The influence of motion pictures on public opinion is, in the long run, more indirect and less incisive than the broadcast media. The motion picture brings the individual out of this world. The radio and television never lose the sense of identity. Similarly, the broadcast media offer a stronger sense of the immediate and the personal than does the newspaper. The speech which is heard and seen on television may be read in the morning paper. But the experience is more remote. No news report or reproduction of a speech can produce the emotional response of participation.

If public relations techniques are to be successful, particularly when applied to the broadcast media, they must produce some sense of participation and of social obligation, along with some stimulus to eventual action. And to insure the achievement of these objectives, public relations techniques, when applied to the broadcast media, should evoke from the receiving audience at least:

1. An implicit—or explicit—agreement that the receiving audience will *consent* to participate, i.e., to view or listen.
2. An implicit agreement that others in the social group will also consent to participate.
3. An implicit agreement that the receiving audience will not be a passive one but will, although indirectly, act as though it is a participant in the event.

# CHAPTER 13

## The Motion Picture

The motion picture industry, and its component parts of production, distribution, and exhibition, comprises more than a medium of communication and an instrumentality of public relations. The industry, in each of its phases, has unique public relations problems of its own. Although all the media are peculiarly sensitive to public opinion, no particular area has been beset with as many strictures as has the film business. This is particularly evident in the distribution area where motion picture advertising and publicity come into play. For sheer promotional and exploitation techniques and for the exercise of press agentry, the movies, by their very content and by the intramural competitive problems which they face, are far and away superior to any of the other media. The stunt, the gimmick, and the tie-in probably originated in the flamboyant merchandising of motion pictures.

But the content of motion pictures, and some of the devices by which themes, titles, and personalities are exploited, generated problems for the industry in the arena of public opinion. Another causative factor, too, was the fact that in motion pictures many of the special pleaders, the do-gooders, and the pressure groups found a powerful agency for influencing the habits of the receiving audiences and, therefore, a vulnerable target for censorship and for criticism. More than any of the other media, the screen has been subjected to rather harsh censorship, sometimes justifiably so and sometimes without any foundation except the zeal of the professional reformer of public morality. A glance at the industry's advertising and publicity problems reveals that the motion picture industry is the least respected and the most criticized of any of the mass media by political, religious, educational, and other social pressure groups. The motion picture, therefore, must be a most potent medium in terms of its depth and penetration on the opinions, needs, frustrations, and aspirations of its audiences.

As the industry entered the 1950's, it began the second half-century of its existence. The screen has risen from a free-wheeling competitive infant to a gigantic monopoly and back again to a state of fierce competition and uncertainty as to its survival and its ultimate guise as an art form and a medium of mass communication. In a literal sense, motion pictures are more directly communicative than either press, magazines, book, or radio. Until the advent of television, they were the most direct of communication devices. But the popular movies, by their very nature, were not intended to generate reflective thought. They sought the common denominator of the median line, of the less literate and the less educated, at least until the use of the foreign film and the development of the "art house" type of exhibition. The printed page, on the other hand, depended upon the more literate public and designed its content for this group. The radio brought public service, information, and education into its orbit. But the appeal of the motion picture, from the standpoint of public opinion, was to the emotions and to the sensoria. And, as competition grew from television and from within the industry itself, the more titillating the content and the more flamboyant the merchandising, the more successful the product. No other medium has searched as relentlessly for its story content, and no other has put as much tension and drive into its advertising and publicity.

One of the reasons for this emphasis on publicity and promotion is, of course, that the industry always has a product which is ostensibly new. Each company is faced with the overwhelming task of launching a big new picture on an average of at least sixteen times each year, and this in the face of extremely fierce competition. It would be a Herculean task were it not for the fact that, partly by virtue of advertising expenditures and partly because of the public interest in movie personalities and stars, the motion picture has fairly wide acceptance in the press from a publicity viewpoint. At the present time, the industry's public relations problems have been accentuated owing to the decrease in attendance (and the corresponding decrease in the number of extant theatres).

## HISTORICAL HIGHLIGHTS

Sooner or later, in the evolution of communication, some form of expression such as the moving picture was bound to happen. Man had always sought, from the days of the Egyptian hieroglyphs and before, a graphic means of expressing himself. While the evolution from simpler forms into the motion picture involved basically the transference of a simple image from the static to the animated, the *mode* of presentation has become increasingly more involved and more scientific. Studies in the problems of tricky photography and of optical illusion, as well as research in the chemistry and physics laboratories, have given rise to such technical phenomena as the anamorphic lens, three-dimensional viewers, variable screen ratios, and so forth.

But the motion picture, despite experimental efforts toward art, artistry, and complexity such as in *Moby Dick,* has remained basically a simple form of communication; and its public relations has involved the more obvious and less subtle techniques of press agentry, promotion, and advertising.

Although there was some sporadic research in the preceding years, the development of moving pictures began in the last decade of the nineteenth century. The device was called a "kinetoscope," invented by Thomas Alva Edison, and its operation was of the peep-show type. Significantly, this first experiment at the Edison laboratory in West Orange, New Jersey, used the Eastman process, a technique which is still in use in its present highly perfected form.

The invention did not create a furor in the arena of public opinion, either among the consumers or among the research personnel. In the Edison scheme of things, the motion picture kinetoscope was a mere by-product of other, more important devices. However, tentative efforts were made to demonstrate the moving picture at the Kinetoscope Parlor on Broadway, in New York City. Only one person could look at the peep-show apparatus at a time. The invention was not an immediate and tumultuous success, although it aroused interest among promoters both in the United States and abroad.

Since one viewer at a time hardly presaged a mass market, arrangements were perfected to process the moving picture on a screen so that a group of persons could view it simultaneously. This improvement led the moving picture to become, for some time, an added attraction to the growing vogue of vaudeville. The improvement, however, was significant because it attracted promoters and investors. The result was a flagrant period of pirating of plots and content and of copyright infringement—a frenetic beginning for an industry which has never been free of intramural problems and internecine strife.

Historically, America's first literal *motion picture* was *The Great Train Robbery,* presented in 1903. It was to become the progenitor of a long line of exciting westerns, based traditionally on the twin themes of banditry and the exhausting chase. It later played, at the price of one nickel, to capacity audiences at the Nickelodeon Theatre in Pittsburgh. This "first" in bona fide motion picture production gave impetus to a number of similar ventures throughout the country. Significantly, they were of great interest to the foreign-born, for this rising tide of immigration brought thousands who could not as yet read or write but who could understand and enjoy the moving pictures.

The business, while highly competitive even in its early days, developed a pattern and a form. Studios, of a sort, sprang up in Fort Lee, New Jersey, and in other environs of New York City. Plots were repeated ad nauseam, and stories were stolen without scruple from authors and publishers. The screen, from a public opinion and public relations standpoint, was free with regard to choice of content, but there was some tentative censorship which plagued the more suggestive attractions. Meanwhile, the financial world cast an eye on the industry, a move which accelerated its growth and continued until the present period when banking and other financial interests have a firm grip on the finances and destinies of many of the major companies. A company formed earlier and known as the American Mutoscope and Biograph Company was reorganized. A patent and licensing arrangement was established to bring some order into the chaotic state of affairs. The precursor of the current National Board of Review was set up in an organization called, formidably, The National Board of Censorship.

Production growth was followed by the development of a system of exhibition. The General Film Company, for example, established a system of so-called exchanges where films could be marketed—a system which has persisted until today's critical days where the companies speak of pooling distribution methods as an economy measure. The General Film group flourished. Each member of the organization was allocated one day weekly for showing film. Meanwhile, the Biograph Company, under the leadership of one D. W. Griffith, was also finding favor. Audiences for motion pictures were growing. The medium was reaching across all strata of society. Admission prices doubled from five cents to a dime—considerably less than the admission tax which prevails today. And the movies developed artistically, as Griffith introduced the close-up and other techniques. From about 1912 until 1918 or 1920, there were more than 25,000 flourishing theatres. The number today is slightly more than half, including drive-ins.

This second decade of the twentieth century has seen the most signficant development of the motion picture as a business and as an art form. Griffith, the artist, was followed by Adolph Zukor, the businessman. The screen evolved from a series of pictures to a single motion picture, the feature film. Personalities began to emerge as Famous Players Lasky organized under the slogan, "Famous Players in Famous Plays." And the screen was given its strongest impetus with the production, in 1915, of D. W. Griffith's *The Birth of a Nation,* a true milestone in the development of the motion picture industry.

As the public for motion pictures grew, the theatres also grew larger and more plush. Rising public interest and support inevitably gave rise to a need for information and merchandising devices. Newspaper publicity began to take shape. Some papers, as a circulation-promotion effort, began serializing stories simultaneously with their exhibition on the screen. Publishers such as Joseph M. Patterson, a potent name in journalism, were early devotees of the screen. The newspaper, facing potential competition from the screen, not only met the "crisis" by using more pictorial material in its pages; it was forced also to cover screen events and personalities in order to meet the demand on the part of the public for news of the screen world. And out of this growing need developed the screen press agent and the techniques of publicity, promotion, and exploitation.

The motion picture not only developed creatively, but also became one of America's burgeoning industries. Star salaries soared to astronomical figures, far beyond the stipend which players conceivably could command either on vaudeville or on the legitimate stage. It was the high cost of star salaries, paradoxically, which was to cause a reversal in policy after World War II when rising costs and the competition of television forced the studios to rescind expensive contracts and to make arrangements for a percentage basis, predicated on talent for each picture, rather than on a per annum contract basis.

## MOTION PICTURES AND PUBLIC OPINION

The acceptance of the motion picture on the part of the public—an acceptance which was accelerated greatly by the high-pressure publicity techniques and the front page news of the escapades of the stars—resulted in the building of large and sumptuous "showcase" theatres for the Hollywood product. Theatres capable of seating capacity audiences of several thousand, such as the Roxy and the Radio City Music Hall, flourished in major markets. But the marketing of films was not restricted to the United States. World War I proved a tremendous impetus to the growth of the American motion picture, for the screen found a world market which continued unabated until the economic freeze which tied up currency until well after World War II and caused many American companies to make films abroad with so-called frozen funds.

The motion picture became more than a luxury, at least until the advent of television. It became a week-in, week-out necessity for millions of families. The money was available for this kind of luxury spending, and the dollars poured into the box office of the theatres and also into the distributing and producing centers in New York and Hollywood. Enormous budgets were set up and spent lavishly on advertising and promotion. The publicity and exploitation for one picture, for example, involved a cross-country special train tour for a group of Hollywood luminaries who were starred in the film.

But the industry, however able and flamboyant its publicity techniques, could not escape the opinion and propaganda machinery of pressure groups. For, it was realized that the screen, as a medium of mass communication, was capable of influencing the habits, morals, needs, drives, and aspirations of millions. The so-called fan magazines, with their inside stories of the private lives of the stars added grist to the publicity mill but did not escape the notice of those who were concerned with the influence of the stereotype of "Hollywood" on the youth. In 1922, after much pressure, a trade association was formed under the direction of movie czar Will H. Hays. Now known as the Motion Picture Association of America, and headed by Eric Johnston, this organization is the official voice, in the area of public opinion, of the major motion picture companies. The setting up of a trade association was followed by the establishment, largely under the guidance of Martin Quigley, Sr., of the so-called Production Code, the tenets of which were predicated largely on the use, or the misuse, of morality and sex. By and large, as a public relations measure, the studios have abided by the code, but there have been instances of late where more intrepid producers have flaunted the code as anachronistic and spurious.

In the past decade, the industry has seen decidedly rough sledding. The chief reason is, of course, the competition from television which uses, in a large measure, the technique of the moving picture on a screen but which does so under the auspices of a "live" entertainment situation—and for free. Another factor, however, was the germination of the government antitrust action. The government, before the war, filed suit against the "majors" in an effort to force a divorcement of production and distribution from exhibition. Under the terms of the so-called consent decree, the government succeeded. A third, though quite minor, cause of travail was the growth of the art houses and the influx of a fine group of foreign films, made far more inexpensively, and in many cases more realistically, than the product of the Hollywood studios. All of these factors forced a period of retrenchment and of stock-taking which is still under way and the final results of which cannot, as yet, be predicted.

As a medium of mass communication, the motion picture has been, literally, all things to all men. Because it has attempted to reach a median line or a common denominator, the movie makers have been accused of setting up a false criterion known as the twelve-year-old intelligence. Fortunately, the foreign film has exploded that myth, as have several more mature Hollywood efforts in recent years. Except for the art house audience, however, the screen requires, by its very economic structure, a mass audience. It is not an intimate art form, for motion pictures offer what is basically not an intellectual, but an emotional experience. And because the screen is an emotive rather than a cognitive or directive medium, its influence on the receiving audience has been a powerful one. It has reflected the daydreams and aspirations of its viewers and, conversely, has been responsible for fomenting those very daydreams and aspirations.

# CHAPTER 14

## *International Communication*

One of the paradoxes of modern communication and, incidentally, of public relations techniques is that they have not succeeded, despite their efficiency, in ameliorating the constant state of international tension. It might be argued that tensions between countries are not reduced or eliminated by the proficiency of mass media, but by a long evolutionary process in the areas of social, political, and economic education. But each of these areas must accomplish its objectives by means of mass communication; and the mass media can exert as great a potential for international mischief as for good, particularly when they are used *only* as instruments of political propaganda as in the case of the Russian infiltration into the Middle East and Europe. Similarly, public relations techniques can be as effectively employed along divisive lines as they can toward the end of international cohesion. The paradox lies in the fact that, in an age when mass communication and public relations are close to their peak effectiveness as avenues and techniques of persuasion, many countries of the world are even more divided in basic philosophy than they were when the mass media were not as ubiquitous.

## HISTORICAL HIGHLIGHTS

There was always, in a sense, some degree of international communication. Prior to the twentieth century, however, the communicators relied upon word of mouth, the personal courier, or the letter as a mode of conveyance and dissemination. The early newsletters and newspapers filtered through, but there was no true state of *international* communication until the science of electricity and electronics perfected the means of immediate transatlantic and transoceanic relaying of the message or content. But, even today, the personal courier or emissary still functions in the diplomatic and intelligence services of various countries.

Toward the middle of the nineteenth century, a man named Paul Reuter began a service, by means of homing pigeons, among the various countries whose link to England was the English Channel. As newspapers grew and increased their coverage of foreign news, Reuter made a deal with the London *Advertiser* for the inclusion of continental news, culled by a staff of so-called foreign correspondents. The astute English political leaders, always brilliant in matters of Empire prestige, discerned that Reuter could be a valuable source, as well as recipient, of important news content. Reuter, a German, became a British subject and established a continental news service of some importance. His only formidable competitor was Havas, of France, who attempted to establish a similar foreign news agency for the French government. Between them, they settled on areas of divided coverage and authority, with Reuter arrogating coverage in the United States to his agency.

Reuters became established in the 1840's. But, in the United States, the formidable Associated Press was also beginning to take form at the half-century mark. And, from about 1850 onward, the news agency became an established institution throughout the civilized world. The basic difference between the early Reuters and the AP was that the former was obliged to disseminate an official government viewpoint, while the AP was not an agency of the government, but an independent news agency, servicing an increasing number of newspapers under the familiar credit line, "by the Associated Press."

What ultimately freed news agency reporting from the shackles of official control was not so much the integrity and the demands of the editors, but the growing power of the media of communication. The scientific achievements in transmission by transoceanic cable, by radiotelegraph, by telephone lines, and by other subsequent electronic developments created a need for additional news-gathering services. And this need led ultimately to the establishment by Scripps of the United Press in the first decade of the twentieth century, thereby providing a powerful competitor for the heretofore exclusive AP. At the present time, there are three major news-gathering services—the Associated Press, United Press, and International News Service.

What these developments in syndicated news gathering and dissemination meant was not only the breaking down of exclusivity, but also the smashing of cartelization and of the use of news agencies as instruments of propaganda. Independence, except in such agencies as Tass, triumphed over authoritarianism and government control. UP, INS, and AP began to rely upon the so-called foreign correspondent who became ultimately one of the most widely read and romantic journalistic figures of the century. Such names as Vincent Sheean, John Gunther, and Cecil Brown were, literally, known to millions. Indeed, in the years following World War I, a breakthrough took place in the foreign news field, with AP and UP correspondents covering the globe. Areas heretofore the exclusive domain of government-controlled agencies became open sesame to the correspondents who gathered news for such papers as the New York *Times* which, in many instances, made the news content available to smaller papers. And, as a consequence, the intensification of international news coverage increased the opportunity for space for those publicists who were interested in the global news market. Today, the coverage of international news includes not only press associations, but also news magazines, press photographers associations, newsreels, radio and television commentators, and free-lance writers of books and magazine feature articles. Many public relations firms, representing industries with interests around the world, have joined forces with foreign concerns or have set up agencies of their own abroad.

The underlying reason for this internationalization in public relations activities is the nature of communication itself; for the growth of international communication allowed many large industries to establish closer contact with subsidiaries, or with similar agencies, around the world. In addition, however, the impact on public opinion was a formidable one. The development of wireless pictures, of transatlantic telephone communications, and of other devices gave writers, public relations experts, and correspondents an opportunity to delve into issues which impinged on the public opinion areas and to write interpretative accounts of significant events—social, political, business, or ethnic. And, although the paradox of international differences is a glaring one, the fact is that the easy accessibility to thousands of words and to quick newspictures has given the peoples of the world an unparalleled opportunity to indulge in a mutual exchange of opinions on the issues which are of paramount importance.

One of the problems which is restrictive and which explains the strange paradox of a hunger for understanding amid the plenty of mass media is the fact that, although the *tools* for dissemination are available, much of the news has not been permitted to filter through that great part of the world under the direct or indirect domination of the Soviets. In these areas, a strangle hold is exercised over the dissemination of outside information not merely through government agency control, but also by a censorship over what is written for relay by foreign news correspondents. Therefore, despite the available facilities on a worldwide basis, many countries have had to resort to the business of prohibiting other countries from setting up their own electronic receiving units within their borders.

There are other difficulties which impede the flow of international news not only at the receiving end, but at the source. The rigid controls exercised in Russia, China, Spain, and Egypt are striking recent examples. Until the need for greater colonial independence became clear to Britain and France, their colonies were frequently subjected to restrictive news censorship necessitated by the political and military events of the period.

Some of the officials of countries which have placed restrictions on news coverage dissemination and receipt offer a rebuttal to the criticism of such censorship. Why, they ask, should news gatherers be given free access to information when there is no iron-clad guarantee that they will handle the material fairly. How can one tell that each correspondent will abide by the creed of his profession and the tenets of a free and *responsible* press. There is, of course, no categorical answer to this question, except that, in the case of those writers who have been trained in a democracy, one can reasonably expect a high sense of responsibility and an ethical attitude toward their work and toward the news service to which they report.

International censorship, wherever it may be pinpointed, works pretty much as follows:

1. It may restrict the internal flow of news entirely.
2. It may change or delete significant copy.
3. It may deliberately and categorically deny the correspondent the privilege of conveying the news.

Obviously, censorship itself is a device which falls in the area of public relations and propaganda. It cannot be ignored, for it poses a grave problem in that public opinion is affected by what it does or does not accomplish in the way of restricting or censoring content. But censorship, many experts believe, will never be eliminated, either. When a public relations man, acting on behalf of management, tells a reporter, "No comment," he is resorting to implicit, if not explicit, censorship. When an executive says, in effect, "I'll tell you what you want to know, but don't use it, it's off the record," he is also exercising a form of restriction on the news. But there is a subtle difference in this kind of domestic censorship. It is, in a sense, an enlightened one and subject to a basic agreement between the public relations man and the press. It is not a blanket effort to restrict the news but in many cases is an example of confidence in the integrity of the editor.

Foreign correspondents face other problems. The basic problem is to gain access to the sources of news. The second problem is to achieve the right to relay the news. And the third, which applies only to the receiving end, is to see that the news is printed and made accessible to the public. An article on Russia in an American magazine, for example, may never reach the Russian people. Even more formidable an obstacle is the shortwave broadcasting of information by such agencies as the Voice of America. Critics of this effort do not deny the quality of intent; they simply ask whether such broadcasts reach their destination with sufficient impact, and in sufficient numbers, to exert any major influence.

Technically, the means of accessibility to foreign news are available to almost everyone in every land. During World War II, the Office of War Information demonstrated the potential in foreign news coverage. Today, such magazines as the *Reader's Digest* reveal what can be accomplished in the way of foreign translation and distribution. The potential of international news exchange is limited only by the interest and literacy of a rapidly growing world population. The problems of translation, format, and distribution are easily overcome, but the problem of restrictive censorship, in some countries, remains the greatest obstacle.

All of the mass media are important, from the viewpoint of public relations, in the field of international communications. Such magazines as the *Reader's Digest, Time, Life,* and *Newsweek* have rapidly growing foreign editions. The broadcasting industry crosses the oceans by means of short wave and radiotelephone. Until World War II, the flow of motion pictures was from the United States to the foreign countries. But the war, and the subsequent freezing of currency, changed the picture considerably and forced many American companies to use the monies to make pictures abroad. At the same time, foreign films began to create a new art house market in large metropolitan cities in this country. Now, with domestic grosses declining because of television, the foreign department has become the bulwark of most major distributing companies, and this situation, incidentally, has offered many screen publicists an opportunity to work abroad.

Apart from the media and their content, from a technical viewpoint, the facilities for international communications are almost perfect. But the mode of operation is not uniform in all the countries which are linked by the various telecommunication devices. Almost every country, with the exception of the United States, owns and operates its own telegraph and telephone lines, either by direct or indirect control. That is, some are overtly controlled, others partially controlled. The United States and Great Britain predominate in the field of telecommunication *facilities,* either owning or controlling miles of cables under the oceans' waters, wireless facilities, radio communications, and other devices.

The facilities for communication, throughout the world, offer at least the *technique* for furthering understanding and rapport between countries and peoples. But technical facilities must be supplemented by responsibility and volition. Certainly, one major responsibility of publishers, editors, public relations men, and, indeed, of all who deal with the mass media is to become increasingly aware of the importance of telecommunications as an instrument for furthering international understanding. The devices of international communication offer an opportunity for an exchange of views and for a project in educational exchange unparalleled in the history of the civilized world.

*Part IV*

# Public Relations
# in Practice

*Functional definition of public relations—Organizing for public relations activity—Policy and practice—Publicity and promotion*

# CHAPTER 15

## *Organizing for Public Relations*

Thus far, we have considered the mass media in their historical or developmental context as well as in their general relationship to the act of communication and to public relations. But the relationship between the arts of mass communication and public relations is not the same as that between the *technique* of public relations as applied to, and within the framework of, the mass media. What *is* the relationship between the activity of practical public relations and the media or avenues which it employs to influence public opinion?

It must be pointed out immediately that the techniques of public relations, such as publicity and advertising, most frequently employ the mass media at the terminal stage of a campaign, not at its inception. Among the four phases of a public relations campaign in practice—analysis, interpretation, implementation, and action—the final, or action, phase is the one in which mass media are employed specifically. In the preliminary phases, the communication media exert an indirect influence. That is why public relations men steadfastly refuse to equate public relations with publicity; for, while publicity is an integral part of public relations, it must not be confused with public relations itself which functions most frequently on the level of management philosophy, or policy, and not on the level of action.

Generally, public relations executives function in either of two ways—as company directors or as outside counsel.

## THE COMPANY PUBLIC RELATIONS DIRECTOR

In its determination of the *kind* of public relations executive it wants, management must decide, first, what role it expects to assign to public relations in its overall management structure and function, and, second, what function, purpose, or objective it is expected to perform or fulfill.

Most of the enlightened company managements have learned one thing: The public relations director with his division must function as an implicit part of the organization if he is to serve a useful and creative function. He must do more than release publicity. He must help fashion company policy and must determine how, i.e., by what techniques and via what media, policy is to be promulgated in the restless arena of public opinion. One of the important ways in which the public relations director works on the policy-making level, for example, is by serving as a barometer of public opinion and by keeping management advised of prevailing opinions, tastes, and attitudes. On the basis of this knowledge, public relations, as part of the management function, can help to set up criteria for company behavior which will rectify unfavorable opinion and insure that favorable opinions stay that way.

A wise company management, therefore, asks that public relations become a coördinate part of its function. It consults the public relations director on the wisdom of important decisions and significant actions. When it does not do so, it sometimes faces unnecessary difficulties. Here is a recent example of what happened when management failed to touch base with its public relations department. A motion picture distributing company found that one of its films was censored in a major city by the local censor board. Foolishly, the vice-president thought that this could be kept secret, and, when queried about it, he disclaimed any knowledge of it. At the same time, he failed to advise his public relations director of either the censor board action or his own decision. The public relations man learned about it through an inquiry from an enterprising reporter. When he discovered the facts, he knew that the only mode of action was a frank admission of those facts, along with any additional data or message which he thought might shift the emphasis toward a favorable story in the press. It took considerable persuasion to convince management, however, that such a situation could not be suppressed or denied and that the only action was a statement of admission of fact *plus* a statement of company policy or attitude in the matter. In this case, the public relations man suggested that the company statement point out that the city in question was the *only one,* among several hundred, which had insisted on censoring the film. By and large, the press carried this statement in a most favorable manner.

In this case, as in most others, the public relations director functioned on two related levels. First, he determined—on the policy level—what should be done, how the problem could best be attacked. Second—on the level of action—he *communicated* the policy, by means of publicity, to the public through the media of the press and radio. What the public relations man did, therefore, was to interpret the problem to management and explain its ramifications and, subsequently, to convey management's attitude to the public by means of the established media of communication.

Public opinion is interpreted to management by many means at the disposal of the public relations department. Basic, of course, is the instrument of public opinion polling or measurement. But, there are other ways of keeping abreast of opinions. Most enterprising departments have at least one person constantly engaged in a study and evaluation of organs and journals from which important kernels of public opinion can be extracted, i.e., the daily press, the trade papers, business publications, national news magazines, and direct mail. Significant items are culled and filed for cross reference so that when issues or problems arise the necessary data are available for consultation. The motion picture company, for example, would have profited from an up-to-date clipping file on the question of censorship. The automobile industry representatives keep a file of data relating to road legislation and safety regulations. In most industries it is possible to subscribe to various special organs or newsletters which highlight and discuss management problems within the industry. *Public Relations News,* for example, covers the field of public relations from the management viewpoint. Various other organs are replete with valuable information. One such organ, Leonard Spinrad's *Day and Date Service,* keeps a running log of all important events—anniversaries, special days, historical events, and so forth. By consulting this log, the enterprising public relations man can find any number of events which will prove useful both to management and to the public relations operation.

One of the key functions of public relations within a company is to evaluate, interpret, and predict public opinion to management. In other words, the public relations man, once consulted on a possible move, must be able to say, in effect, "If you take this step, this is what will *probably* ensue, both in terms of the press and other media and, ultimately, in terms of public opinion." Public relations, therefore, functions to predict the possible outcome of projected activity. It serves as a guide to management in making policy decisions as well as a restrictive force in diverting management from acts which will have negative results in the market place of public opinion. The latter activity is often a thankless one. Many a company president, upon being urged to abandon a favorite project, has asked his public relations man, "Whose side are you on—ours or the press and the public?" But intelligent public relations frequently must stand *against* a management decision, not only because the stand is in the public interest, but also because it is in the best interest of management. In this area, particularly, ethical public relations can be of unique service to management by showing that enlightened policies in the public interest are, ultimately, in the best interest of the company—an idea which is hard for management to swallow at first and still harder for the public relations man to sell. Too many companies, large and small, still look upon public relations as a simple publicity function, to be called upon when management wants a statement published or broadcast but never to be elevated to the level of helping to establish policy. Frequently, it takes a major crisis to educate management to the fact that *all* of its activities have a public relations coloration and that public relations is not a segmented function but an organic company attitude.

One of the most difficult of the tasks which face many company public relations directors is internal liaison between the publicity-promotion department and other company divisions. In one particular company, for example, there was practically no regular contact between the sales department and the public relations department. The publicity unit frequently sent out blanket news releases to a mailing list of newspapers in areas where the company's products were not even on the market!

In another—and, incidentally, a major business operation—the sales vice-president tipped a newspaper editor to a big deal without checking with the public relations director. The lone paper printed the story, and when the other editors pounced on the publicity department, no amount of pleading could make these competing papers believe that the "exclusive" was a fortuitous and unfortunate accident. In both of these cases, fortunately, an enterprising and firm public relations director taught the sales heads the value and necessity of constant liaison. The lesson learned in both instances was that public relations is not a haphazard function but an integral part of the entire company's operations, ramifying into every area at one time or another. In a large, departmentalized operation, the public relations director, or his staff heads, should be in constant touch with each of the following operating divisions:

1. *Advertising department:* Publicity and advertising are best separated, but each should report to the public relations director or vice-president who will coördinate policy.

2. *Personnel department:* Publication of employee handbooks, bulletin board materials, newsletters, and house organs should be tied in with the public relations department. The public relations head should be advised of union problems and negotiations because public opinion is involved, and one can never tell when publicity, favorable or otherwise, will appear in the mass media.

3. *Financial department:* The public relations director and staff should work with the controller and treasurer in the preparation and timing of stockholder reports, press releases, dividend announcements, etc.

4. *Legal department:* This division should keep the public relations director advised of important litigations and, conversely, the public relations department should clear legal rights, certain exploitation procedures, and policy statements with the legal department.

5. *The advertising agency:* The agency should work with the public relations department so that advertising campaigns are not at variance with publicity and exploitation campaigns.
6. *Sales department:* Constant and close liaison should be maintained between public relations and distribution. Not only is this division a source of publicity because of what it offers in terms of important sales announcements, but it is also an excellent source of business items, interviews, and other publicity "angles."

Within the public relations department proper, the division of labor depends upon the size of the company and the emphasis placed on public relations activities. Although this is an age of specialization, there is still a respectable group of general practitioners in public relations, as in medicine. The most capable public relations men can accomplish almost any assignment, whether it be writing copy, planting a story, or devising a special event. But the trend has been toward the development of specially trained individuals, particularly in large companies where public relations is actively a key part of the general operation of the business.

There is no classic chain of organization which will apply to any company in a literal sense. Departmental structure will vary, depending upon the kind of organization and the public relations objectives. A motion picture company will emphasize spot news, column items, and pictures. Large industrial concerns, such as steel, may emphasize stockholder relations because of the large number of shareholders. In general, however, a well-organized public relations department will be divided into four major areas:

1. *The executive echelon:* On this level are the vice-president and director who are part of top management and participate in policy-making.

2. *The administrative heads of publicity and advertising:* These men will supervise the functioning of each division and carry out policy.
3. *The subheads:* These consist of men in press relations, promotion, etc., who both supervise and handle day-to-day working assignments.
4. *The general staff:* This group is assigned to specific functions —news writing, features, pictures, magazines, special events, promotion, etc.

In smaller companies, the table of organization may be reduced to two or three of these categories, and, in these cases, the department heads and administrators usually do a greater amount of writing, planting, and leg work, in addition to their duties as staff supervisors. Very large industrial organizations, on the other hand—such as General Motors—have a number of subdivisions and regional organizations, each with a high echelon official and all reporting ultimately to the top vice-president in charge of public relations. At the Columbia Broadcasting System there is a separate and fully staffed press information department for its radio division, its television division, and its record company, and each is self-operating and autonomous of the other.

The public relations department, on the internal level, has many functions which it is expected to perform for management. These functions include:

1. Studying and interpreting public opinion, although outside agencies are usually called upon to perform measurement surveys.
2. Reporting on public opinion trends as well as on the content of the mass media to management.
3. Setting up and revising company policies in terms of its needs and objectives and in consideration of the climate of opinion.
4. Determining and establishing it, by means of advertising, pub-

licity, and promotion a symbol, creed, or stereotype of what the company stands for and represents to the public.

5. Preparing news about the company to the publics involved.
6. Coördinating its work with the function of other company departments.

On the external level, the public relations department, through its publicity staff, functions to translate many of its internal operations into language which is acceptable to the public and to convey various ideas and concepts *to* the public by means of the mass media. This operation involves a number of active procedures, involving writing copy, placement, and the following:

1. News releases are written for dissemination to the newspapers, syndicates, radio, and television.
2. Pictures and feature stories are set up with the national magazines.
3. Specialized pictures and stories are provided to trade journals.
4. Additional special materials are prepared for special publications—farm magazines, women's publications, house organs.
5. Material is prepared for company publications which have both internal *and* external distribution.
6. Company reports are prepared.
7. Speeches are written, along with accompanying releases, for various company officials.
8. Interviews are set up for company executives with the daily press, trade press, radio, television, and magazines.
9. Still pictures, motion pictures, slides, clips, kinescopes, and transcriptions are prepared for specialized use, such as in schools.
10. The department works with the advertising department in coordinating advertising concepts with relevant publicity.
11. Liaison must be established with civic, religious, and philanthropic institutions.
12. Promotion materials must be prepared—brochures, posters,

booklets—for distribution to special groups, such as colleges and libraries.

13. Exploitations and special events are set up for special occasions, such as anniversaries.
14. Public speaking engagements occasionally are attended to by the public relations department.
15. Appropriate liaison is maintained with the industry trade association.

Obviously, in a large company, these activities cannot be handled by a few persons. They are usually assigned to various subdepartments. One group may handle all news writing. Another may be assigned to speeches, reports, and presentations. Still others may be responsible for research activities, educational liaison, motion pictures, radio and television, magazines, special services (such as women's clubs), promotional tie-ins, and community relations.

Supervising all of these internal and external activities is the public relations director who is responsible for the setting of policy and for all liaison with top company management.

## THE OUTSIDE PUBLIC RELATIONS COUNSEL

The outside public relations counsel may function in two related ways. He may be retained by companies which do not maintain their own departments, other than a skeleton staff, or he may work as an advisory adjunct to the established public relations department.

The question frequently asked is why should a company find it necessary to employ outside counsel at great cost when there is a permanent staff available? Public relations counselors are called in much the same as doctors call upon consultants for specialized problems. But the outside counsel is not always used as an emergency measure. Many company heads believe that the independent counsel is valuable *because* he is independent.

They feel that the outside counsel can offer a more objective viewpoint, a perspective which is difficult to attain within the confines of the internal job. Again, many management executives tend to listen more seriously to the voice of an outside specialist than to that of the internal public relations director. Another reason offered is that the outside counsel has specialized stature in certain areas, just as doctors and lawyers have in special phases of medicine or law. Finally—and this is true of giant corporations—the increase in the size of a company seems to increase its vulnerability to pressure and criticism, and frequently the outside counsel offers a healthy system of checks and balances on projected policy and procedures.

The contribution of the outside public relations counsel is similar to, but not identical with, that of the company director. The former inclines more to policy; the latter is responsible for both policy and the promulgation of it. Although many outside agencies are equipped to handle the techniques of publicity, their major concern is with broad attitudes and problems rather than with specific techniques. They tend to be most helpful in the areas of opinion measurement and evaluation and in recommendations and reports which can be activated by the company departments. While the inside director is concerned with company patterns and with various internal restrictions, the outside counsel has no such encumbrances. He is in a position, because of his many accounts, to offer a diversity of viewpoints and possibilities. He can, in a word, offer an independent and unbiased point of view which is not fettered by internal policies, politics, or personal considerations.

Small companies, unless they do not have their own director, do not need an outside counsel. Large companies may derive benefit from his help and advice. The independent counsel can help in establishing and directing internal policies, in clarifying the thinking on major problems, and in constructing sound public relations policies and objectives. Outside counsel has been found to be particularly helpful in legislative matters, in opinion measurement and interpretation, and in liaison with troublesome special interest and pressure groups. The independent counsel is often helpful to the company director in suggesting various alternatives to campaign plans which have been drawn up for activation.

In addition to company matters, however, there is a recent tendency for companies to call upon the independent public relations agency on an industry basis when the trade association is involved in an important and intricate problem. These special situations may require specialized techniques whereby, through public opinion polls and evaluations of data, the counsel can provide information and ideas which are of benefit not only to one company, but to all the organizations within a given industry. For example, the various bus lines may form an association to bring their particular mode of transportation to the attention of the public in such a way as to demonstrate its superiority to other carriers. Such a campaign, if it is to be successful on a nationwide basis, obviously requires considerable planning before it is put into action. In this situation, the public relations counsel is best equipped to handle the campaign by advising and coördinating with the trade association and with the public relation directors of the various large companies involved. Public relations counsel has played a major role, too, in devising strategy to handle various monopoly actions, union problems, rate increases, and adjustments and in other delicate and critical areas. Particularly in emergency situations, the counsel can serve as an objective guide and adviser to management and to company public relations directors. Specialized agencies also are called in to assist with financial and stockholder reports, with personnel problems, and with various approaches to effective community relations.

Usually, the outside counsel stops short of actual publicity techniques, although some are called upon to promulgate campaigns. The basic work of the counsel, in most cases, involves measurement of opinion, evaluation of findings, preparation of a report which defines the necessary ends, and recommendations for ways of achieving the ultimate objectives. Company directors frequently find the outside counsel of great assistance in helping to inculcate top management with the basic truths that publicity must not be confused with public relations and that public relations is not concerned so much with immediacies as with long-range objectives. On the other hand, management must be receptive. It must agree to listen to the recommendations of the counsel, both with regard to its internal as well as external activities.

The outside counsel, therefore, is a valuable adjunct, but not a categorical necessity. It can supplement the public relations department as a consulting agency. It can be retained to set up and carry out a complete program. Or, as most often happens, it can be called upon, at a stipulated fee, to attend to a special situation or project.

# CHAPTER 16

## *What Public Relations Is—And Is Not*

Every public relations counsel has his own definition of public relations. And almost every definition is different! In fact, one student of public opinion has collected more than fifty definitions from fifty experts in the field!

Although practitioners rarely agree on a single, precise definition, there is an area of general agreement. Public relations is that specific operating philosophy by which management sets up policies designed to serve both in the company's and the public's interest. It is, further, the *basis* of communication techniques which management employs to achieve good relations with the public. These techniques include, among others, publicity, promotion, exploitation, and advertising. But the "operating philosophy" concept is hardest to define, because this involves the whole complex matter of policy and the basic aims behind that policy. A good public relations campaign requires a sound basic policy and the application of sound publicity techniques to achieve the desired goal. That goal may be good will, sales, company prestige, or individual prestige—or it may be a combination of all of these. Usually, it *is* all of these. Ford

Motors, for example, is an industrial institution. It is, therefore, interested in creating and maintaining good will. It desires the good will of the public as a basis for sound sales policy. Sound sales policy and a satisfied buying public enhance company prestige. And company prestige enhances the individual prestige of the industrial leaders who head up the management of the company.

## A FUNCTIONAL DEFINITION

Public relations men themselves find it difficult not only to talk of their work but also to describe exactly what they do. A conversation between a public relations counsel and a curious layman might yield the following:

Layman: Just what is it that you do, Mr. Smith?

P. R. Man: I do public relations.

Layman: Oh, that must be fascinating work.

P. R. Man: It is. And hard work, too.

Layman: I've got a vague idea of what you do, but public relations has always been a somewhat mysterious profession to me. Just what is it? What do you do? And for whom?

P. R. Man: Well, that's rather hard to say. You see, the top public relations men are accustomed to speaking for and about their clients, not about themselves.

Layman: What do you mean by clients?

P. R. Man: Clients are the people we represent. A private counsel may have several clients or accounts.

Layman: Like an advertising agency?

P. R. Man: In a way, yes. But the public relations man frequently helps set a whole way of thinking, or pattern, or philosophy that involves *all* of the activities of the client that impinge on the public—including sales, packaging, product design, and lots of other things besides advertising. In a specific company, the director of public relations works with many people, including the advertising agency, and he may set in motion plans or policies that the advertising agency carries out.

Layman:          What's the purpose?

P. R. Man:       The purpose is to gain and maintain the support of the public, for one thing. To build sales, for another. To develop institutional prestige, for another. To transmit important information about the company to the public and to the media that serve the public, like the press, for still another. You see, nobody lives in a vacuum. We must understand the public and must develop patterns of exemplary behavior that will elicit good opinions from it.

Layman:          Well, now we're getting somewhere, anyway. You tell people how good your clients are by getting publicity for them in the newspaper. That explains it quite simply.

P. R. Man:       Truthfully, it *can* sometimes boil down to that. But, if it were a question of telling the world how good our clients are by means of straight publicity, we wouldn't be doing public relations. We'd be capable press agents, or publicists, or advertising copy writers—all of whom, incidentally, play a vital part in carrying out public relations programs.

Layman:          Then, you devise the *basic* program or policies?

P. R. Man:       Under ideal conditions, that is exactly what a public relations man does. It is our function to study public opinion at all times, to relate our findings specifically to a given problem, to analyze the situation from within our company and from without, to interpret correctly the data available to us, to predict possible outcomes, and to devise a program of constructive action—again from within and without.

Layman:          What does "within" and "without" mean?

P. R. Man:       "Within" means anything relating to the company or client from an internal or operating standpoint—the plant, the employees, the company policies. "Without" involves just about everything external which is affected in any way by the company—in other words the company's public, or publics.

Layman: Then, you're a combination trouble-shooter, adviser, and good will ambassador.

P. R. Man: That is just about right. And if you insist on a definition, let's say that public relations means developing and maintaining good relations with the public and with the media of communication that service—and serve—the public.

Layman: Basically, for a business concern or large industry.

P. R. Man: For a business, for a college, for a trade association, for a symphony orchestra, for a politician, for a movie producing unit, for a church group, for a medical organization, indeed, for *any* person or group that must in any way depend upon the support and good will of the public. That's public relations!

## FUNCTIONAL PROCEDURES

Is there a precise definition of public relations which will both describe and delimit the range of its activities? Since the best definitions are verbal and necessarily arbitrary, and since public relations is a dynamic rather than a static procedure, perhaps a functional approach is the best in describing public relations. For public relations is best defined not by what it is, but by what it does. Its purpose is to create a favorable climate of opinion among those publics upon which the activities of an organization impinge. The achievement of this end involves a set of functional or operating procedures which include:

1. A study of the prevailing climate of opinion, based on research data.
2. An interpretation of these data and findings in terms of their meaningful impact on the management function.
3. Based on this interpretation, a setting up of policies or programs which will relate the management function favorably to the public interest.

4. A program of information to the public about these policies by means of the mass media of communication.

These specific steps are related, in fact, to the social and economic conditions which created the need for public relations techniques in the first place. Public relations as a management function grew out of need, as public opinion became informed and articulate. Once the social need was established, it remained to determine what would constitute sound management policy. The *why* of public relations is explained, therefore, on the basis of economic and social need, plus a more informed opinion resulting from information and education obtained through the mass media. The *how* of public relations involves a study of the best ways and means to utilize the mass media in order that management's policies may be communicated to the public for the purpose of creating a favorable climate of opinion.

A public relations program in action, then, attempts, first, to relate the policies of the organization to the best interest of the publics involved, and second, to devise ways and means of telling the publics involved about these policies and activities by utilizing all available and relevant media of communication. Public relations is not publicity. It is not advertising. It is not promotion. It is not exploitation. But all of these activities are, when they are properly and skillfully employed, integral parts of the carrying out of a public relations concept, objective, or program.

# CHAPTER 17

## Policy and Practice

There is an articulate and critical minority who view any definition of public relations—either theoretical or operational—with a degree of suspicion. To some, public relations is an elaborate and cleverly contrived whitewash or cover-up for some of the nefarious practices of both business and labor. To others, it is a form of not too subtle propaganda—the inference being that propaganda is, by some arbitrary standard or definition, always an unsocial or unethical activity. Public relations is an effort to present big business interests to the public through the hue of rose-colored glasses. It is, in the political sphere, an attempt to make the worse appear the better reason. It is headline hunting, it is opportunistic, it is sheer sophistry.

Practiced badly, public relations can be all that its critics say it is. But that is equally true of other professions, such as the law or medicine, practiced badly. The public relations field has not cornered the market on charlatans.

From a more realistic vantage point, however, the practice of intelligent public relations has restrained many a management, many a political group, and many an individual who is in the public eye from running afoul of public opinion. And, beyond its preventive facets, intelligent public relations has made these groups and individuals not only aware of the power of public opinion, but also aware of the necessity for maintaining the good will of the public by decent and constructive acts in the public interest. Beyond the philosophical or sociological principles involved, however, is the claim by its proponents that there is a legitimacy in the publicity and advertising phases of public relations because merchandising and marketing are legitimate activities of a competitive and free economy. Naturally, the publicist will be prejudiced in his client's favor. He will not be expected to demean the institution, product, or idea which he is retained to espouse. But this bias need not lessen the integrity of his operation.

## A SOURCE OF INFORMATION

One reason, among others, for the growth of public relations as a profession is the constant demand on the part of an increasingly well-informed public for information. The public wants information, to which it feels entitled, about industry, educational institutions, political figures, and social agencies. Part of this information it receives directly, by mail or by group meetings. But most of the information is disseminated through the media of mass communication, and the public relations man is the catalyst or transmitting agency. Checks and balances are available, therefore, not merely by the self-regulating code of ethics of public relations men, but in the media themselves—newspaper editors, newscasters on radio and television, and the other communicators. Significantly, the press and other avenues of transmission recognize in the public relations expert a source of timely, interesting, and newsworthy material.

Practiced ethically, therefore, public relations has a valuable and useful function in modern communication. The trained and professional public relations counsel recognizes and helps management to recognize that the good will of either press or public cannot be bought, that it has to be earned by constructive deeds in the public interest. Good public relations, practiced by qualified experts, can contribute greatly to the improvement of the policies of management. Good public relations can convey sound management policies to the public by using the established media of communication. Public relations is a social science, involving skilled diagnosis of the client's or organization's problems, careful interpretation of public opinion data, and successful communication of information and ideas through all relevant channels. Its basic concern is with the *effect* of the activities of the client, directly or indirectly, on the public. The public relations expert is, in even a more literal sense than a lawyer, a counselor to his client. He is a barometer of public opinion climate, an interpreter of findings in the area of opinion formation, a guide to constructive management policies, and an expediter and transmitter of these policies to the public through the mass media of communication.

To regard public relations merely as headline-hunting publicity is to disregard the long, painstaking preliminary studies which every good public relations counsel makes before devising a special event or writing a release that will mean space in the newspapers or magazines. A good deal of fine public relations, in fact, is practiced negatively, that is, with the contradictory purpose of actually keeping a client out of the public eye until there is something positive and constructive to talk about.

The successful practitioner recognizes a primary objective: to dissuade his client from engaging in any activity which will bring a negative response from any of the publics affected by his operation. His next function is to advise the client on ways and means of generating public support and good will.

## PSYCHOLOGY AND GEOGRAPHY

To accomplish both objectives, the public relations expert must constantly be measuring public attitudes in two related areas. One area is psychological. It is concerned with the temper of public opinion on the specific problem at hand. The other area is geographical. It involves the delimitation of the problem to the specific localities affected by it. Different communities not only pose different psychological problems, but geographical differences frequently underscore the public relations problem. The advertisements of southern states in northern newspapers, outlining the economic and social advantages of moving industry to the South, is a simple example of a public relations message which underscores both the psychological and geographic aspects of a campaign. The public attitude on racial discrimination in North and South is a more complex example of the psychological and geographic differences which must be taken into consideration in any public relations appraisal of this problem. But, whether simple or complex, an understanding of the psychological attitudes and of the geographic area is essential for a sound public relations approach to any problem— whether it be industrial, educational, social, or cultural. Each problem has a unique psychological or attitude aspect, as well as a geographical pattern, which cannot be ignored in planning a campaign to influence public opinion.

Having studied both of these vital areas, the public relations counsel may devise a single event or a whole series of events which are then communicated to the public through such channels of information as press, radio, motion pictures, magazines, brochures, or any other appropriate promotional or publicity medium. The Pennsylvania Railroad, for example, is interested primarily in those geographic areas which the road serves. A specific public relations problem in one area may affect only that area, or it may affect the entire geographic area covered by the railroad. Depending upon the nature of the problem and the prevailing public opinion about it, the public relations counsel will determine what steps to take, and he may then communicate these policies to the public through the instruments of press, radio, and the other mass media.

Unfortunately, the most active, or the publicity phase, of a public relations program is too often confused with public relations itself. When this happens, the operation becomes at best obvious publicity and at worst mere press agentry. In the case of certain industries, such as the entertainment industry, publicity is the primary objective. "Spot news" stories about casting and production notes, as well as features, go out to the newspapers daily. In the world of motion pictures, the theatre, and broadcasting the role of the press agent is important. His prime objective is to bring a title, a star name, or a special exploitation stunt to the public eye and to accomplish this quickly and with as much fanfare as possible. In other fields, however, press agentry, publicity, and promotion are subservient tools in a complete public relations program. They serve as means to an end, not ends in themselves. This is true of such companies as General Motors or the Pennsylvania Railroad; of various trade associations; of educational and philanthropic institutions; and of any number of medium-sized business and industry units.

## A PUBLIC RELATIONS CONCEPT

In a special public relations bulletin, prepared for employees by its Eastern Division, the Pennsylvania Railroad had this to say about public relations:

What do we mean by public relations?

Public relations is the impression carried away in the mind of every person with whom you talk—by telephone or in person—today. It has been said "to make a friend, be one." If you were friendly in your contacts today—and we don't mean fresh—then you probably made a friend for yourself and for the company as well, for in the mind of that person you are "the Company." If every employee of the Pennsylvania Railroad made one friend today for himself and for the company, then we are all richer by more than 150,000 friends! Multiply this by 365 for every day of the year and what have you? You have a vast army of friends raising their voices loud and strong in praise of the Pennsylvania Railroad. With this good deed you have done a good job of public relations.

You may ask, why should I concern myself with public relations? Why not let the other fellow worry about it? I'll get along just as well without concerning myself with that problem. You may not realize it but the very fate of the Pennsylvania Railroad rests squarely on a foundation of good public relations. Unless our customers, the investors, the press, government agencies—even the employees themselves—have a friendly feeling for, and interest in, the Pennsylvania Railroad, the Company's business will suffer, and the conditions under which its operations are carried on will become so burdensome that it can no longer remain in business.

For the Pennsylvania Railroad, as well as for countless other American businesses, public relations is, obviously, not an optional procedure to be employed or discarded as a casual whim of management. It is recognized as a vitally important day-in and day-out aspect of every single phase of the company's activities. A company can flourish in business only if it has sound public relations, for sound public relations can help see to it that the company's business functions at the optimum level of success and efficiency.

## BASIC PROCEDURES

What technical operations does public relations involve? In a literal sense, of course, any company activity which affects any of the numerous publics dealt with by that company has a public relations aspect. Technically, however, public relations does involve a number of specific operations, all utilizing, at one phase or another, the media of communication. These can best be described as four mutually related procedures: (1) analysis, (2) interpretation, (3) implementation, and (4) action.

## Analysis

Analysis of the problem, or problems, confronting the institution is the first step in devising a public relations campaign. It involves a survey and appraisal of the specific and general nature of the problem and of all relevant factors which have any bearing on it. Here, the psychological and geographic aspects are important. What, for example, is the prevailing temper of public opinion with regard to the issue at hand? Is the majority for it or against it? Is the minority disinterested or articulate? And what geographic factors must be considered, i.e., what localities are involved? Are they urban or rural, industrial or agrarian? For example, a large industrial company which decides to move its plant, and thereby affect the living habits of hundreds or thousands of people, would certainly consider these problems if it were at all interested in good public relations— both among employees and the community. Analysis, therefore, involves an understanding of the causal background of the problem. It involves a study of the climate of public opinion and of the possible effect of a projected act upon it. Public opinion surveys play a large role in analysis.

## Interpretation

Interpretation of findings follows the public relations man's analysis of the problem under consideration. Here, all data which have been gathered, both from the psychological and geographic areas, are weighted and evaluated. As accurate an appraisal as possible is made of all the implications and alternatives. And this information is then readied for presentation to management as the public relations man's interpretation of the prevailing climate of public opinion. In the case of the removal of a vital industrial plant, the public relations man may find that, while the employees are largely against it, certain key opinion leaders in the community can be enlisted to support the move. He may discover, too, that the employees are against it because they fear what they do not understand or what has not been explained.

## Implementation

Implementation, based on the data discovered, is the third step. In other words, having made an interpretation from the information at hand, what is to be done about it? This is an internal problem and involves the setting up of immediate or long-range policies and plans. It involves the vital decision, upon the part of executive management, to act upon the recommendations of the public relations counsel. Old procedures may be altered and new ones set up in their place. The management may find itself faced with the need to give up certain policies which it has held with selfish zeal. A constructive blueprint to win good will may be set up, both from within the company and from without. A company, for example, may decide to forego moving the plant in return for some important concessions on the part of the civic officials.

## Action

Action is the fourth and final phase. And here the public relations campaign is tested pragmatically. For, if management has made its decision and set its internal house in order, the time has come to "talk it up" with the press and public. Some, or all, of the media of communication may be utilized to get an informational message across to the public in the hope of winning its good will and support. It is at this stage that the techniques of publicity and advertising play so important a part in an omnibus public relations campaign. For the purpose now is to inform and influence public opinion through successful utilization of the mass media. Through the use of various media of communication, company policies may be promulgated in several public relations areas—employee relations, consumer relations, stockholder relations, press relations, dealer relations, and many others. Stories, explaining that the company has decided *not* to move its plant, in the public interest, may be disseminated by means of the mass media. Press interviews may be arranged to explain why.

Naturally, these four procedures are not hard and fast. Public relations men do not set about to schematize each campaign arbitrarily, nor do they apply such a blueprint rigidly in all situations. It is, however, a useful guide in approaching most public relations problems—and most public relations problems are amenable to analysis, interpretation, implementation, and action.

For example, assume that an established manufacturing company has decided to produce and market a new product and is planning to build and operate a subsidiary plant in a new territory. What are the public relations aspects of the problem? The public relations counsel, under ideal conditions, will have a potent voice in every single step of the operation. Undoubtedly his approach to the problem will involve an analysis of the problem, an interpretation of findings, and a specific course of action. He will undertake most of the following procedures:

1. A survey of general market conditions in the area. What other businesses operate there? What is the buying power of the con-

sumer? What is the nature of the general population of the area?

2. A survey of the community: its educational, recreational, housing, medical, and religious resources. Who are the community leaders in these fields? How may their good will be earned?

3. An investigation into the civic factors: political parties, city authorities, tax situation, labor unions.

4. An interpretation to management of the prevailing situation, and a recommendation of the preliminary steps to be taken to set up an operating public relations policy.

5. An advance internal educational program (preparatory to launching the new product) to the employees, dealers, distributors, and others affected by the company and its activities.

6. An advance announcement to stockholders, couched in terms of their interest in the company.

7. An external program of practical publicity and promotion to launch, exploit, and merchandise the new product and the new plant. This will include:

   (a) News releases of facts and information about the new product and the company to the press.

   (b) Institutional advertising in newspapers, magazines, and other media.

   (c) Advertising and promotion tie-ins—novelties, testimonials, endorsements, e.g., pictures of well-known actors, actresses, or other public figures shown using the product.

   (d) Trade association recognition and support.

   (e) Slogans, symbols, identification phrases to help the consumer identify the product.

   (f) Promotion to dealers and consumers—brochures, posters, dealer aids, merchandising devices.

   (g) Special events to publicize and exploit the product, the company, and the manufacturer—exhibits, fairs, special luncheons, awards, ground-breaking ceremonies.

   (h) Special feature stories and pictures for house organs, trade papers, business journals.

   (i) Feature story ideas for newsreels, national magazines, Sunday supplements.

(j) Promotional and institutional materials to special groups—women's clubs, and schools—booklets, teaching aids, charts, film strips.

One very important fact stands out in this preliminary outline of a public relations campaign. Long before practical steps were taken to publicize the project, a period of analysis (or survey) was undertaken and an operating policy was set up. Successful and efficient public relations operates on the highest level by a primary concern with overall policy, based on a careful survey of relevant geographic and psychological areas. And it is from the preliminary steps of policy and planning that the practical implementation steps of promotion, advertising, and publicity develop. A public relations program succeeds or fails on the basis of the overall management policy of which it is an integral part.

# CHAPTER 18

## *Tools of the Trade*

Twenty-five years ago, there was the untutored and rather flamboyant press agent seeking the publicity "plug" from the newspaper editor. Today, there are informed, well-trained public relations men whose function it is to make pertinent and factual data about their clients available to the editor for dissemination to the public by means of the mass media. The press agent or publicity man of the roaring twenties was an extra hired hand whose sole function was to dream up some unique stunt that would result in a picture or a story in the newspapers. The equipment of most publicity men was some newspaper experience, plus a flair for adroit ideas that would achieve free space in the papers for the client. While this still prevails today, to some extent, publicity for its own sake has been subordinated to its rightful place as an important tool of overall public relations. Publicity, promotion, and exploitation are structural elements, resting on a firm public relations foundation and using the mass media as instruments of communication between management and the public.

As a result, modern management looks upon public relations not as a casual operation, but as a vital center of its operating policies. It calls upon public relations to revise poor planning and to devise constructive programs, both in *client's and the public's* interest. The public relations attitude extends into every phase of management's activities. Publicity is thought of as essential, but not as an end in itself. Policies affecting personnel, planning, stockholder reports, advertising, dealer and consumer promotion, employee programs, educational liaison, and other areas are subsumed under the heading of public relations. In short, every direction of the company's activities has a public relations aspect, and this public relations aspect is taken into consideration in planning operating procedures in each category. Public relations is part of company policy. More and more it is becoming part of the thinking and planning behind individual businessmen's daily operations. Effective communication with the public is essential to good business procedure. Public relations is the catalyst.

As public relations came to occupy a unique place in management, its status rose from the level of the simple publicity release to the vastly more important and difficult policy-making level. Management sought people who had the newspaper-publicity touch, *plus* broader professional equipment. If public relations men were to aid in directing policies, they must have adequate training and experience. Consequently, professional public relations has had to organize, to set standards, and to provide trade media for the exchange of ideas. Experienced public relations men deem certain training and professional equipment essential for the practice of sound public relations. For, despite the individual variations in different enterprises, practically every specialist in the field works with a set of more or less standard tools.

## PREREQUISITES FOR PUBLIC RELATIONS MAN

Even on the highest level of policy, for example, a knowledge of communications and the communication media is vitally important. If the essential job of the public relations man is to interpret the public to the client and the client to the public, he must be on familiar terms with the instruments of interpretation. For public relations, as a professional career, embraces the many fields of public information. And information efforts today require the use of mass media.

The skilled public relations man, therefore, should have as thorough training as possible in a complex of subjects which are relevant to his work. The top public relations men are profound students of public affairs. The more thoroughly the public relations man understands contemporary economic and political trends, the more fruitful will be his contribution to the basic construction of sound operating policy. An equally thorough grounding in general psychology and in sociology, plus some knowledge of statistics, is tremendously helpful in the important business of understanding public opinion and group motivation. The public relations man need not be a statistician, but an understanding of surveys and methods of opinion measurement is important. The broader the base of general culture, the broader will be his comprehension of the human relations aspect of the problems he must resolve. And an understanding of marketing and selling is of tremendous help, because a good part of practical public relations is to merchandise, whether the item merchandised be a product, an idea, an institution, or an individual. Public relations men, at one time or another, are asked not only to publicize, but to promote any one of these, or a combination of all of them, to the public.

One of the most challenging questions asked about preparation for a public relations career concerns journalism training. Actually, there are many organizations which will not consider an applicant unless he has had newspaper experience; and certainly this training is valuable. But it can also be a two-edged sword. Well-staffed public relations departments usually include among their personnel one or more persons whose job it is to handle news and to write releases. These individuals have usually had formal training in journalism or active experience on a newspaper. But, publicity is not all of public relations, however important it may be. A sense of timeliness and an understanding of current events frequently add up to a better public relations man than a strict adherence to the journalism-newspaper-publicity standard. Some of the greatest public relations men started as newspaper writers or as publicists. Some of the greatest have not. Journalism training is an asset in publicity writing; it is not an absolute essential in public relations. Many public relations men have been teachers or lawyers, and at least one was the dean of a liberal arts college.

The public relations man is vitally interested in just about everything that reaches the public through the media of communication. He is concerned with public trends and attitudes and with ways of measuring them. Therefore, he will be interested in various methods of the poll or survey. He will follow business trends, labor regulations, and insurance programs and study current economic, educational, and political events. All of this is essential for his daily work.

## INFORMATION SOURCES FOR PUBLIC RELATIONS MAN

The big question for the newcomer to the field is where to find this fund of information, outside of the daily newspaper, the magazine, television, radio, and newsreel. Fortunately, the growth of public relations as a recognized profession has also seen the rise of a number of specific trade and professional journals which cover significant developments in most phases of public relations, public opinion, and mass communication. Practically all of these publications, at one time or another, will prove useful to anyone engaged in public relations, publicity, or promotion. They carry material which is as essential to the public relations man as the latest medical journal reports are to the physician.

In the general field of business and industry such excellent publications as *Nation's Business, Forbes, U.S. News and World Report* and *Business Week* offer stimulating analyses of economic and social trends as well as coverage of labor problems, government regulations, industry analyses, stockholder developments, and other information of interest to public relations practitioners. Similarly, the *Wall Street Journal* and the *Journal of Commerce* are daily business newspapers which contain a wealth of important information about business and industry trends. All of these publications, incidentally, touch on specific phases of public relations activity at one time or another.

Supplementing these specific business reviews are the trade papers and trade journals. There is scarcely any organized activity—industrial, professional, or educational—which does not publish several trade papers. A survey of representative basic industries shows that there are anywhere from five to thirty-five varied trade papers published in each category. The automobile industry, for example, has about twenty-five intramural industry trade reviews, with circulations varying from five thousand to more than one hundred thousand. The picture is similar in such industries as railroads (a half a dozen major journals), steel (about fifteen large industry papers), chemicals (about ten, exclusive of the university and academic publications), and building trades (about fifteen key journals). The titles are of typical trade paper flavor: *Automobile Topics, Railway Age, Iron Age, Coal Age, Food Field Reporter, National Grocers' Bulletin, American Fabrics, Motion Picture Daily, Radio and Television Daily,* and many others in various fields of business and industry.

This material serves a twofold purpose for the public relations counsel or the publicity director. Primarily, it covers the news in his own field and gives a trade view of those activities that are under way by competitive or related companies or organizations. Secondly, these journals are themselves important media for communicating publicity, advertising, and promotion about company and industry activities. They are, from the trade point of view, clearinghouses of information and ideas within a specific industrial frame of reference.

Since public relations problems frequently demand contact with various government agencies, the *United States Government Manual* offers a complete listing of who, what, and where in government. An equally important reference item is the *Directory of Trade and Professional Organizations in the United States* which lists every trade unit and organized professional group in the country. In the field of education, a category too frequently overlooked by public relations counsel, there is *Patterson's American Educational Directory,* a listing of public and private schools and colleges in each state, supplemented by an invaluable roster of educational associations and boards.

Periodicals are also listed in annual up-to-date catalogues. *Editor & Publisher Yearbook* is a compilation of all daily newspapers throughout the United States, along with a listing of key editorial personnel. Weekly newspapers, an important medium for reaching grassroots with both advertising and publicity, are listed in the *American Press Association's* directory of small-town and county newspapers. The *Columbia Scholastic Press Association* is helpful in reaching school papers, and the *Col-*

*lege Paper Rate and Reference Guide* has both advertising and
publicity data on college newspapers throughout the country.

Two other reference volumes are essential for the successful
operation of a public relations department. These are N. W.
Ayer's *Directory of Newspapers and Periodicals* and the *Standard Rate and Data* guide. Both include a careful and complete
record of newspapers and magazines, along with current circulation figures and other vital data.

Pertinent information about the entire field of radio and television is included in the *Broadcasting Magazine Yearbooks*
and *Radio Daily Yearbook*. Here the public relations man can
find data on the location and personnel of broadcasting stations
from coast to coast, Federal Communications Commission documents on radio and television, regional network operations, advertising information, trade associations, newspaper-radio ownership affiliations, and other pertinent information.

Finally, there is the field of public relations itself. Although
still in an organizational stage, public relations has developed
its own trade units, and its activities are recorded in several
media. Professional public relations is now represented by
the American Public Relations Association, a national organization of public relations counsel; by the Public Relations Society
of America; and by the Financial Public Relations Society and
the American College Public Relations Association. The purpose
of these units is to aid in the development of professional public
relations, to serve as a clearinghouse for the exchange of ideas
in the field, and to advance the standards and ethics of public
relations as a profession.

A weekly barometer of news and events in the field is found
in the special public relations section of *Tide* magazine, while
publicity and public relations are frequently discussed in
*Printers' Ink, Editor & Publisher,* and *Advertising Age.* A

week-by-week account of activities in public relations, along with editorial comment, is contained in *Public Relations News,* a valuable weekly newsletter intended for the public relations executive on the management level but of interest to all students of public relations activities and techniques. Leonard Spinrad's *Day and Date Service* offers an invaluable survey of forthcoming national and area events of interest to public relations practitioners.

The area of public relations is, therefore, no longer a circumscribed one. It has become a full-grown profession, with its own trade associations and its own media of exchange, supplemented by a well-organized system of data and reference guides. At one time, the publicizer stood outside the door, seeking the so-called plug from the press. Today, public relations is an integral part of America's magnificent network of communication through which *information* is brought to an increasingly well-informed public.

Following is a listing of some of the important press syndicates, photo syndicates, and other special outlets:

1. *News syndicates and wire services.* The Associated Press, United Press Association, International News Service, Chicago Tribune Press Service, Dow-Jones News Service, NEA Service, Inc. (Newspaper Enterprise Association), Scripps-Howard Newspaper Alliance, Associated Negro Press.
2. *Photo syndicates.* The Associated Press, United Press Newspictures, Globe Photos, Inc., International News Photos.
3. *National special syndicates.* AP Newsfeatures, The Bell Syndicate, Inc., King Features Syndicate and Central Press Association, North American Newspaper Alliance, Inc., Religious News Service.

# CHAPTER 19

## The Publicity Phase

There are relatively few fields of business endeavor which rely *exclusively* on publicity techniques to get their message over to the public. The motion picture distributing companies are an example of the direct publicity approach, but even in this area there are broad corporate and public opinion problems which require a public relations as well as a publicity orientation. In general, the distinction between those companies or business enterprises which rely on publicity alone as opposed to those which utilize publicity techniques as part of a complete public relations approach is a distinction between the long term and the short term, the institutional and the "hard sell."

A motion picture company, for example, must exploit, publicize, and promote a new film within a given period of time. To a lesser degree, the television networks must publicize aggressively the new shows and stars and must do this continuously because of the necessity of maintaining large audience interest. Industries such as steel, automobile, railroad, electronics, chemical, and others occasionally have a short-term campaign, but more often they work on a long-range public relations program which is established as part of the general effort to build and maintain good will. These companies are as interested in their company name and reputation as they are in selling their products, and many do not sell directly to the public at all.

There is a point in all public relations campaigns when the preliminary work of analysis, interpretation, and implementation must be resolved in the period of action. This is the publicity phase when the *news values* engineered or inherent in the individual, institution, product, or idea are conveyed to the public through the mass media. The purpose is to create a demand to buy, a pattern of good will, or some thought or deed which will redound positively in favor of the person or thing publicized. The basic purpose of publicity is to achieve an affirmative public reaction because of favorable or provocative mention in the newspaper, radio, television, magazines, or newsreels.

Publicity has been referred to by countless public relations counsel as a public relations tool. This means, simply, that public relations and publicity are not one and the same thing. Public relations is concerned with basic policy in the various areas which impinge on public opinion formation. Publicity is a specific technique. The science of publicity is the mechanical expertness by which the content is serviced for transmission through the media of communication. The art of good publicity is the expertness with which the publicist wins the friendship, good will, and faith of the newspaper editor by means of his rendering a dependable service at *all* times, not just when the need for a specific story is acute. Those with aptitude and training can master the science of publicity. But the art of being a good publicist or press agent (i.e., respected by the editors) is a more subtle equation involving personality, personal integrity, and emotional maturity. The best publicists build and maintain the respect of the editors by rendering a service, by being regarded as part of the fourth estate. The better an understanding they have of the needs of the press, the greater the chances of securing successful publicity.

At one point or another, there is a time in the practice of public relations when publicity techniques must be employed in order to transmit a concept, fact, or idea to the publics involved by means of one or more of the mass media. The purpose is to bring the data to the *conscious attention* of the viewer, listener, or reader. Publicity is the catalyst by means of which public relations policies are transmitted to the public. The mass media are the transmitting agencies. Publicity is the most direct way of transmitting the content or message, apart from paid advertising.

For the purpose of clarity and simplification, publicity may be said to consist of *mention*, bringing to the conscious awareness of the receiving audience the name and deeds of an individual, institution, product, thing, or idea. It is incorrect, however, to regard mere mention, in the newspaper for example, as a completed job. The ultimate purpose of publicity which serves the public relations master is more than name dropping in print, although some publicists regard a clipping service and tear-sheets as sufficient. From a public relations viewpoint, the mention must be a positive and affirmative one. It must elicit a response which is *positive* either in an emotive, cognitive, or directive sense. It must create a favorable climate of opinion, a desire to buy or to vote or to discuss, a feeling of liking. It must help to create consent.

Publicity as such is not sufficient, for it may elicit negative reactions as well as positive ones. It may create dissent. The newspapers in a large city have printed reams of copy about the notorious habit of late arrival of one of its servicing railroads. The situation became so bad that even the most direct and forthright publicity release was treated humorously in print. An astute public relations director called off all routine publicity releases but managed at the same time to get across the idea to the editors that the affairs of the road called more for sympathetic understanding than for humor. This was done by notices to passengers, by the issuing of reports, by scheduling special meetings with officials of various civic organizations, and by other deeds which convinced the press—and through the press the public—that the lateness of the trains was not capricious but was due to many formidable problems which the road officials were trying earnestly to resolve.

Unless, therefore, publicity can create consent and, when indicated, positive action, it has not accomplished its purpose. The public relations director, as well as the publicity manager, is responsible for determining and defining what any given publicity venture is expected to accomplish. For example:

1. What, on the basis of a careful analysis of the problem and a subsequent establishing of general policy, is the specific publicity objective?
2. What is the specific form in which the message is to be couched?
3. What is the kernel or news peg which makes the content acceptable for transmission by means of the media of communication?
4. When, how, and where is the content to be transmitted? How will the release be timed? What technique will be used—speech, press release, press conference, report? To what media is it to be directed?

These are some of the basic or root problems in publicity as a tool of public relations, and they cannot be emphasized too vigorously. For publicity, improperly used, is a two-edged sword. Too many impetuous press agents have rushed releases to the press without regard for purpose, timing, or content. And the consequences have been disastrous. It should be remembered that not all publicity is handled as written, that editors have the prerogative of rewriting or asking for additional information or digging for more facts. Many reporters have sensed that there is more than meets the eye in a routine release and have discovered data which is both embarrassing and unfavorable in print. The seasoned publicist and public relations director will caution management against a hasty effort to achieve the dubious immortality of a story in the paper without due regard to the possible public relations consequences. One example of this is the publicist who learned that his company was about to receive a favorable contract. He leaked the story to an editor who gave it prominent space. This so angered the negotiating agency that they withdrew from the deal and ultimately contracted with another firm. The publicist could not understand this reaction, until he learned that the company which was about to award the contract did not want any publicity given until the announcement was made by mail to its own stockholders. Its public relations concept was sound. It wanted its own family serviced internally before any stockholder read about the project in public print.

## THE RELEASE

The publicity release is the statement or story which contains the publicity material, or peg or angle, presented in the form of news or information. The release is the specific technique or tool by which the communications content is serviced to the mass media for transmission to the receiving audience. It is the instrument which, from a public relations viewpoint, puts policy and planning, purposes and objectives into linguistic form. Some releases are of the policy, report, or interpretative type.

Some are written to obtain a mention or plug for an individual, institution, product, or idea. But, regardless of purpose, *all* releases should conform to the accepted standards of good publicity writing and the criteria of good, acceptable journalism. Faced by a plethora of daily releases, with sufficient verbiage to fill a full-length novel, the editor is in a unique position to demand that all publicity releases be professionally styled, written, and presented. Certain specific procedures should be adhered to in all publicity writing which is earmarked "for release." These include the following:

1. The release should follow the accepted style of newspaper writing, the best example of which is to be found in any major newspaper, particularly the New York *Times*. Understandably, every release will include mention of the individual, institution, product, or idea which is of paramount concern to the publicist and which he hopes will appear in print.

2. The sound news release should put first things first. It should open with a lead paragraph which summarizes succinctly and interestingly the kernel of the message, while the succeeding paragraphs should contain additional information in order of *descending* importance. The reason for this is logical, because it allows the editor to exercise his prerogative of pruning. But, in any event, the lead *must* sell the editor the idea that the story is newsworthy.

3. Some publicists use heads or captions on stories. Some do not. Many editors would prefer to have the story released without a headline, since they invariably compose their own. On the other hand, publicists claim that a good head gives the editor a quick grasp of the message and helps to sell it by arresting his attention and instigating further reading.

4. The oft-repeated rubrics of *who, what, why, when, where, how* is the staple of good release writing. The only change in concept has been in varying the emphasis in line with the nature of the story. Some releases will emphasize the *who* or personality involved, others the *what* or the idea or project,

and so forth. If the release concerns a nationally known name, such as the President, the lead should begin with the *who*. If the story concerns an atomic development, the *what* should be in the lead.

5. In any event, the lead should contain as much relevant information as possible. For example: "A new discovery called Camera Scope, which will revolutionize methods of screen technique through wide-screen projection, was revealed yesterday (date) by Professor John Smith in a special demonstration showing at the Acme Studios in New York City." Here, in about forty words, is the *what*, the *who*, the *where*, and the *how* of the story. Succeeding paragraphs should tell more about the technique—how it works, what will be demonstrated on the screen, who is Professor Smith, how long has the research taken. The story might conclude with a quote from a company official predicting what Camera Scope will accomplish for motion pictures in the future.

6. If feasible, quotes should be used in those publicity releases where policy is involved or where an important announcement is made. It is useful, from the standpoint of style and reader interest, to vary quotes from direct to indirect and, in addition, to vary the language. Editors appreciate variations of "he said" to "he stated," "he asserted," etc. But they do not look kindly on such rhetoric as "he mused" or "he asseverated"; nor do they react kindly to releases that open with a quote.

7. Publicity release style should be newspaper style. The advice "Write as though you were a newspaper desk rewrite man" is sound. And rewrite men do *not* employ such phrases as "Financial interests involved estimated . . ." or "The opposition were conspicuous by their absence" or "The meeting room was filled to capacity."

Dr. Benjamin Fine, education editor of the New York *Times* cites five major reasons for the rejection of publicity releases by editors:

1. The release editorializes and is not newsworthy.
2. The lead is not fully explanatory.

3. The writer does not cite authority for statements.
4. There is too much plug or puff for the client.
5. The paragraphs are too long, complicated, or involved.

In addition to style and content, however, the publicity release must be professional from a mechanical point of view. The effect of the work of a public relations operation on the press is a total one. Such elementary factors as the mechanics of the release should invariably be letter perfect. A release which commands the respect and attention of the editor, even before a reading, is one which adheres to certain basic preparatory principles. It is necessary to type, mimeograph, or multigraph the release. It should be double spaced and written on one side only. It should indicate a release date or be marked "for immediate release"; it should include the name, address, and telephone number of the source; and the story should begin about halfway down the page. Certain special releases need a more specific date. If, for example, the president of a company is making a major address on Tuesday evening, the release and text should be serviced to the papers Tuesday afternoon, but with the indication that the release is to be held until after the start of the speech.

The desirable size for release paper is 8 1/2 by 11 so that the editor can determine quickly the number of words for his column. White or yellow paper is standard, and carbon copies should not be used, except in emergencies. All pages should be numbered, and the release writer should try to end paragraphs on one page so as not to run over. If additional copy follows on the next page, the term "more" should indicate this fact. And the conclusion of the story should use either the symbol—30— or # # # to indicate that no more copy is forthcoming.

One of the most important aspects of publicity is the planting or servicing of the story. Many companies service regular spot news and features by mail. But very important stories should be preceded or followed by a phone call to the editor, and the timing of the service should be accomplished with some knowledge of the newspaper's deadline. A story which is intended for the following morning is best serviced by about two in the afternoon, in order to give the editor time to evaluate and plan for the following day. Sunday papers must be planted four or five days ahead, particularly when the material is serviced to specific departments such as drama, movies, radio and television, or books.

Exclusive planting means simply that the publicist is giving one paper the story to the exclusion of all others. This procedure is appropriate for feature material, but so-called "spot news," such as an important announcement, should be given to *all* papers and not restricted to any one. The only variation in timing involves the difference between local or national release. Local release includes the papers within a given city. National release includes the syndicates and wire services as well as a mailing to newspapers on the company's national mailing list. Publicists vary the release timing, depending on the story. Some favor a release to all local papers with a specific date line, followed by a national "for immediate release" mailing. Those who hope for a simultaneous news break service the national list a day ahead of the local one.

In very important announcements when it is thought that the editor will want follow-up material, it is advisable to have additional background or fact-sheet data on hand. On occasion, this may even be serviced with the release. For example, a press release may summarize the commencement address which an individual is making at a university, but the full text should also accompany the release. The release announcing the signing of a famous personality to write a book should also be

accompanied by a biography and by pictures of the individual.
The most seasoned publicists have learned that there is no
way of predicting whether a story will get into print. Many extraneous factors and variables are involved. Even the most important news release may be crowded out, depending on "what
else happened that day." But the careful and trained publicist
can see to it, at least, that all the following amenities are observed:

1. The daily press and the syndicates do not want to be held up
   on release of newsworthy events. They want the story as quickly
   as possible.
2. Radio and television newsroom editors and commentators usually pick up stories from the United Press or Associated Press
   wires, but they should be serviced with additional filler copy,
   containing background and color material.
3. The trade papers within the industry can receive the identical
   release as the dailies, but they will tend to do less editing, and
   will also be more amenable to personality pictures.
4. The national news magazines (*Time, Newsweek*) should be
   serviced, through the appropriate department, if the story has
   national interest.
5. Other national magazines (*Life, Look,* etc.) must be serviced
   well in advance and invariably on a direct contact basis. If the
   editor is interested, these major publications will assign a researcher, writer, and photographer to engage in extensive background preparation.

There are other ways of breaking or planting a story than
the news release, but they should not be used as routine procedure. On occasion, the publicist will manage to leak a story
by alerting the editors to what is in the wind. Another procedure is to call a press conference and have the company
executive release the story verbally and directly to the press.
This procedure is helpful when the public relations objective is

such that questions from the press are welcomed, but it should not be used for routine items. It is not considered good taste to write a letter to the editor along with a release, unless the individual involved is a personal friend of the publicist. In case of a very special story, the publicist can call the city desk or the department editor and alert these individuals to the story. And, where the release is of great topical importance or of unusual news value, it is wise to wire the respective editors as well as the press syndicates.

Timing is a vital aspect of all publicity planting. An intelligently handled story, from the standpoint of day and date of release, has a much greater chance of breaking into print than one which is sent out with no regard for deadlines or for the requirements of the various papers and their respective staffs. Routine spot news presents no particular problem, but important stories must be timed properly in order to assure that at least they arrive under the most favorable circumstances. Where there is ample opportunity to time the release, the best days seem to be Sunday, Monday, or Friday in the opinion of many seasoned publicists. Saturday is a notoriously light day for the papers, but it may also be the best time, because the chances of use in certain departments, such as radio and TV, are greater. The author's experience has been that the best days for releasing publicity stories have been Monday, Tuesday, or Wednesday. The reason is that the editor is given an opportunity to evaluate the story without the pressure of the weekend rush. From the publicist's viewpoint, too, this procedure offers a chance to resubmit the story for Saturday use if it fails to run during the week. This is particularly true of departmental news, such as motion pictures, radio, or business, but it is not as valid for city-side or run-of-paper stories which usually run the day indicated for release or not at all.

Probably too much conjecture has been made over the question of release to morning or afternoon papers. Much depends on the story. A business story for the New York *Times, Herald Tribune,* and *Wall Street Journal* should be timed for these papers specifically. If the evemng papers use the story, so much the better. Some stories which break importantly in the afternoon papers may have little holdover value for the morning editions. Usually, however, an important story will be accepted and used by all. The experienced publicist will take a bird-in-the-hand attitude and gather his publicity in the most feasible way, unless there is good reason to be concerned about a break in one particular paper, such as the New York *Times.*

Nothing can be quite so annoying to editors as releases which go to the wrong desk and have to be rerouted. The general news story should be directed to the city desk or city editor. It is best to eliminate specific names unless one editor has been alerted and is looking for the release. In stories where there is a question whether to plant city side or a specific department the release should go to both, e.g., city desk and radio. Otherwise, it should go directly to the city desk if the story is a city side story; or to the department desk if the release concerns news of specific interest to the department editor. When a story has been cross planted, it is wise to advise the department editor of the fact that it has gone to the city desk.

Two factors should be borne in mind when servicing department editors: the policy of the paper *and* the needs of the specific editor. A story about educational television, for example, conceivably can be used both by the radio and TV editor and by the education editor, depending on whether the greater emphasis is on communications or on education. The best procedure is to check the editor who is regularly planted. If he rejects the story, he may be helpful in directing it to the attention of the other department. Special stories to the education or science editor should be checked in advance, as more information may be requested. Women's page releases should be timely and, of course, should talk about the woman's angle in connection with fashions, food, parents, and children, and related subjects. The appointment of a woman attorney to a high post in business, for example, may not only make news for this page, but may suggest a follow-up pictorial feature about the personality.

Radio, television, drama and motion pictures departments will run items about personalities, new shows, schedules, engineering developments, etc. They will also use, on Sunday, feature stories and interviews, pictures, and roundup pieces. The sports pages offer occasional opportunity for ingeniously engineered publicity, such as a company golf tournament, an industry physical fitness program, speeches by sports celebrities, youth fitness programs, and similar ideas.

Three other areas are important from the publicist's viewpoint: the columns, letters to the editor, and the editorial page. Columnists, as a rule, must have exclusive items; and the chances of a specific item breaking are much greater if the press agent has serviced the columnist regularly with variegated material which may have no immediate publicity value but which builds confidence and good will. Occasionally, columnists will attend a press conference, luncheon, or special event, and they should be invited as a matter of course if there is a remote chance that the subject will be of interest. Columnists have wide syndication and enormous readership.

Letters to the editor may be used if they are timely, provocative, and germane to some specific issue which is currently in the news. For example, the *Times* printed an account of a study which was generally critical of educational television.

Several days later the same paper printed a letter to the editor, written by a leader of the educational TV movement, in which the original story was commented upon in terms of a critical appraisal and rebuttal.

Editorial space is rare, but it is worth the effort to obtain it if it seems feasible. An editorial may be suggested in many ways: by phone calls to the editor, by letter, by sending special reports or other background or documentary information to the attention of the editor. A few years ago, a motion picture company prepared a short film on the Springfield Plan for Intercultural Education. The editors of the papers were invited to see the film and were briefed in advance by letter and by background fact sheet. One of the leading newspapers printed an editorial commending the film, as well as the company which produced it, for its social usefulness.

Every story, regardless of type or the department for which it is intended, must have a news peg. This is the prime requisite of all publicity release writing. The story need *not* be exclusive, although stories marked "exclusive" invariably receive greater attention than general releases. A distinction should be made between an exclusive story which is intended for one specific paper and a story marked "Special to the New York *Times*" which is simply a variation of a basic story which has been serviced to other papers. Before any story is marked either "exclusive" or "Special to . . . ," the publicist should determine the policy of the particular newspaper involved; and by policy is meant the general attitude toward, and handling of, the news from several significant viewpoints—political, sociological, economic, educational, etc. What, for example, is the attitude toward humorous items, toward crime, pictures, sex, children, religion, business, personality features?

There are frequent occasions when the publicity release will summarize an annual report or a special document such as the New York University Self-Study Report. This type of story should include a special memo to the editor, along with the original document, if possible. For example: "Dr. John Jones, president of the Jones Foundation, today made public the results of a six-month survey, conducted throughout the country, on the use of atomic energy in medical research. A summary, as well as a copy of the report, is attached."

Publicists who are attached to the public relations department of large institutions often have an opportunity to interest a specific newspaper in a series of stories of a semifeature nature. These are news stories in series, such as the convention of the National Association of Radio and Television Broadcasters or the annual meeting of American Association for the Advancement of Science; or there may be a narrative series of reports such as "Your Community Resources"; or, finally, the publicist may interest the editor in a series of feature stories which combine news quality with human interest material. The possibilities for this type of story are many and varied: a feature series on a newly elected official, a new stage or screen personality, a story about some unusual hobby or invention, and others.

News items which are printed in the newspaper or mentioned by radio or television commentators may not be publicity; but all publicity releases should be *news*. The capable public relations and publicity men render a distinct service to the mass media, for they are directly or indirectly responsible for a very great part of the material which is covered in the press and over the air-waves. The crucial determinant in a publicity release is that special kernel which makes it *news* and therefore worthy of coverage. The kind of publicity which the editor accepts for publication is the kind which makes news.

What is news from a publicity standpoint? It is that which

the editor considers worthy of printing in the paper, or the commentator deems worthy of mention on the air, or the newsreel editor thinks worthy of coverage *because* it will probably be of sufficient interest to the receiving audience to engender a desire to read, hear, or see it. The public relations director may set policy, but the publicity man must devise, engineer, or discover the news out of the welter of activities that surround the individual, institution, product, or idea which he is representing. Out of this fabric he must create the event or the story that will become news. There are occasions when the news simply happens, such as accidents or other unexpected events, but by and large the publicist must find or devise the news and see that it gets into print.

There have been many estimates of what makes news, depending upon the nature of the project under way. There are, however, certain *basic* areas which are sources of news and which have proved to be substantial and important from a publicist's and an editor's point of view. The publicity "pegs" most commonly used as sources of news are:

1. *Spot news:* This is a straightforward announcement of some activity of interest, e.g., the announcement of a new appointment, a new program, or project, etc.
2. *Special survey:* This is exemplified by such surveys as the New York University Self-Study, the Ford Foundation Surveys, etc.
3. *Reports:* These consist of annual reports and special studies, stockholder reports, particularly when issued with the document or a summary of it.
4. *Current events:* These are items in the news which may suggest a "peg" to the astute publicist. For example, a book on economics may suggest some statement from the head of a large corporation, either in rebuttal or as additional comment.
5. *Meetings and conferences:* These are of some interest to the daily press and of particular interest to the trade papers,

e.g., a stockholders' or directors' meeting, or a special meeting to set up some new project or program, as the building of a new civic center.

6. *Speeches:* Frequently the public relations director will arrange for a company official to speak at a convention. The publicist takes over from that point, working with the speaker and the public relations director on the speech as well as on the preparation of the necessary release. There are scores of conventions—educational, scientific, advertising, or business —which offer a springboard for public speaking if the speaker and subject are germane to the meeting topic.

7. *Formation of a committee:* This announcement may be either serious or semihumorous. Serious stories include political committees, civic groups set up to achieve some reform, religious groups or committees formed for the express purpose of achieving publicity. One example of a semiserious one was the formation of a committee to promote a love of piano music, formed by a famous popular pianist.

8. *Anniversaries:* These are actually long-range special events, involving promotion and advertising as well as publicity. But they offer excellent possibilities for reiterative publicity through releases, features, and picture spreads. Examples are the Anniversary of the Electric Light and the Twentieth Anniversary of the Talking Motion Picture.

9. *Holidays:* The publicity value of holiday dates depends upon how feasibly the project can be related to the event. The National Safety Council, for example, secures considerable space by issuing a safe driving story prior to every major holiday when many cars are expected on the road.

10. *Awards and degrees:* The arranging for an award, or for the receipt of an honorary degree, offers opportunity for publicity releases as well as pictures.

11. *Drives and campaigns:* Special stories announcing a fundraising drive for some reputable institution are usually carried, particularly when important names in business, education, the arts, and society can be used in the release.

12. *Donations:* Any large sum of money, donated for some edu-

cational or philanthropic purpose, is usually worthy of an item in the press.

13. *Scholarships:* These announcements, such as the annual Westinghouse Science Scholarship program, achieve considerable space not only for the sponsor, but also for the schools or institutions from which the recipients are chosen.

14. *New products:* These are many and varied—new motion pictures, new plays, new industrial products, new fabrics, new cars, new inventions. Issued to the proper department, they are sound newsworthy items.

15. *The Exposé and demand:* This concept includes several variations—a revelation showing need for remedial aid to some organization or individual, a denunciation of some project as injurious to the general welfare, a demand for more aid to schools, etc.

16. *Research:* This subject is of particular importance to education and science editors, e.g., a new experiment in psychology, a study in fluoridation, etc.

17. *The debate:* Of some importance to the press, this device is of particular interest to radio and television programs. If the subject is of sufficient interest, and the names suggested of recognizable value, the publicist may be able to arrange for a discussion of some topic on a TV forum. For example, the head of a college may debate federal aid to education with a member of some committee which has issued a report on the subject.

18. *The special event:* This area is a particularly important one for the creative publicist. It involves, literally, the setting up of a specific project or event for the purpose of *making* or *creating* news. Special events are of various kinds, depending upon the nature of the institution involved. They include: dinners and banquets, conventions, the arranging for a crowd of teen-agers to greet a singing star, a rally, a fair or exhibit (such as the General Motors Futurama), a planned series of events (such as the Boy Scouts Annual Jamboree), special exhibits, contests (such as Miss America), and fashion or industrial displays or showings.

Special events require long and painstaking work, but if they are done carefully and with an eye to the news values, they can achieve important coverage in the press, radio, TV, magazines, and newsreels. Publicity releases are not sufficient if used alone. The publicist must have pictures, feature stories, background material, fact sheets, and other paraphernalia available in order to insure proper service to the mass media. At a special convention, for example, facilities should be provided for complete press coverage. These should include, at a minimum, the following:

(a) A press representative in attendance at the press room where there should be paper and typewriters.

(b) Western Union wire facilities, if possible.

(c) Advance copies of projected speeches and addresses.

(d) A log of events or a fact sheet.

(e) Background and filler data.

19. *Common denominators:* Stories, pictures, or column items which find a common denominator of public interest make news. In other words, statements, pictures, or events should be allied in some way with an area or topic that touches directly on the audience's sphere of interest. Money is such a common denominator, as are sex, religion, children, and animals.

20. *Promotion tie-ins and publicity:* The promotional area is, in one sense, a distinct part of public relations. In another, it is an important adjunct of publicity. Most companies with fully staffed public relations departments have a separate promotion unit which functions in conjunction with publicity and advertising. But, in a larger sense, promotional activities are part of the publicity operation for, while they may function separately, they nevertheless can contribute in an important way to the publicity achievement.

Promotion efforts are concerned with specific steps to build the product, institution, individual, or idea. They frequently render a service in addition to promoting the product. In general, promotions are of four kinds:

(a) *The tie-in:* In this area, the promotion man works to secure endorsements or testimonials, either for the purpose of advertising or publicity. The principle on which this activity is based is the tendency of the receiving audience to climb on the band wagon, the idea being if so-and-so, who is a famous personality, does it, why not everyone else? Prizes for contests are frequently promoted by tying in a mention of the manufacturer; and the television quiz shows reveal the tie-in technique when they announce that the contestants have been flown in by a designated airline. This, then, is a *quid pro quo* promotion in which both participants benefit. Another tie-in involves the awarding of scrolls or other accolades whereby both the award giver and the recipient garner favorable publicity. For example, a well-known radio program was given an award by a national organization and, as the case turned out, the president of the organization appeared on the program and was able to get across a fine plug for his own institution. Recently, a well-known television star took his program down South to cover a motion picture premiere, and, by the same token, the movie company not only secured publicity for the event, but took some formidable advertising, mentioning the star in the copy.

(b) *Direct mail*:  This effort is as important in publicity as it is in advertising, but the lists are more specialized. The national distributors of motor cars, refrigerators, and other items do a great deal of dealer promotion in the form of brochures, posters, contests, and similar efforts. Direct-mail promotion is also important in sending out information about new products and ideas to editors, dealers, and community leaders.

(c) *Special mailings*:  These promotions are valuable in specific areas, such as schools or colleges. For example, the CBS Radio Network prepared a special discussion and study guide on one of its series of current events programs and sent it to department heads in high schools. The material, while legitimate promotion, sold no product and was carefully educational or institutional in nature. It was designed basically to render a service to the teacher. At the same time, it told the educator that the broadcasting network was not disinterested in education. The project was not only successful from an educational viewpoint, but also received favorable publicity in the press and in educational journals. Similar public service brochures are prepared by many other industries and are widely accepted in the educational world.

(d) *Exploitation promotions:* In this area, promotion functions to exploit a favorable event, a good publicity story, or an important advertisement. It involves reprints of news stories or good critical reviews, mailing of proofs of an advertisement, and the preparation of special flyers or broadsides which tell dealers or other affiliated publics that the company has received or achieved something of importance. A big picture story in *Life,* for example, is reprinted and mailed to all possible outlets which might be interested.

## PUBLICITY AND PUBLIC RELATIONS

Publicity may be called successful *if* it carries out, in a practical and sensible way, a total public relations objective. It is neither press agentry nor public relations but includes something of both, depending upon the nature of the project or campaign. The skilled publicity man, whatever the objective, will avoid certain pitfalls in his releases. He will avoid sending news to the wrong department. He will not oversell the plug in his story. He will cooperate with editors who follow up the release for additional data. He will try to be specific, factual, and straightforward. And he will service the editors by careful captioning of pictures and by including a summary of long and involved reports.

The purpose of public relations is to convey to the public a concept of good deeds in the public interest. By means of publicity, the public is kept informed of the policies, objectives, and deeds of an organization. At best, publicity serves to inform the public, by means of mass media, and its legitimate purpose is to espouse or advance the cause of an individual, product, institution, or idea. Publicity *must* have a news key in order to further its chances of breaking into print. If it is successful, publicity will not only service the editor but also achieve the public relations objective of building good will and creating consent.

Two caveats should be noted in connection with publicity writing and planting. First, the publicist must not expect to see his release printed as written. Following is a release issued to the press:

### USE OF RADIO SHOULD HELP IN TEACHER SHORTAGE
### HAYES TELLS 7,000 EDUCATORS

Teachers have failed to make the most complete and effective use of the various mass media of communication, Arthur Hull Hayes, President of CBS Radio, told an audience of 7,000 Catholic educators today. Mr. Hayes made the principal address at the closing session of the National Catholic Educational Association Convention in Milwaukee.

"Particularly in a time of critical need, such as the present teacher shortage," Mr. Hayes stated, "mass media such as the press and radio can be of enormous help to the educator. I am not suggesting that these are to be substitutes for the able and dedicated teacher, but I do believe that they can provide an effective bridge in times of need, and a very useful supplement at all times. A radio broadcast of a talk by a distinguished personality, a forum, or a broadcast of a symphony program reaches millions of students simultaneously, whereas even the most brilliant of classroom teachers can reach only a limited number."

The educators, Mr. Hayes told the Convention audience, are the true directors of the content of mass media. "You, the public, are the true program directors. In your hands rests the ultimate power either to listen or to turn the dial."

Mr. Hayes stated that educators have failed to exercise their unique franchise as the real program directors. "As program directors, have you done anything positive about improving your program content?" he asked them. "You must exercise this responsibility to yourselves, to your students and to the general public. The educator has as much responsibility to the mass media, as the purveyors of mass communications have to you."

Mr. Hayes charged that educators have not taken full advantage of the considerable amount of educational and informational programming which is available. "Do you listen to symphonies? Do you discuss them in the classroom? If the New York Philharmonic Symphony came to your city, certainly you would urge your students to attend the concert. Yet, your students—all of them—can hear the Philharmonic every week over the radio."

"It's not possible for your students to attend the Presidential Press Conference, but you can hear it at regular intervals on the radio. You can also study it in the press. Yet, how many of you are encouraging this kind of activity on the part of your students? These programs are offered to you at great cost and at considerable effort. But, if you and your students do not listen, they must inevitably go off the air."

One of the basic reasons for continuing this kind of programming, Mr. Hayes said, "is our sense of responsibility, because we put these programs on the air even when many of you do not listen."

Mr. Hayes urged the assembled teachers, supervisors, and other administrators to take advantage of the mass media so that they would continue to remain free and competitive. "The best encouragement you can give us is to listen. What will be on the air or in the press four or five years from now depends, in large measure, on you and the students whom you are training."

Each of the newspapers which printed the story did so in terms of its own formula of presentation. The New York *Times,* in the course of a complete story of the meeting, printed the following:

The principal speaker was Arthur Hull Hayes, president of Columbia Broadcasting System Radio. He told the educators they had not been taking advantage of many of the great educational possibilities offered by the mass-media communications.

The press, radio and television, he said, could help alleviate the current teacher shortage but are being neglected.

Shortly after Mr. Hayes' talk the convention adopted some resolutions prepared many weeks before. . . .

The New York *World-Telegram and Sun,* however, ran a complete story, devoted to the address:

SAYS SCHOOLS NEGLECT TO USE
CULTURAL PROGRAMS ON RADIO

Special to *World-Telegram and Sun.*
*Milwaukee, April 29.*—In a time of critical teacher shortage, educators have failed to make effective use of the various mass media of communications, CBS Radio president Arthur Hull Hayes told an audience of Catholic educators over the weekend.

Speaking at the final session of the National Catholic Educational Association he further charged that the men who direct the nation's schools do not give the proper support when the entertainment media try to present cultural programs.

"It is not possible for your students to attend the Presidential Press Conference, but you can hear it at regular intervals on the radio," he said. "You can hear the Philharmonic every week on the radio. You can hear a man like John Mason Brown discuss modern poetry. Yet, how many of you are encouraging your students to listen to these programs?" he asked.

Mr. Hayes said that, while he did not propose to substitute radio or TV "for the able and dedicated teacher," he did believe that "they can provide an effective bridge in times of need and a very useful supplement at all times."

The New York *Daily News,* in the course of a news roundup, printed the following:

Educators have failed to use mass media such as the press and radio effectively, CBS Radio prexy Arthur Hull Hayes said yesterday. Addressing a group of 7,000 Catholic educators in Milwaukee, Hayes stated that the nation's teachers are "the real program directors." "You must exercise this responsibility to yourselves, to your students and to the general public," he said. He urged the assembly to listen to the radio, particularly to the information-type programs on the air, and to discuss them with their students.

A second caveat relates to the problem of planting or servicing the press. There are occasions when even an important story cannot be sent routinely and in the same form to all local and national newspapers. This across-the-board servicing can be done with an official announcement, but special events and promotional efforts require so-called pinpointing. In other words, in addition to the routine service story, the publicist would do well to have prepared "Special to . . ." pieces which are planted directly with many of the respective papers. In this way, the event itself receives greater chance of being handled in an important way.

Publicity, then, is not public relations. It is a *tool* of public relations, a technique which promulgates policy through its active dissemination of information to the public by means of mass media.

# Part V

# Areas of Practice

*Areas in which public relations is applied—Business and management, the stockholder, the consumer, the employee, government, education, the community*

# CHAPTER 20

## *Publicity Areas*

As public relations, advertising, and publicity grew in importance in an expanding industrial economy, the departmental director and the private counsel concerned themselves with matters of management function in relation to public opinion and with the establishment and delineation of policy. Areas of specialization were demarcated. To many veteran publicists, this development into specialization was not a happy event. A public relations man was supposed to set policy, handle publicity copy, and plant it with the speed and ability of the best press agents. Most capable publicists can handle almost any phase of activity, but there was a rationale behind the development of the specialist. As the mass media grew and as business became more acutely aware of the need for, and value of, public relations, the territory to be covered expanded. Handling of the press became a full-time job requiring a staff of several writers and planters. The many national, fan, and special magazines also required the full-time services of at least one person who could work constantly with the editors and become familiar with their needs and idiosyncrasies. The need for specialization, particularly in organizations with many possible publicity outlets, made itself felt, and, as a result, the profession acquired its specialists in various areas. The fully staffed department, in addition to its publicity manager, usually is equipped with news and feature writers and planters and individuals who are responsible for magazines, columns, radio and television, pictures, motion pictures, special events, and promotion.

### SPECIAL FEATURES

More important than spot news publicity is the feature story, the prearranged article, or the combined picture-story. Features for the newspaper are usually of three related kinds: the news feature which combines both a news peg and a special human interest aspect; the department feature, such as an interview or special by-line piece on the amusement page; and the magazine feature which is an article, written on assignment to a staff writer, and sometimes illustrated by pictures or line drawings.

The communication content of any one of these features is essentially *thematic*. In other words, it is built around some creatively contrived idea such as one of the following:

1. An unusual anniversary story, e.g., twenty-five years of service as a radio newscaster.
2. A retirement story, e.g., fifty years as conductor on a railroad.
3. A special plan, e.g., a foundation grant to a university for medical research.
4. A new building development, e.g., story based on the personality behind the project.
5. An unusual idea, e.g., the origination of a television quiz show.
6. A human interest idea, e.g., story of a lawyer who writes novels in his spare time.

Feature publicity, then, is more than news. It develops *out of* some news event or special event and is an elaboration of a thematic idea. It is the most difficult kind of story to arrange, first because each publication develops its own ideas for features out of editorial conferences, and, second, because the newspaper and magazine editors are literally flooded with feature suggestions from publicity men. Yet, in terms of enduring value and depth and penetration into public opinion, it is the kind of publicity which is most significant from a good will or public relations viewpoint. This is so because feature publicity helps to shape public opinion in a more permanent mold than spot news. For example, a major magazine feature on a process of bread baking not only brought the product to the attention of its millions of readers, but also created an unprecedented sales demand. Features, particularly in Sunday supplements and national magazines, are a significant public relations aid and a tremendous boost to prestige, good will, and tangible public action. They create consent.

Arranging for the feature story, however, requires much more than a theme or idea, particularly for the magazines. The newspaper department editor may use a feature on some timely personality or subject *if* that subject or person is tied in with an immediate event, such as the opening of a play or a new plant or the publication of a book. But magazines must take a longer view. The thematic idea must have a more universal significance and a longer range of interest span for the readers. In addition, magazine features must be planted as much as three or four months ahead. For example, a publicist succeeded in securing a news feature on a radio performer who was celebrating her twenty-fifth year as a daytime serial player, and the story ran almost on the day of the event. But magaines, which might have run a story on the personality, turned the publicist down because he came to the editors too late. The story would not have appeared in print until two or three months after the event.

Feature writing and planting require more than a basic idea. They require considerable preliminary research and documentation which are then presented so convincingly and colorfully that the editor will urge the story on his colleagues and ultimately assign a special writer to take it on. Probably the most successful achievement in modern publicity is the prestige of a story or picture in such publications as the New York *Times Magazine,* the Sunday supplements such as *Parade, This Week,* and *American Weekly,* or a story in *Life, Look,* or the other great national magazines, as well as in such news weeklies as *Time* and *Newsweek.* The latter, incidentally, are departmentalized and offer a tremendously important outlet for newsworthy material in such fields as business, education, radio and TV, books, motion pictures, science, and other related areas. The key to almost any of these publications, more so than to the daily paper, is the degree of human interest inherent in the theme or idea, along with the documentation of it. Many publicity men attached to the radio networks have complained about the emphasis on television features on the part of the editors. But the editors' rebuttal is a simple and conventional one: "Give us an interesting theme or angle and we'll use it." There is no premium on publicity ideas, particularly in the feature field.

The kernel of feature publicity is, simply, the discovery of an interesting theme. And, while certain staples always make for feature possibilities, the staple must be garnished with a provocative theme or idea. The staples of interest are romance, religion, money, children, health, and animals. But no one of these *as such* makes for a feature, unless it is built around an idea. For example, the story of a famous art director who trained for the ministry until he discovered his artistic talent is a good feature idea; or the story of a college instructor who amassed a fortune in the stock market; or that of a mechanic who is an authority on Elizabethan drama; or of an opera star who spends every week end experimenting with the preparation of new culinary delights. All of these are human interest stories, based upon a theme.

With the exception of those newspaper editors who welcome them, features should not be written by the publicist except by request or by prearrangement. Wherever possible, they should be accompanied by interesting pictures. But the enterprising publicist can suggest many creative possibilities even in the most mundane topics. The subject of silk, for example, suggests the following:

1. New scientific developments in processing.
2. Style features.
3. "Cheese-cake" pictures.
4. Educational features on the history of the product.
5. Business and political features on the problems of export and import.

The best method of successful feature servicing is a study of the media which use feature stories and pictures. Certain newspapers and magazines will place emphasis on specific themes. Some newspapers rarely run features; others run them on a daily basis. And, in addition to the daily newspapers and magazines, the press syndicates should not be overlooked, for they service hundreds of newspapers with daily features. For example, a story on the one-hundredth anniversary broadcast of a famous radio program, based on an interview with the sponsor, was syndicated via the Associated Press, and the resulting tear-sheets revealed that several hundred newspapers had printed it. Feature publicity, once achieved, is worth the necessary effort made to achieve it. Its public relations impact is tremendously important.

## PICTORIAL PUBLICITY

Probably every teacher of journalism has had occasion to
mention the axiom "One picture is worth a thousand words."
This, literally, is true of a major part of newspaper and magazine publicity. Most publicists would settle for a two- or three-
column captioned picture, with appropriate credit, rather than
a story, unless they achieved both a news story *and* a concomitant picture. From a practical publicity viewpoint, however, most newspapers use very few pictures in comparison to
copy; and most of the pictures are of the spot news variety.
Even those organs which use a daily picture page or a two-page
picture spread will include only one or two planted pictures
among the group. Editors are watchful of the picture space. A
picture must be enormously newsworthy or interesting to be
considered, and it is usually selected, again, on the basis of how
interestingly it varies one of the basic human interest themes—
religion, health, sex, money, children, animals. The public opinion impact of a good picture, with a strong head and caption,
is far more powerful than a whole paragraph, or even a column, of type.

The problem which every pictorial publicist must resolve
in order to plant pictures successfully is simply this: What, in
the opinion of the picture editor, is considered a "good" picture, either for the specific paper or for the photo syndicates,
such as International News Pictures?

First, editors are almost unanimous in asserting that the
best pictures, and those most likely to be used, are those with a
theme. In other words, a good picture, apart from explanatory
text or caption, tells a complete and interesting story. It arrests
the attention of the reader.

Second, the most desirable pictures, from the point of view

of the editor's choice, are those which are embellished with a human interest aspect. They do more than *record* an event. They tell something active and creative about people in terms of what they are doing.

Third, desirable pictures are not static or posed. They look alive because they record some human action which is timely and interesting and which, above all, has narrative value. In other words, a good picture is worth a thousand words because it tells the story graphically and completely.

A careful study of the kinds of picture used day in and day out by the press and picture services reveals that certain basic requirements have been met. To be acceptable, a picture must:

1. Record a news event of genuine significance, e.g., an important dedication by an important personality.
2. Record an event of local or national interest and of genuine excitement, e.g., a flood, an unusual football victory, a big campus event, the signing of an important contract.
3. Record a news event which features a personality, e.g., a dignitary or celebrity arriving, or leaving, aboard ship or at an airport.
4. Be of specific human interest, e.g., one thousand children on an outing, a star returning from entertaining European royalty, a famous personality engaged in an off-beat hobby.

Pictures eventuate in the press in three ways: the editor uses one from the files in connection with a news story; the photo editor assigns a photographer to cover an event; the publicity man services the pictures to the paper. Although photo editors should be invited by wire to cover events which appear to have picture possibilities, it is essential that the publicity department also have its own staff photographer on hand. Even though the papers have been covered, there is always extra insurance in servicing pictures. These should be developed, captioned, and serviced to the newspaper's city or photo desk as quickly as possible. Most papers will use 8- by 10-inch glossy prints. Some prefer mats, because they are less expensive, but timely events must be covered by glossy prints. Local weekly papers may ask for cuts, which are made from the prints, and this is worth doing if there is assurance of use. All serviced pictures should have a caption pasted along the bottom of the photograph and *not* written on the reversed side. The caption, depending on the event, can be a brief explanation or a longer news feature.

It is advisable to service pictures only to the specific local press, i.e., those which can be reached by messenger. Pictures which have a chance of national use in many papers should be serviced to the photo syndicates which may syndicate the picture to the many member papers in much the same fashion as a news story is distributed. If possible, each syndicate should have a different picture on an exclusive basis.

Pictorial publicity has a much greater chance of breaking into the papers if pictures are planned in advance and with the needs of the press in mind. The action in the picture should be carefully planned, as should the number of people who are to be in it. It is not wise to use more than four personalities at the very maximum. An appropriate background should be selected. For example, a photo of an inventor is best taken amid laboratory apparatus because it lends color and thematic texture. Finally, the picture should be so planned as to tell the desired story. What, in essence, does the publicist want the picture to accomplish from a public relations viewpoint? Good pictures are rejected because of lack of space or because they do not tell a story imaginatively. For example, a picture of a conductor who retires after fifty years of service is greatly enhanced by showing him next to a model 1900 train; a cub scout lends humor and human interest to a Boy Scout award picture. Most of the national magazines prefer to take their own pictures if they are interested in a personality or special event. But it is still wise to have pictures on hand. And, at all times, the pictorial publicist should keep an up-to-date file of pictures of all company officials, along with up-to-date biographical material. The need for pictures in this area is frequently unexpected, and a good picture is an important tool to have on hand.

## PRESS RELATIONS

The publicity section of a public relations department may be called, simply, the publicity department, or it is sometimes called the press information division or press relations department. In any event, this section functions specifically to relate the activities of the organization to the press, to service the press, and to be available to answer questions and handle matters concerning general publicity. Press relations, like public relations, is a two-way street. The publicist functions not only to contact the press when he has a story, but also to render service to the press when a reporter or editor requires information or is following a lead.

Apart, then, from the sheer technique of publicity writing and handling, press relations involves what is truly a human relations aspect of the public relations function. For, despite the conviction that newspapermen respect only facts and will pursue a story relentlessly, there is still an important human equation in which personalities are involved and emotional factors come into play. The editors assert that they demand only that the publicity man "level" with them, that he not plant a palpably false story, and that he avoid double dealing and chicanery. They will not respond to contrivance and they will not be touted off the scent of a good story. Furthermore, the top-level editors realize that there are matters of internal concern which management may not want to publicize, although they do not react kindly to the "no comment" technique.

At one point or another, the publicist cannot depend upon the mailing of a release to do a job for him. He must contact the press directly, get to know the editors, and win their confidence. This, in itself, is a monumental task of public and human relations. The publicist will discover quickly that he cannot distort, conceal, or misrepresent information to the press. To do so is not only a violation of professional ethics and a flaunting of the editor's own integrity as a journalist; it is also a black eye for every publicist who works so arduously to achieve legitimate publicity. It demeans the profession of public relations.

Beyond the truthful representation of content, however, there are occasions when the overtures will come from the editor. Some of these reportorial demands may prove embarrassing or difficult to obtain because company policy may prohibit the release of certain data for publication. In these situations, the public relations director may be called upon to discuss the request with the reporter or editor. If it is impossible to service the material asked for, the publicist should remember that the reporter has an obligation to his city editor or managing editor. Perhaps a substitute story of some interest will suffice. As a matter of human relations, it is not wise to turn down the request peremptorily, for the reporter and editor will both appreciate an effort to service them.

In addition to the human relations problem involved in publicity techniques, there are also certain pragmatic do's and don'ts involved which distinguish the seasoned and careful publicist from the careless or inexperienced one. It is not advisable, for example, to direct material to the wrong department. Too many publicity agencies maintain carelessly handled mailing lists and send out across-the-board data only to find that the ultimate disposition is not in newsprint but in the permanent limbo of the wastebasket. Such careless servicing does not build good press relations, and subsequent efforts are less likely to find their way into print. It is advisable, therefore, to determine which department is most likely to be interested in a story. Well-organized publicity departments keep a card index of mailing lists, broken down into people, categories, and papers. In this way, appropriate material can be directed to the appropriate department. The publicist who sends "cheese cake" to the New York *Times* is simply indulging in an exercise in futility. The careful publicist develops a close working relationship with editors, based on their wants and needs, and soon finds that the editors themselves will turn to him as a sound source of news.

The history of public relations and publicity vis-à-vis journalism has never been a story of complete mutual trust and good will, nor will it ever be. There are editors who hand out indulgences with the spirit of an absolute monarch. A month of internship as a working publicist would provide editors with a fine operational example of what is involved in the arduous business of servicing the press against ruthlessly keen competition. There are editors who look upon all public relations men with a degree of suspicion, until they are reminded that a major part of their content is from copy serviced by publicity men.

Since World War II the relationship between the press and the press agent has been greatly improved. Business interests have become more cognizant of the public relations area, and editors have come to respect the public relations man as a willing and able co-worker and not an interloper. While the objective of the plug at any price still exists among some, the contemporary publicist writes and plants with an understanding of the needs of both the press and the public relations policies of his company. The concept of publicity as an integral part of sound public relations developed out of the crucible of experience —the discarding of the "public be damned" notion of business-men, the rise of trade unionism, the growth of public opinion and propaganda studies, and the increasing use of public rela-tions techniques in political campaigning as manifested both by the New Deal and by the astute public opinion campaigns of the Republican party in 1952 and in 1956. The public relations and publicity man of today wants to understand the press and wants to be understood by it. He strives to convince the editor that his material is honest and factual and newsworthy. He strives to become a good source of news. And he works to con-vince his own management that the press is important and that company policies which are not in the public interest will result eventually in poor press relations and, finally, in a nega-tive public opinion.

At the same time, the publicist who has serviced the press ca-pably and forthrightly has a right to expect help and coöperation when it is needed. He has a right to expect a sympathetic un-derstanding of his, and his company's, problems and, particu-larly, to expect that legitimate news will be used. In the long run, the publicist who has won the confidence of the press is most likely to get his story printed favorably.

These seven suggestions may serve as guides to constructive press relations:

1. By and large, the publicist should place his trust and confidence in the press. Rarely will an editor use names if the publicist has asked that they not be used.
2. The publicist should be accessible to the editor at all times.
3. Background material should be available at all times in con-nection with an important release, e.g., biographies, pictures, etc.

4. The press should be treated respectfully but should not be pandered to.
5. Advertising should not be confused with publicity, and the editor should never be asked to run a story because the company is a large advertiser.
6. The editor should not be told what is good about a story. He should, on the basis of data and suggestions, be allowed to make his own decision.
7. The skillful publicist will, on occasion, service the editors with ideas and leads which do not necessarily concern his own operation.

## THE PRESS CONFERENCE

The device of the press conference is one of the most delicate instruments in the practice of public relations. It requires not only an understanding of management function and policy, but also of press relations and publicity techniques. Press conferences can be helpful and they can also do irreparable harm. For example, a new public relations director decided to call a press conference with his company president because he had noted that his predecessor had steadfastly failed to call such a conference. Therefore, he arranged a luncheon at a midtown club and wired the press to attend. What the public relations director did not take the trouble to determine was the reason for avoiding such conferences in the past. The reason was simple: The president was not directly aware of many company activities and concerned himself only with esoteric matters of very high echelon policy. At the conference, reporters asked questions about stock problems and related matters only to find the president in the embarrassing position of being unable to answer their questions. Subordinate officials had to come to his aid.

On the other hand, press conferences can be useful and important. A broadcasting network was about to present an important documentary bearing on an important international *cause célèbre*. In this situation, the public relations director issued a news release and followed with a wire to city desks. At the conference, the reporters were briefed *in advance* of the program highlights, and interested parties were present to answer background questions. As a result, the press ran advance stories alerting the public to the broadcast.

These examples illustrate one major point: Press conferences should not be called unless there is a valid and *newsworthy* reason. To invite the press to an informal luncheon is one thing. But a press conference is an entirely different matter. It should be what it purports to be and not an amalgam of many different techniques. The most timely occasion for a press conference, other than in an emergency, is the issuing of *major news*— news of such importance to the press and the public that a release is not sufficient because questions will inevitably crop up and the answers to these questions by responsible officials may garner additional space. The press group to be invited to a conference depends on the nature of the story. Any combination of the following may be asked to attend, but it is always expedient to extend the invitation to both the city desk *and* the specific department if the story has general, as well as special, news overtones:

1. The city desk.
2. The specific department—business or finance, motion pictures, women's page, radio and TV, sports, advertising, books, etc.
3. The city desks and departments of the press associations—AP, UP, INS.
4. If feasible, radio commentators.
5. If feasible, the newsreel companies.

Any of the above should be invited by wire and/or phone call, and the nature of the story should be described so accurately that the desk will know precisely which reporter to assign for coverage.

If the press conference is to be successful, attention to the following details usually helps:

1. Telephones should be available.
2. Typewriters and paper should be available.
3. Telegraph service should be offered.
4. Releases should be on hand.
5. Background and fact-sheet material should be available.

A press conference obviously requires a spokesman. And no detail is more important than having top management present. This not only adds prestige, but also lends authority to the statements made. In addition, it offers the reporters and photographers an opportunity to use an important name for news and picture purposes. One caveat is in order in connection with the presence of a company spokesman: The reporters should know what is a direct quote, what is indirect, and what is off the record. By far, the most successful press conferences are those which avoid falling back on the phrase "no comment." If possible, the reporters should be allowed also to use names instead of the phrase "a spokesman said." The most forthright way to handle questions which cannot be answered is to have the official state that, while the data in the news release are all that can be used for publication, he will be glad to fill in with background information and explain *why* it was not included in the original release.

Certain strategies are important in handling the conference. The major achievement is for the public relations man to have a top company official present. But, if this is to happen, the official must be briefed in advance, for, unfortunately, few company executives are public-relations-minded. Policy matters should be discussed in advance so that the public relations man can anticipate questions and advise the official regarding alternative replies. At the conference itself, the public relations man's role is best described as a mute, inglorious guide, stepping in only when absolutely necessary—and then only to offer information or fact, not to discuss policy, unless the spokesman is in serious straits with an overly aggressive reporter.

The press conference, finally, is not a routine event. It should be utilized only when, as, and if the occasion demands.

## PUBLIC RELATIONS IN CRISIS

Both public relations as a policy matter and publicity as a technique are also involved when some critical situation or emergency occurs. At one time or another in every large enterprise a crisis will happen, and in such a critical situation the public relations director and staff must act swiftly and surely.

Probably the first determination to be made is whether or not to exercise the dubious prerogative of censorship or to issue a succinct "no comment." Four possible situations may serve as examples.

First, an event beyond the control of the company or its public relations director occurs, and news about it is printed in the press or is voiced over the air; or, a reporter digs up a story which did not emanate in any way from the company publicity department, such as a critical statement from the opposition, an unfavorable resolution at a PTA meeting or some similar event.

Second, an internal crisis breaks, such as a union problem or a strike or accident.

Third, a statement is made by a company head or staff member, or by a faculty member at an educational institution, *without* the prior knowledge of the public relations department. A most unfair result of such occurrences is a situation whereby the company heads score the public relations director because the press did not check with him before printing the story!

Fourth, an unexpected crisis may arise, such as an attack on the policy of a company by a stockholder in attendance at a stockholders' meeting where there are reporters present. In this situation, the company president may ask the public relations man to keep the story out of print. While this is remotely possible *if* the public relations man has excellent press contact, it is neither practical nor ethical procedure. More often than not, it is manifestly impossible. The optimum that can be expected is that the reporters have sufficient confidence in the public relations man and the reputation of his company to make a special effort to give fair representation to the company viewpoint.

These potentially critical situations should not catch a public relations department unaware. It is particularly important that the company executives be made aware of public relations techniques and problems. Officials should understand the possible consequences when questions relating to a release are handled with a "no comment" attitude. More often than not, the reporter will ferret out the answer elsewhere and confront the public relations director with the data. The question of ethics in public relations is nowhere more acute than in crisis where the publicity or public relations director is faced with a need for immediate decision. Frequently, the decision must be made whether to attempt discreet censorship or allow the press to have the requested information. No firm rule can be formulated, but in general it is wiser, as a matter of long-range relations with the press, to allow certain news items to run if the reporter has the facts. A few tenets from the Code of Ethics of the American College Public Relations Association are germane in this respect. Among the guiding principles listed are:

1. Respect for truth.
2. Dignity, good manners, and high purpose.
3. Responsibility to the public.
4. Fairness and sincerity.
5. A progressive attitude.
6. Coöperativeness.

These tenets can be translated into pragmatic and operational situations.

1. *Respect for truth:* Statements to the press, whether scientific, financial, or in some other area, should not subvert the truth.
2. *Dignity and good manners:* In most enterprises, even in the entertainment areas, flamboyant special events should be avoided. In all enterprises involving public relations, the press should be treated with courtesy, and, incidentally, the public relations director must insist upon courteous treatment for his staff from the internal company heads.
3. *Responsibility to the public:* Every institution requires the support and good will of the public, and this support must be earned by specific actions in the public interest.
4. *Fairness and sincerity:* Neither the press nor the public should be given false information.
5. *Progressive attitude:* Public relations should suggest constructive changes in policy when necessary because these are in the public interest.
6. *Coöperativeness:* The public relations director should spearhead a spirit of willingness to coöperate with the press on the part of every member of the company, both executives and rank-and-file employees.

In cases of crisis where the public relations and publicity directors are confronted with decisions which have an ethical aspect, the one avenue *not* to take is that of the so-called defense mechanism. If, for example, a criticism is made by an irresponsible individual, the company president is well advised not to demean himself or his company representation by engaging in a brass knuckles gutter fight. Secondly, hotly worded *post facto* denials always leave an overtone of defensiveness. The rebuttal should be made immediately and in terms of sober, cold, hard facts. And, if misstatements have been made, a factual correction should be made and should be completely *documented*.

Censorship of press information arises when reporters get wind of impending activities which the company is not ready to release—changes or realignments, new deals on the fire, plans for new projects, etc. The problem here is whether to deny the story, make no comment, or affirm the story; and the handling depends upon many factors—how soon will the release be made, what are the consequences of releasing it, who will benefit and who will be affected adversely? If possible, no effort should be made to suppress news which the press already has gotten wind of. The most practical step is to give the entire story to the inquiring reporter.

In dealing with the press on particularly sensitive issues, it is, on rare occasions, advisable to avoid the press altogether. An understanding reporter *may* agree tacitly to such an arrangement, but it is not acceptable public relations behavior. Reputable newspapermen are not prone to print the harmful or the sensational and they will, invariably, give the public relations man every opportunity to present his side of the story. Ivy Lee, founder of modern publicity techniques, insisted that the publicist had no right to suppress any information needed by the press since, inferentially, the publicist and the journalist both must serve the public.

There are occasions when a story will break into print, and the public relations man must decide upon a reply or statement. One important rule should be followed: The public relations man should *not* be panicked by an insistent press into making a regrettable statement. Time must be allowed for checking facts and determining policy. Precipitate and irresponsible statements are worse than none at all. But, after the facts are gathered and policy determined, all relevant data should be supplied to the press. Recently, a major transport company encountered an extremely critical situation. One of its engines crashed in late afternoon. But the company officials refused to talk to the press, and the public relations man did not release passenger information until hours later. The result was not only a critical press, but, in addition, a radio commentator departed from his newscast to score the company for its deplorable public relations.

Finally, the publicist should avoid the precipitation of crisis. An irresponsible press agent decided to send out a story announcing that his client, a movie star, had signed an important long-term picture contract. But the star arrived a few days later and denied the whole story. The result was inevitable. The publicist lost the respect and confidence of the press by instigating his own critical situation.

## RADIO AND TELEVISION

The broadcast media, as arts of communication and avenues for publicity, have given the newspaper its most powerful competition during the past two decades. Spot news reporting by radio, in particular, is a unique reportorial phenomenon unequaled by any other agency. Furthermore, the growth of radio and television, in terms of sets sold and used, has been truly phenomenal. Beyond the home and automobile, the schools and colleges have shown great interest in the broadcast media. Many educational institutions operate their own radio stations. Many are experimenting with closed circuit instruction by means of television. Several hundred educational institutions testified as to the need for their own reserved channels before the FCC on behalf of the Joint Committee on Educational Television.

In industry, in the entertainment field, and in educational circles there is a vital recognition of the importance of radio and television as publicity outlets. Releases which go to the press and syndicates are also sent to news analysts. Plugs are sought on entertainment shows. Philanthropic and charitable organizations have raised huge sums of money by means of telethons and program mentions. Tie-ins have been arranged between quiz shows and air lines which fly in contestants "for free" in return for mention on the broadcast. Some of the major areas for radio and television publicity are:

1. Special press conferences.
2. Interviews or coverage of talks.
3. Guest appearances of personalities on programs—entertainment or public service.
4. Contests.
5. Promotional tie-ins.
6. Coverage of a special event, such as a motion picture premiere.
7. Plugs or mention of an individual, product, or institution on the air.

Working with publicity material for broadcast media demands certain variations from the techniques applied to the newspaper. Radio and television publicity copy, for example, should be shorter, more colorful, more pithy and direct. Word pictures and descriptions are important, because the receiving audience cannot go back to the topic as can be done in the case of the newspaper, magazine, book, or promotional pamphlet. It is essential that so-called spot news material be even more newsworthy than that which is directed to the newspaper; and this copy has a greater chance of use if it is brief and contains some public service aspect. A newspaper release, read on the air, would not conform to broadcast news standards. The extra added-color paragraph, which may be blue-penciled by the newspaper editor, may be used prominently on a broadcast. For radio, publicity writing must be concise, sound as though it is being used extemporaneously, be colloquial and conversational in style, and contain some human interest angle. The publicist should see that radio and TV newsrooms receive relevant releases and reports. He should supply special news commentators with relevant and interesting material. And he should be alert to the possibilities for tie-ins between his organization or client and appropriate discussion forums or entertainment programs.

Radio and television networks and stations, of course, maintain their own advertising, publicity, and promotion departments. This operation offers frequent opportunity for tie-ins with outside organizations whereby the network receives important newspaper publicity in return for program coöperation. Broadcasting companies, however, are careful about the ethics involved in cross plugs and the project must have some genuine entertainment, news, or public service value. Both networks and affiliated stations will devise on-the-air promotions in order to alert the listener or viewer to forthcoming events of importance. But the broadcast media also rely to a great extent on the other media of newspaper and magazine for their own publicity endeavors. Since almost all newspapers maintain radio and television sections and full-time columnists and editors, the press offers a very important outlet for publicity news stories, features, and pictures. The national magazines are interested in color stories and pictures on outstanding new personalities and programs, and the fan magazines use a wealth of popular story and picture material of the human interest variety.

Radio and television publicity must also be devoted to coöperation with the advertising agency which acts on behalf of the various sponsors. The press information department, finally, is responsible for handling all requests and inquiries from the newspapers and for disseminating advance information and copies of important addresses by company officials, as well as information to the daily and trade papers regarding new sales of time and new programming developments.

## PUBLIC RELATIONS AND ADVERTISING

Many companies—in fact, most—subsume the publicity, promotion, *and* advertising functions under the public relations director or vice-president, although advertising copy, art, and placement are usually accomplished by the outside advertising agency which handles the account. Although the public relations director may show greater interest in institutional or the public relations type of advertising, it is nevertheless important that there be a coördinating force between the publicity and advertising functions. Strategically, as well as pragmatically, the best overall public relations is that in which there is some coördination of theme in advertising, publicity, and promotion. An advertising campaign which is slanted for top class or slick magazines should not be matched, generally, by a publicity campaign which is replete with flamboyant and tawdry gimmicks.

Some major companies rely on the advertising agency for assistance in publicity, and this tendency is growing. But, despite the fact that there is an increasing tendency to staff advertising agencies with publicity experts, the contribution of the agency is largely in the direction of promotion rather than in policy-level public relations. A few enterprising agencies are extending tangible help to the client beyond the press release or promotion. And the fact that the same source which places the advertisements also does some or all of the publicity seems to make no difference in the success or failure of publicity placement in the press. Whether the agency handles publicity or not, however, the account executive at the agency should be informed of the general public relations policy of the company. Managements which set up campaigns by consultation with the public relations counsel or company director and then neglect the advertising agency are not integrating a complete campaign. If advertising is to be part of a public relations program, the agency should be integrated with the total effort. In many business efforts, public relations involves a completely integrated campaign of marketing and merchandising; and the advertising approach is part of the complete organic approach toward informing and influencing public opinion.

There is, of course, an important distinction between advertising and publicity, and it is one of kind, as well as of degree. Advertising is, to the extent that it conforms to certain basic standards, a controlled operation. It is paid for. Publicity is basically "for free." What can be sold directly, such as hard sell in advertising, must be couched indirectly in publicity, for the latter must make news. The public relations *concept* may be identical, although the modus operandi may differ. Apart from preparing ads and buying space in the media, the agency can contribute to the publicity effort if it chooses to maintain its own publicity department. It can, in any event, contribute to policy making. The management should bear in mind, however, that an advertising agency's primary interest is in *advertising*. It is important for management to determine the extent of interest in publicity, the kind of staff, and the manner in which the agency is geared to carry out the public relations function. Some agencies carry publicity personnel merely as a supplement or service addendum to the advertising function. And this operation is largely a random one and may even prove deleterious. The best it can accomplish is routine publicity. A few agencies, and the number is growing, take the public relations function more seriously. They have trained staffs and they try to coördinate publicity and advertising. They try to think in terms of public attitudes and the building of good will, not in terms of numbers of press releases with which to impress the client.

The agency which takes its publicity function seriously can be enormously helpful, but it is doubtful whether it can improve on the work of a public relations counsel or internal departmental director. The agency can undoubtedly work up a fine presentation for the client, but the ability to carry it out successfully may spell the difference between agency effort and the work of a department devoted exclusively to public relations. Basically, the presentation will:

1. Reveal what a public relations–advertising program can accomplish in terms of the development of a favorable climate of public opinion.
2. Outline what the objectives and content of the program should be.
3. Indicate to whom (i.e., what publics) the content is to be communicated.
4. Determine what media are to be employed for the communication of the content.

These are classic procedures in any well-planned public relations presentation. They may be carried out entirely by the agency staff, or they may be coördinated with an outside counsel or with the company director. The most *important* function which an advertising agency can accomplish is that of helping to keep the publicity-advertising effort in proper coördination and balance. A capable and ethical agency may, after surveying the situation, suggest a concentration of advertising with little or no publicity; or a concentration of publicity and little or no advertising; or a prudent combination of both. Despite the importance of the agency contribution, however, it is still important for management to be secure in the fact that the basic and final public relations decisions are made by a competent public relations director working within the company and operating in a top-level management capacity.

The problem of advertising versus publicity in the relationship between the press agent and the press is always a sensitive one. There are those who remain unconvinced that advertising space has no relevance to publicity space. The press has been accused regularly of venality, of catering to the implicit or explicit whim of the advertiser, and of being peculiarly sensitive to the strictures of special interests. Certainly, one fact cannot be bruited: The mass media, particularly newspapers, radio, and television, exist on the basis of advertising. Circulation and audience figures do not defray expenses, but they do stimulate the interest of the advertiser. The question for public relations is whether, and to what extent, the mass media subordinate their integrity to the demands of advertisers. If they do subordinate their integrity, how strong an influence does the advertising dollar exercise over content? And, finally, does the company which advertises regularly and heavily receive more, and more favorable, publicity than the company which does not?

There is no *categorical* evidence pro or con on any of these questions. There are newspapers, albeit rare ones, over which advertising can exercise a direct influence. Occasionally, as in the field of motion pictures, advertising breeds better publicity on the amusement page, although it does not in any way change the integrity of the reviewer. In the main, it is virtually impossible to postulate that advertisers truly control editorial or reportorial content. Some capable editors and ethical journalists claim the opposite. They state that the advertising revenues, plus the competitive situation, are guarantees of a free and responsible press. Where there is a *quid pro quo* consideration it is not likely to be in important news or editorial areas. For example, a newspaper may add a special section on education or fashions in the expectation of securing advertising. This, however, is legitimate promotion. A service to the reader is rendered, despite the fact that the section itself offers an opportunity for publicity.

What probably exists between advertising and publicity, between the press and the advertiser is an interaction similar to that described between press and public. The advertiser and the mass media exert a mutual influence or interaction on each other. Advertisers do not select media willy nilly. They research carefully and buy on the basis of circulation, readership, and editorial and news content. They want to know whom they are reaching with their copy and layout, as well as the kind of medium they are using.

It has been claimed that the advertising agency controls broadcasting content. Again, however, the rebuttal is that advertising revenue enables the broadcast media to operate freely and responsibly and, at the same time, permits a considerable amount of time, effort, and money to go into public service programming. All of the mass media must show a degree of sensitivity to the advertiser. But they also have the obligation of exercising their prerogative to select and reject what is printed, screened, or broadcast. Furthermore, the reader is not obliged to read, nor is the listener obliged to listen. The public, too, can exercise its power to reject or accept. These influences, interacting on each other, do work constantly—if not always overtly—to maintain a formidable degree of independence on the part of the mass media.

# CHAPTER 21

## The Business Enterprise

Public relations as a management function is more closely identified with the world of business and industry than with any other area. In point of fact, public relations began as a business function with Ivy Lee, who called himself a "publicist." It is only in recent decades that, owing to the growth of the communication arts, public relations and publicity techniques have been applied more vigorously to other fields, such as education and the arts.

There is some degree of economic logic in the identification of public relations techniques with the needs and objectives of the business enterprise. While business and industry present singularly dominant aspects of American life and culture, and while the symbols of capitalism and free enterprise are peculiarly American, business no longer functions in the spirit of laissez faire. Because business has social obligations to perform, public relations is the order of the day. It is essential, therefore, that public relations practitioners understand the relationship between the business enterprise and public opinion; and such an understanding involves a knowledge of industrial relations;

consumer, customer, and dealer relations; stockholder matters; and other aspects of the business endeavor.

Public opinion still responds, emotively if not cognitively, to the Horatio Alger stereotype. Business is still looked upon as a dynamic institution in which office boys can, and do, become corporation presidents. The concept of free enterprise, particularly in the past few years, is strong and resilient, although subject to the checks and balances of public opinion. It was, in fact, out of this perennial sense of crude strength that there developed a need for an understanding and interpretation of the function and aim of business to the public, and from this need there developed the public relations expert. Such events as the Sherman Anti-Trust Act, the New Deal, the Fair Deal, and the consequent regulatory measures created an urgent need for business to defend and/or explain itself to a public which could no longer "be damned." At one time, the corporate executive had but two interests to consider—his own advancement and that of the company. Now, he must add a third—the public interest.

## PUBLIC RELATIONS AND BUSINESS

Today, business requires public relations to perform on the policy-making level because of, and as a result of, its always implicit problems in the areas of labor relations, government legislation, tax matters, social security, pension plans, and other manifold considerations. In a century and a half, the national income and the population have grown to incredible proportions, and they are still growing. Technological developments and changes have created a new kind of relationship between management and the employee. The expansion of the business world was so rapid that business, for a long period, had no occasion or need to seek the support or good will of the public.

But the crash of 1929, the subsequent development of what some have termed the "welfare state," World War II, and the tumultuous changes in the international scene created concomitant changes in education and social orientation. Private enterprise found itself no longer free to proceed with abandon, if it wanted to. A creed of public interest and public service developed.

Public relations experts who studied the situation found, for example, that the attitudes toward business could be delineated into a pattern of popular belief that management was totally disinterested either in the employee or the other publics; that exploitation, rather than service, was the motto; that all business, in general, was vigorously opposed to trade unionism; and that company executives hoarded all of the available profits.

Obviously, if these opinions were correct, one of the internal tasks of public relations was to give management a new and more enlightened orientation which would not be inconsistent with the normal profit motive. To the external publics, however, public relations also had the task of showing how business made a seminal contribution to the American standard of living. For it was also found that, by and large, the public was not critical of business when it functioned on the community or so-called plant-city level. The public was critical of business as some remote and mammoth entity, operating out of Wall Street. This concept, because it was remote, was not easy to understand and was, consequently, easy to mistrust and to fear.

The purpose of public relations as a management function, therefore, is not only to effect a change in the attitude of business toward the public, but also to *interpret* this attitude to the public by means of the mass media. The operating philosophy of good public relations is to convince management to undertake constructive deeds in the public interest and to convince the public that what business accomplishes *is* in the public interest. For example, the automobile industry, in addition to its interest in selling cars, can be interested in safety and good roads; the broadcasting industry, in addition to selling time to agencies and sponsors, can present programs of educational and informational interest; the motion picture industry, in addition to attracting customers to the box office, can use its resources to sell bonds and raise funds for important drives.

Public relations, from a business enterprise viewpoint, means every single act performed by everyone associated with a company which impinges on the public and elicits a reaction or opinion from that public—from a report by the president to the manner in which a switchboard operator handles a phone call. As a management function, public relations is expected to help create an atmosphere of consent by setting up certain basic criteria for company behavior. Good public relations functions to:

1. Build good will and create consent for an institution, product, individual, or idea.
2. Build public understanding of the company, out of which should grow confidence in the actions of the company.
3. Help sell products to dealers and consumers by establishing the conviction that the company behind the product is sound and trustworthy: "The priceless ingredient of any product is the honesty and integrity of its maker."
4. Effect a harmonious working liaison between management and the trade union.
5. Win and retain the confidence and support of the stockholders as well as the dealers, the consumers, and the employees.
6. Build a reputation for integrity with the press through its publicity operation.
7. Build the concept of an institution which is contributing to a dynamic program of economic productivity which is helping to build a better country for everyone.

These are not abstract concepts. They can be applied concretely and with pragmatic success in the arena of public opinion. A company can offer its resources to the community for civic and educational projects. It can contribute to worthy causes. It can encourage its employees to take part in community events by offering the incentive and making the time available. It can establish fair employment practices as well as a pension plan, insurance, and recognition of meritorious service. It can coöperate with the press and with educational and civic organizations.

A company which acts constructively and which implements its public relations gives the publicity staff something to talk about through the media of communication. And the talking phase should do more than create publicity for its own sake. It should convey the idea that the company is one that renders a constant public service. This is a story that can be told continuously and ingeniously in all available media. It can be told by features in the press which grow out of interviews and special events; in the house organ; in published reports and speeches; and by word of mouth through the employees themselves.

Not every company functions in the same way or with the same objectives. Policy and practice will vary according to the nature of the business and the kind of publics it serves. What public relations must accomplish on the policy level is to determine, by a process of internal evaluation, the criteria of good service and public interest. The publicity activity will then be determined by a consideration of the desired ends or goals. Publicity which functions merely to get a product *known* does not achieve a public relations objective; it must also achieve the purpose of getting the product and the company behind it *accepted*.

Some have asked, would not an institution flourish without

the expense involved in the public relations effort? At one time, it probably would. But today, such factors as competition, a more enlightened electorate, more vigilant minorities, and powerful media of communications make public relations not only advisable but necessary. In addition, since most business enterprises are now doing a constructive job, why not tell the public about it? If this is done continuously and evaluated periodically by measurement devices, the facts show that public relations can be a positive and dynamic force both in directing business in a constructive manner and in influencing public opinion. Business and industry, as well as other fields, utilize public relations techniques because they have proved to be of institutional and practical worth. The influencing of public opinion is not, as such, either good or bad. Its goodness or badness depends upon who is doing the influencing and toward what end.

Business uses public relations techniques, such as advertising and promotion, in two directions. Mass media are employed either to effect direct sales or to develop company prestige. In very large companies, both of these objectives are combined. In a large and complicated economic structure, the chasm between producer and consumer grows ever greater. The possibility of any direct contact with the public is remote, and this fact, incidentally, is one reason for the plant-city operation and for the tendency toward decentralization. But there is always the need for a bridge between the producer and the ultimate consumer. Does the consumer know the essential contribution which many companies and their products make to the finished material? Probably not, and this is one reason why International Nickel, for example, tells the story of nickel as "your unseen friend." Such remoteness is the reason for much institutional activity. A survey interviewer questioned a consumer, and the discussion may be paraphrased as follows:

Q: Do you select known or unknown brands?
A: Known ones.

Q: Can you tell me why?
A: Because the known brands are better.

Q: Why?
A: Because most people have heard of them and accepted them as the best.

Q: How do you know a known brand from an unknown one?
A: Known ones are advertised in the paper or on radio and TV.

Companies, in addition to "hard-sell," engage heavily in institutional public relations. Radio and television are used, for example, to present a symphony orchestra or to illustrate some highlight in science or history. Educational films are prepared for schools as an educational service. Various public service brochures are distributed, such as the informative health pamphlets of the Metropolitan Life Insurance Company. Various visual aids, such as recordings, charts, maps, and teaching guides, are distributed as a public service. Most of these ventures are, of course, very costly not only to produce, but also to distribute. They have encountered criticism from some quarters for this reason because, it is claimed, only very big business can afford them. From a public relations and public service viewpoint, however, this does not detract from their worth if they are intelligently planned and executed. An educational promotion is poor when it subordinates its public service aspects to a commercial plug for the company or its products.

In addition to its institutional public relations, a company may have to engage in the kind of campaign which specifically undertakes to explain its position. This occurs in moments of crisis, such as a strike, an accident, a widely publicized critique, or an antitrust action. Such a campaign is usually presented by means of the press conference, supplemented by such advertisements as "The public is entitled to the facts." Such procedures, too, have been criticized because it is claimed that the opposing faction frequently cannot afford to pay for a massive advertising campaign. In the long run, however, public opinion usually makes a wise decision; and, when it is wrongly advised, opinion is not irrevocable. It can, and does, change—usually in the right direction. No phenomenon is wiser or more formidable than public opinion.

Many business enterprises engage in indirect as well as direct public relations. This more oblique activity comes under the heading of the dual promotion or tie-in, in which two organizations work together for their mutual interest. Movie companies will display a certain make of car in their pictures, although it is not mentioned by name. A star personality will speak at a business organization luncheon in return for the publicity received. Contests, talent searches, scholarships, and other promotional devices involve more than one company. For example, a contest among dealers for the best local selling campaign may net the winner a free trip to some Caribbean resort; but the company does not pay for the transportation or the hotel expenses. By illustrating the hotel and the travel medium in the promotion and advertising, the company has effected a promotion tie-in by which all parties benefit from a public relations viewpoint. Recently, to cite another example, a publisher agreed to put out a cookbook by a well-known television personality provided that the sponsor of her program would mention the book on the air and illustrate it on the box top of its products. Some promotions may be profitable ones. Motion picture companies will arrange for paper-back publishers to make novels from original screenplays in return for an illustrated credit on the jacket and either advertising or royalties from the prospective sale.

Business will frequently engage in public relations on matters affecting its own general welfare. The automobile industry has a stake in better highways. The producers of commercial films have a stake in finer theatres. It is not unheard of for business enterprises to establish separate public relations organizations for the purpose of promoting some activity which will redound ultimately to their own interest. These organizations function as distinct entities, with their own executive secretary, their own direct-mail and educational campaigns, and their own publicity staff. It should be emphasized that, from an ethical viewpoint, the validity of these organizations depends upon what they are set up to accomplish and by whom. The criterion for judgment is, as always, whether the public will be duped or whether the organization will render a positive public service. Frequently, a trade association will undertake a campaign for an entire industry in the course of which the respective members will declare a temporary moratorium on competition on the conviction that what is good for one is good for all, and vice versa.

## THE MATTER OF MONEY

Even very large companies are not oblivious to the cost factor in public relations activities. Many companies distribute advertising mats for which *both* the manufacturer and the local dealer share the costs. This is advantageous because local advertising rates are cheaper than national advertising charges. Other cost-saving devices are the production of so-called "open-end" transcriptions, i.e., records or tapes with space for a promotion by the local sponsor; the distribution of calendars and pamphlets which leave space for the dealer imprint; and the preparation of a key publicity release from which the local outlet can adapt the copy for an area-directed message. Some companies, in fact, concentrate a major part of their promotional efforts on the dealers who are urged to pass the content on to the public. A book publisher may find it more advantageous to offer prizes to bookstores for sales achievement than to concentrate on consumer advertising. This dealer promotion procedure is particularly effective for smaller companies which do not have the budget to reach everyone effectively—dealers, jobbers, and consumers.

Practical public relations demands that a decision be reached as to which public to concentrate on without too reckless an expenditure. Is the biggest audience always the most effective? Or, should not some promotion be developed through concentrated efforts toward a specific public? Should a company which sells baby foods spend the money, time, and effort on an evening television program; or would it not be wiser to buy a daytime radio serial program which reaches the housewife directly? Should a company marketing a product intended for older persons sponsor a crime or western program; or should it concentrate on the type of content most likely to find favor with persons in this age group, such as music or biographical drama?

While even the giant companies will watch the expenditure on advertising and promotion, some very large enterprises have set up expensive foundations. It is true that such foundations have tax advantages. But there are public service and public interest aspects that are operative as well. No one can demean the remarkable contribution of such foundations as Rockefeller, Ford, Carnegie, Sloan, and others. Some have argued that other, less interested, agencies should assume these responsibilities, but this argument does not lessen the scientific and educational contributions of the foundations or their assistance to many significant research projects. The long-range public relations value is great, of course, but the contribution is equally significant. Medical research and educational television, to name two areas, have been helped tremendously by the contributions of the Rockefeller Institute and the Fund for Adult Education.

Business public relations obviously is predicated on a point of view. It is prejudiced in favor of business. Business is not immune from criticism, nor should it be allowed to forget its obligations to the public. But public relations, intelligently performed, can show business how to meet its obligation and benefit by doing so. The healthiest control is a combination of an alert and informed public opinion along with a sense of responsibility, on the part of business, to the public it serves. Public relations should function to develop that sense of responsibility and to communicate it through the mass media.

### "SMALL" BUSINESS

Small business is, of course, a relative term. Some very large corporations are small business compared to the giants of industry. One automobile manufacturing company may be small compared to another. An independent motion picture producing company is certainly small compared to the five so-called major producing and distributing organizations. A great retail department store, employing ten thousand persons, is small compared to a steel company that employs fifty thousand. Yet, any company which uses public relations on even a moderate scale, including the tools of advertising, publicity, and promotion, is not a small company in the sense that a local factory or an operator of three or four retail stores is a small business.

From a public relations operation, the basic difference between small business and big business is one of centralization.

The scope is circumscribed or limited, geographically and psychologically. The large industry tends to be decentralized into many units. In the smaller company, management usually is in closer proximity to the staff and is not a remote and absentee operation.

Smaller companies do not tend to engage in as extensive a national advertising and promotion campaign as do the giants. The principles of public relations, however, remain the same. There is still the internal objective of creating a working rapport between the supervisory group and the rank and file; and there is still the objective, within a limited budget, of creating good will and sales by means of the mass media. Both small and big business have identical purposes in the realm of public opinion. Both produce and/or distribute products for the purpose of making a profit. Both need public relations as a practical and institutional tool. From a public relations standpoint, the small business competes, in a sense, for publicity and advertising space with the larger-budgeted business enterprises. In a way, public relations is more of a challenge to the small business because it can accomplish a very successful program by using its advertising, publicity, and promotion tools to the best possible advantage. It cannot afford to waste money and make costly mistakes in the promotional budget.

The smaller company can, for example, stress more vigorously certain areas of its public relations. The word-of-mouth endorsement of the employees can be enormously effective in a centralized operation. Management, which is closer to the community, can be more overtly active. The company can foster closer ties with the educational and civic agencies of the community. Internally, the public relations department can accomplish its work in the same areas as in the larger companies, but less lavishly and expensively. There is the identical need for effective liaison between management and the levels subsumed under the top echelon. House organs, newsletters, forums, pension plans, and employee handbooks can all be set up effectively, although some may be printed and others mimeographed or multigraphed. If there are stockholders, it is probably necessary to prepare an attractive report. The bulletin board and the direct-mail letter are two inexpensive devices which can be employed aggressively and successfully.

Externally, the problem is sometimes more complicated. The extent of the public relations activity and the amount expended depend upon the nature of the company, the kind of product, and the modus operandi of distribution. Usually, the smaller business will try to avoid extensive advertising, for this is the most expensive part of a public relations program. Small companies will stress the direct sales and the sales promotion which can be accomplished by personal contact, direct-mail letters, and a well-trained sales force.

The smaller business can accomplish, on its own level of activity, as successful and significant a job of good public relations—and sometimes a better one—as can the large company. What the public relations director should avoid is an attempt to compete with the giants as well as the conviction that his activity is futile because he cannot compete with them. Because public relations for small business is more direct in its operation and its contacts, it can frequently accomplish a more active and successful program than the larger and more impersonal operation.

## THE TRADE ASSOCIATION

The industry association, or trade association, represents the sum total of the public relations goals and activities of its member companies. A trade association is, as the term implies, a federation of companies within a given industry, and it is set up to act on behalf of the industry as a whole. While individual companies are competitive, each gives up some of its independence of action by joining the trade association because it is in its own best interest to do so. The member company realizes that the industry must have some total representative agency if it is to tell its story with conviction. The basic reason underlying the formation of the trade association concerns coördination with the general public *and* with special interest groups. The association handles problems of antitrust legislation. It marshalls public opinion in periods of industry crisis. It tells the story of the industry as a whole to particular audiences, such as educational groups. And, most important, it meets the threat of competition from other analogous industries. Air lines, buses, and trains are all competing for the same public, and each has a trade association designed to foster the interest, respectively, of air-line travel, bus travel, or train travel.

The trade association does not undertake specific public relations for any of its members. It functions to represent the industry as a unit and to supplement the efforts of each member company. Ford, General Motors, and Chrysler are all competing companies as are TWA, American, and United Airlines. But the industry associations act to protect and further the interests of automobile sales and air transport in general so that all members may benefit. The Motion Picture Association functions to set up and administrate the production code, to help in foreign currency problems, to promote films to educators, and to secure a favorable hearing on tax legislation. Similarly, the National Association of Radio and Television Broadcasters represents the commercial broadcasting stations on such matters as presenting the case of the broadcasters in the recent hearings before the FCC on the move to allocate broadcast frequencies exclusively for educational institutions.

Each member company is concerned primarily with its own advertising and promotional efforts. Its activities are determined by its budget, the nature of the product, and the marketing problems. The trade association's efforts are sparked by problems common to a majority, or all, of the member companies. It meets a group rather than an individual need. While the individual company must necessarily restrict its public relations and merchandising to specific areas, the association can range widely, without regard for *specific* marketing considerations. The company, in other words, emphasizes the virtues of its product over other products within the same industrial area; the association does not promote the virtues of one company or product, but of all companies and of the industry product as a whole.

These distinctions seem quite simple, but they are not easily established. The public relations director, or executive secretary, of the trade association has a formidable job of internal public relations. It is, basically, to create consent among the members of the association by educating each to the point of view by which the association is accepted as working in the best interest of all concerned. A trade association has no need to move with the galvanic speed of the individual company. Its competing problems are usually (although not invariably) not that keen. Its purpose is to act objectively, to rise above intraindustry factions, and to decide on a long-range objective. A trade association can be a strong and closely knit unit, able to do an effective job, or a loose federation whose every move requires a meeting of individual company public relations heads.

Specifically, the association contributes importantly to the members by acting as a clearing house for information and,

particularly, by engaging in frequent studies in opinion measurement. Through such soundings, the trade association is able
to delineate those areas in which public relations is effective
and in which it needs strengthening. And, in addition to providing valuable information to each company, the results of surveys offer a directional signal for public relations objectives and
needs on the part of the association. On the basis of survey information, the association is in a position to orient the member
companies toward an understanding of industry-wide problems
and to reveal not only how individual companies may contribute
to the total effort, but also how they can avoid acts which will
reflect negatively on the industry as a whole. If, for example,
the association is empowered to speak for the industry on matters relating to government, then individual companies must
not engage in activities which will prove embarrassing to the
association when matters affecting legislation must be promulgated. An association must develop a basic philosophy of management for the entire industry which it represents. Its approach
is a unitized, not a discrete, one. It must function to prevent
crises and to handle them when they occur. In a major industry
accident, for example, the association should have the statistics
to prove that the safety record of the company involved—and
of the industry in general—is as good, if not better, than that
of any competitive field.

The story of industry activities, as told by the association press
department, embraces all media that will accept and disseminate newsworthy material. Publicity releases should include results of industry surveys, research projects, and other matters of
statistical interest. Advertising, almost invariably of an institutional variety, is employed both as a general tool and, specifically, when an issue arises on which the industry is obliged to
defend its position. The advertising that meets a crisis, such

as an antitrust action, is best placed in the daily press; while long-range institutional or public service advertising is more effective in the large circulation, national magazines. Promotional literature, a very important aspect of trade association activities, should be available on historical, research, and general educational aspects of the industry. The educational brochure has become increasingly important as an informational and promotional aid. These are distributed either by the association or by the member company or both. For example, "The Story of Coal" may be mailed by the association, or space may be left for individual company imprint. Educational brochures are of value if they are truly *educational* and if they avoid commercialism and stress the fact that they are published as an informational service. The association can also develop an effective public relations program by enlisting the coöperation of radio and television for special events coverage, such as an anniversary; and by setting up an active speakers bureau which services schools, women's clubs, and other civic and fraternal organizations. All of these avenues offer an opportunity to tell the industry story dramatically and effectively. In addition, most associations make 16-mm motion pictures available to schools and offer their coöperation, in terms of advice and assistance, in setting up community projects such as theatrical events, forums, and various public services.

Within the industry, the trade association can be of assistance to each of the member companies in setting up special events and in arranging for conventions and seminars at which common problems in public relations and promotion are discussed. A report of the meeting is subsequently distributed to each member company. Some trade associations, in fact, offer an annual prize for the best public relations effort undertaken by a member company.

The trade association is, then, an important industry public relations organization, both internally and externally. The possibilities for public service, both within and outside of the industry, are great. The association can do an effective job on internal orientation and education and an equally effective external one on public information. A progressive trade association serves as a barometer and a guide to its members by keeping them informed on matters of interest to them; at the same time, a progressive association can also accomplish a very effective educational service by making relevant information available to the press and other media as well as to the schools and other interested community agencies. The vistas of trade association public relations are broad, and the possibilities for genuine public service are limitless.

# CHAPTER 22

## Internal Public Relations

There are two vital areas of internal public relations. One is the relationship which develops between the public relations director and management; the other is the relationship between management and the employees. More than any other public —management, dealers, consumers, or stockholders—the employees *are* the company. They, by doing the spade work, promulgate the productive end of a business. They are the most important word-of-mouth organ of public opinion about the organization to the community at large. And, as a consequence, employees constitute a tremendously significant public relations area.

### EMPLOYEES AND PUBLIC RELATIONS

A sound employee or industrial relations program invariably stems from a sound management policy; and a sound management policy stems from a regard, on the part of top echelon officials, for the advice of the public relations counsel or director. In no area can intelligent public relations work more effectively than in employee relations. The only proviso is that management place public relations on a policy-making level, listen sympathetically to the suggestions of the public relations director, and allow these suggestions to be carried out in the arena of employee relations. In some less enlightened company managements, the major problem for public relations is to convince management that good deeds in the public interest begin *at home,* that there is no group more vital to the social and economic well-being of an organization than those who work for it. Intelligent employee relations programs attempt to change the employee concept of working *for* a company to working *with* the company. A successful program in this area makes of every employee an enthusiastic ambassador of good will in the arena of public opinion formation.

Obviously, in these days of labor unions and general enlightenment about industrial relations, Pollyanna messages will not be effective unless they are supported by the firm foundation of a truly effective employee relations program. For this endeavor is a vital aspect of general public relations, and it is concerned with setting up and carrying out policies designed to establish and promote good working liaison between management and the employee, including the labor organizations which are the employee's representatives. But the basic problem for the public relations director is not so much the employee group as it is the supervisory group. Theoretically, the public relations director should work with all departments of the company on questions affecting employee relations—with the personnel department on matters affecting policy; on employee booklets; on training and educational programs; on grievances, etc. What happens all too frequently, however, is that these department heads guard their domain zealously and look upon the advice of the public relations people as an intrusion. That is why top management must support public relations by explaining that intelligent public relations can help to avoid many pitfalls in employer-employee relations and that, at the same time, it can be constructive by showing how a positive personnel program can earn dividends among both the employees *and* the other interested publics.

The immediate objective of public relations, therefore, is two-pronged. From a management viewpoint, it should insist upon a fair and enlightened employee relations policy by explaining that inspirational talks and inspirational literature are frauds unless basic working conditions are clean, safe, and pleasant. Once this foundation is set, public relations can turn toward an honest and constructive representation of management to the employee, designed to show each member of the company how he can help carry out a total public relations objective.

Public relations, as part of industrial relations, serves as a communicator as well as a catalyst between management and the employees and between the employees and their bargaining organization. As a catalyst, the public relations department is in a position to record the public opinion pulse of the employee, to discern and analyze trends in employee behavior and attitudes. These findings are communicated to management; constructive policies are decided upon; and such policies are put into action by devising and carrying out a specific program.

Historically, the need for public relations intervention in the sphere of the employee grew out of the same sociological context as the need for public relations in business. Public relations, through the efforts of Ivy Lee and others, taught business the need for a sense of responsibility toward press and public. Similarly, public relations is teaching management to recognize that the employee is not a casual phenomenon; that he spends a major part of his daily existence within the confines of the office, showroom, or plant; and that his entire social and economic orientations are affected by what happens to him, physically and psychologically, in his daily working environment.

Unfortunately, one of the concomitants of the growth of business enterprise was the development of a communication barrier between employer and employee. The growth of business and, paradoxically, of mass communication threw up roadblocks between management and the employee public and developed a creed of impersonality whereby the executive group and the employee group were each in a separate universe of discourse. The public relations man's entry into the picture served to set up a communication bridge between these two ever widening publics. If public relations could not always bring about a physical rapport, it could work to establish a psychological one. The growth of trade unionism as a powerful bargaining agency is also due, incidentally, to this concept of bigness, for as the gap widened and absentee ownership became more common, the union stepped in to represent the employee public as a bargaining agent.

The legitimate purpose of ethical employee relations is not to whitewash an untenable situation but to ameliorate it; not to compete with the trade union but to work for a spirit of coöperation between management and the employee representatives. Equally legitimate is the function of public relations, in times of crisis, to bring management's position before the general public by means of publicity and institutional advertising. It has been said that management has the advantage in this situation because it has more money to work with as well as the support of the owners of the mass media. This may be true, but it is also true that public opinion reaches its own level of understanding. In the long run, management will lose its case in the court of public opinion unless it has a *positive* argument to offer, unless it gives public relations a backlog of good deeds and good will to build its case upon. A company which has been concerned with the morale of its employees, which has shown regard for such matters as recreation, pension plans, insurance, incentives, vacations, and recreational outlets has a fairly solid foundation on which public relations can build a case in times of crisis.

The basic operating principles of public relations—analysis of the problem, interpretation of survey findings, implementation of a policy or plan, and overt action through the mass media—apply, as well, in employee relations. There is, however, no more difficult area for opinion measurement, or analysis, than in management-employee relationship. Employees simply are not good subjects for direct interview. Despite the evidence of suggestion boxes and other devices by which their complaints and ideas are invited, the employee group is loath to express opinions unless foolproof protective machinery is set up. Employees are not keen about putting their grievances in writing, even where there is a committee on grievance available. They are not eager to talk freely to sociological or psychological experts, although management gives the assurance that these people are trained and objective and that they are present to supplement the work of the personnel department.

Probably the most effective device for opinion measurement among employees is the questionnaire, *provided that* the survey is conducted with absolute anonymity for the employees and under the auspices of a reputable outside organization. It may be asked, if employees are timid about participating in the survey, is it worth the time and effort involved? It is, because it is the only device which gives an indication of the attitudes, aspirations, complaints, and objectives of the employee. As a preventive measure, it is far less expensive than a long union wrangle. In purpose the objective employee survey accomplishes at least two things. First, it delineates the general attitude of the employees toward the management and second, it helps to outline and determine specific problems in various departmental areas.

On the basis of the contributions which public relations has made toward a more enlightened concept of the management function, management itself has taken a forward look at the employee and industrial relations aspect of its operations. The result has been a new concept in which the disposition and resolution of problems are not left to the devices of the personnel department alone but are jointly discussed, both from a personnel viewpoint and from a company-wide public relations aspect. Intelligent employee relations, by acting upon the findings of frequent soundings of opinion, can direct a smoother course in the entire company chain of command from top-level management through the supervisory group and down to the employee level. Public relations, in this respect, is important at all levels of action. It helps in securing and disseminating facts and information, in adjudicating problems, in avoiding critical situations, and in handling a crisis when the inevitable cannot be avoided. Among the various strata or levels on which public relations can operate positively is first, the level of top management. Here the public relations man may operate by sitting in directly on matters of company policy, *including* those affecting the employees.

Another level on which public relations can operate is the supervisory group level. The public relations department should function in two directions with this group. First, it should explain to management why it is important that the supervisors be taken into management's confidence. Second, public relations should indoctrinate the supervisors with the idea that *they* are the chief source of passing on the management viewpoint; and ways and means of promoting this viewpoint should be illustrated. Indeed, part of the function of the employee relations division of a public relations department should be centralized around the training and function of the supervisors. This group should be made to feel that they belong, that they are an integral appendage of management. And public relations techniques can accomplish this purpose by arranging for direct meetings with management and by writing and distributing pamphlets and newsletters in which this group is kept sympathetically advised of management's problems, functions, and objectives.

There are, in addition, certain basic principles of good public relations which apply specifically to the area of employee relations. Probably the foremost is the indoctrination of management with the idea that, since employees are a potentially loyal and important public relations area of the company, they should be kept informed and told the facts about company activities. Secondly, all departments which are concerned with employee activities should be orientated to consult with the public relations director on questions that might involve policy and public opinion. And third, public relations should be so integral a part of the general management function that all decisions affecting company personnel should be determined and carried out with an eye toward their effect on the employee relations and the overall public relations of the company.

No phase of company public relations is as important as employee and industrial relations. For no amount of concentrated publicity or promotion or advertising will find a favorable public opinion reaction if the good will of the employees is not developed and maintained. The company's most potent public relations content is carried by its employees. Conversely, the most dangerous and inimical factor in developing a poor climate of opinion toward the company, from both press and community, is a group of dissatisfied employees.

## EMPLOYEE RELATIONS

Collective bargaining cannot be avoided, and, indeed, there is no reason why a company with an enlightened and realistic attitude toward industrial relations should want to avoid it. But, apart from wage and hour negotiations with employee representatives and trade unions, the company management can take certain basic steps to secure a loyal and enthusiastic employee body politic. Acting on the advice of an alert public relations director, management will see to it that the employees feel a sense of security, of permanent belonging to a growing and productive enterprise. Management, through the supervisory group, will assure the employee that his contribution will not be neglected or treated cavalierly. And, management will find tangible ways of taking cognizance of and publicizing unusual employee efforts or contributions.

What are some of the positive steps which management can take in the interest of bettering its employee relations program? From a public relations standpoint, management can try to humanize the routine working situation, not by such artificial devices as "canned" music or blaring announcements over the public address system, but by developing a feeling of mutual trust and confidence between the supervisory group and the employees. Management can call in experts to develop forward-looking and progressive pension plan systems, employee group insurance plans, and health programs. It can offer tangible rewards in the way of recognition and meritorious advancement. And, apart from the specific values received in greater output, management will benefit because the company becomes recognized, by press, government, and general public, as a good place to work.

These broad concepts can be promulgated by specific steps in the way of practical publicity and promotion. The public relations director who is kept informed about employee problems can indoctrinate the employee group with a healthy attitude toward the company which will be reflected, ultimately, in a healthy climate of public opinion toward the company. Among the concrete, internal public relations devices which can be used in the employee area are:

1. *The employee handbook:* This booklet is an introduction to the company in terms of its history, what it stands for as an institution, its objectives, its obligations to the employee, and the responsibilities of the employee toward the company. In addition, the handbook should be informative and should delineate specific information regarding working hours, overtime, insurance, sickness, pension plans, merit increases, special recreational outlets, etc.

2. *Visual aids:* Motion pictures and slide films are also important devices for orientation and indoctrination, both from the point of view of training and from a general public relations orientation.

3. *Official reports:* Various company reports, such as the stockholders' reports and other announcements, should be sent to the employee; and it is frequently expedient to include a special memorandum from the company president, explaining items which might arouse employee interest.

4. *Publicity releases:* From time to time, the employees will be interested in publicity concerning new products, expansion plans, etc., and copies should be distributed to them.

5. *Bulletin boards:* This is a device frequently overlooked or handled carelessly. Yet, the bulletin board which is kept up to date will elicit considerable interest and provoke lively discussion, both in and out of the plant, or office.

6. *Publications:* These include direct-mail letters which are use-

ful on occasion, the house organ, newspapers such as *General Motors Folks,* and an occasional institutional advertisement. All of these, incidentally, should be sent to the home.

## THE HOUSE ORGAN

This publication, more recently known as a company publication, is the most important single tool in an employee relations campaign. Just why some public relations directors should see fit to deprecate the term house organ is not quite clear, for these publications are literally published as organs of the house, and they are useful for external as well as internal public relations. In recent years the house organ has expanded to a great degree, in content and format, and its circulation, in the large companies, has grown to imposing proportions.

It is interesting to note that, apart from the public relations aspect, such important national magazines as *Harper's* and *The Atlantic* were once known as house organs, as was also the famous *Poor Richard's Almanac* of Benjamin Franklin. The latter, incidentally, is probably the true precursor of the organ of today, since it was representative of the printing house which Franklin established in Philadelphia in the eighteenth century. The house organ, as a company publication, began in earnest in the nineteenth century. The *Lowell Offering,* published by the personnel of the Lowell Cotton Mills in Massachusetts, may have been one of the first. But the house organ did not become a bona fide public relations tool until well into the current century and, in fact, did not grow to its present estate until the last two decades. The first house organs were literal *company* publications. The current house organs are true organs of public relations. In recent years, the concept, tone, and content of the house organ changed from a trade viewpoint and acquired the look of a publication designed to create a favorable climate of opinion both among employees and other related and peripheral publics. It became a communication medium which implicitly stressed the company as a good place to work. It showed, by copy and illustrations, why the company was a leader in its field. It ranged beyond routine affairs to broader items of general welfare and public service. It identified the growth and aspirations of the company with the growth and expansion of the American economy. And, in the area of industrial problems, it became a necessary adjunct to management-labor relations.

The house organ of today is, then, a true organ of public relations and public opinion, and it may be considered one of the important adjunct media of mass communication. House organs are, in point of fact, of two varieties. There is the internal organ, published for and edited by the employees themselves; and there is the external organ, produced internally but directed toward dealers, customers, and trade press. In some instances, there are both economic reason and editorial justification for the preparation of an organ which will cover both areas. Some of the best publications do just that.

What *specific* public relations value inheres in the house organ? First, it is the only authenic printed presentation of the goals and achievements of the company and its personnel. Second, it depicts graphically what the company and its employees represent in the court of public opinion. House organs are much more than publicity releases because their purpose is not merely to secure mention in print, but to reveal an attitude, a sense of pride in achievement, and an identifying symbol of solidarity.

In format, house organs offer a very wide variation. Some are simply stapled sheets which are mimeographed. Others are elaborate rotogravure magazines or large newspapers. Some companies publish one organ for all the relevant outlets. Others vary the form and content slightly for different distribution, particularly where a company has several regional offices or plants. Every well-done house organ, however, aims to secure the loyal readership and interest of employees and their families, customers, dealers, editors, and numerous other publics. The best publications are truly organs of adult education. Internally, they aid in developing a sense of company cohesiveness and good will between management and the employees and among the employees themselves. Externally, they contribute toward an understanding of the company by editors and other opinion makers.

From a public relations viewpoint, the house organ should have a specific policy or point of view. It should be more than a rambling presentation of items. A publication with a public relations *theme* is one which stands a better chance of developing sound public relations for the company. And public relations themes can be developed out of many areas—the history of the company, the biography of its key figures, pictures of people and their activities, news events of management and employee activities, information about new company developments, and general information about related industry activities. In addition, of course, the house organ will include the kind of item which is of legitimate news to the employees—new appointments, births, promotions, pictures, interesting activities, and other special events and items of interest.

From a copy and picture point of view, certain specific public relations objectives should be borne in mind. Skillful copy should stress the importance of good liaison between personnel and management. It should present a symbol of management as significantly interested in the employee and his problems and objectives. It should give a total impression of the company as a substantial institution. And beyond the company and its activities, the house organ should also find occasion to include items of community interest as well as information on the adult education level.

The point of view expressed in house organ content depends, of course, on the nature of the enterprise and its objectives. Some companies will stress the adult education angle, others will use the publication primarily as a sales promotion device. Some will emphasize hard-sell, while still others will be thoroughly institutional in form and content. The kind of publication which will be produced depends upon both these policy considerations and the question of budget. Some inexpensive organs will do a better institutional job than many on which expensive art and production have been lavished.

The cost of a house organ depends upon many factors—the number of copies as well as the number of pages; whether it is produced in black and white or in color; and the style of publication, i.e., offset reproduction, mimeographed, or letterpress. But by far the most important aspect of the house organ is its communication content. And, in general, the content should be an amalgam of contributions from the public relations staff as well as from the publication's editorial staff. Specific data which might feasibly be considered include:

1. General adult education material of interest to the employee, e.g., current events.
2. A public relations message about the policy of the company in the employee area as well as in the broader area of community relations.
3. A frank discussion of any existing management-labor problems.
4. Specific company plans concerning matters of interest to the employee, e.g., health and recreation, insurance, pension plans, working conditions, etc.
5. A regular editorial in which viewpoints are presented on specific issues.

6. A presentation of important advertising or publicity on the part of the company, e.g., reprints of recent advertisements.

In this content area, too, certain pointers should be noted. The publication of a house organ should not attempt to duplicate any other organ, newspaper, or national magazine. It should be indigenous, in form and content, and recognized as representative of a particular organization. It should include a sympathetic outlet for grievances and for employee viewpoints. It should seek the widest possible distribution in the widest possible areas—schools, libraries, community leaders, and opinion makers. The best house organs will accomplish the major purpose of inculcating a genuine sense of employee pride in the company as well as providing a stimulus to act as ambassadors of good will.

# CHAPTER 23

## Special Publics

Although it is a convenient simplification to speak of the public, and although the term does appear to be all-inclusive, from a public relations viewpoint there is rarely a total public. There are, rather, publics; and public relations applies policies, principles, and techniques to each of these as they are germane to a specific problem or frame of reference. Employees, for example, comprise an internal public whose good opinions constitute valuable public relations. Similarly, stockholders, dealers, customers, consumers, and jobbers—depending on the nature of the business—constitute important external publics, although the stockholder, as a member of the corporate "family," is an internal public to some extent. Public relations is as important with each of the groups as it is with the press, and frequently more so, for press relations, however skillful, cannot whitewash a negative public opinion from employees or customers or consumers.

### THE STOCKHOLDER AND THE ANNUAL REPORT

A stockholder, unless he decides to attend annual meetings and take an active interest in company affairs, is actually a member of the family by remote control. In a literal sense, however, the holder of even a few shares of a major company has a *share in* the company. The public relations man's approach must be predicated on a candid acknowledgment that the stockholder truly belongs and that he is not part of an incidental or extraneous public. The stockholder is more than a face in the crowd. His opinions count.

In recent years stockholder relations have undergone a new look. Prior to the time when investment in the market became popular among average wage earners, the holder of stock was looked upon as one of a wealthier group, remote from the general public. Recently, however, investment in the market has been looked upon as a method of securing income in the form of dividends, or as a means of planning for the future by purchasing shares of stock on a long-term, dollar-cost averaging basis. Public interest in the market is due to a large extent to the change in the stereotype of Wall Street from a remote and millionaire's domain to one in which the public has a genuine financial stake. The stock exchange, as well as many of the large brokerage houses (such as Merrill Lynch, Pierce, Fenner and Smith), have popularized the concept of investment by the average man through the monthly investment plan, the advertising copy line that no sum is too small, and the concept that stockholders are buying shares in America's productive future. The rise of the mutual funds, by which the purchaser gets both diversification and professional management, has also tended to increase interest in buying common stocks.

These events, plus the stockholder relations efforts of many companies, have erased the idea of the stockholder as a unique economic symbol of wealth. Stockholders *are* the public. They represent a cross section of the many heterogeneous socioeconomic groups that comprise the wage earning population of the

United States—housewives, teachers, doctors, lawyers, truck drivers, and white-collar workers. The public relations director who is responsible for the supervision of a company's stockholder relations program has, again, both an internal and an external assignment to fulfill. Public relations functions as a two-way street, interpreting the company to this important public and, in turn, interpreting the opinions of the public to the company.

The major task of the public relations director is to convince management that stockholders are an important public, not a select and different group set apart from others. Stockholders, management should know, are not only investors *in* the company; they may also be customers *of* the company. They are, to some extent, an internal as well as an external audience. Above all, stockholders constitute a key part of the public to which the company directs its practical and institutional communication content. Stockholders are not a different breed.

On the other hand, public relations must design a positive external program, aimed at the stockholder, which is friendly without being patronizing and which is clear and understandable without giving the impression that the company management is a benevolent autocrat talking down to the children in the corporate family. No phase of corporate public relations is as important as the attitude toward the people who own shares, not only because the stockholder is entitled to know about the company affairs, but also because his attitude toward the company spills over in his peripheral relations with other publics such as the press and those consumers who are not shareholders. All publics who are affected by the company's activities, whether directly as employees or indirectly as consumers and stockholders, are potential ambassadors of good or ill will for the company. They influence other publics, and this influence penetrates to the mass media through editors and columnists. Since the good will and support of the stockholder is important to the well-being of a corporate enterprise, public relations functions to orient management to a healthy attitude toward those members of the corporate family.

For example, company decisions affecting the stockholders can be made cavalierly or, at best, with a token regard for their opinions; or the management can take earnest consideration of the point of view and welfare of the stockholders, both as a source of investment capital and as potential public relations ambassadors. Company decisions should be arrived at with an eye toward stockholder attitudes and with the objective of building stockholder good will. Recently, a major company decided to sell its home office building, which it owned, and to rent quarters in a new building under construction. The public relations director, anticipating that some stockholders might question why the company should sell a building it owned in order to pay a high rental for new quarters, discussed this situation with management. His suggestion was to arrange an interview between the company president and the business editor of a prominent newspaper. The result was an imposing feature in which the company point of view received most sympathetic press handling. Reprints of this article were mailed to stockholders, along with a letter from the president in which he enlarged upon the strategy of rental versus ownership and showed that the former was more feasible from an economic viewpoint. It should be noted, incidentally, that the public relations man did not wait for the Sunday feature to appear in the press. Stockholders were informed in a preliminary announcement, with the reprint mailing as a follow-up.

The role of the public relations director in the area of stockholder matters is somewhat anomalous. He cannot be expected to know the complicated facts of auditing and accounting, profit and loss, balance sheets, and other vital economic matters. These are best left to the company's legal department and the business office. But intelligent public relations can make these figures interesting and intelligible to the public. Public relations steps in when the figures are ready for distribution. It functions to plan the format and style of the annual report, adding promotional copy and pictures that make dull figure columns come alive; it works on the president's introductory statement, on a résumé of company activities, on a concluding prediction for the future. When the report is ready, the public relations department arranges for distribution to the press by sending it to editors along with a covering release in which the facts of the report are summarized.

In general, stockholder relations should be served by a running liaison between the public relations office and the legal and financial officials of the company. The function of the latter is to determine what, how, and how often the company's legal and financial problems and affairs are to be brought to the direct attention of the stockholder by a letter from the president or to his indirect attention by a story released to the press. All too often, the problem of public relations rests not with the stockholder but with the company management and directors who must be persuaded that stockholders should be kept informed because they can be of incalculable value in the area of public opinion formation.

In the external area of stockholder relations, the public relations director is concerned with the geographic and psychological environment in which the corporate family is to be found. This involves the informational phase of stockholder relations, and it includes the basic annual report, along with interim reports and statements, the annual meeting, and the distribution of proxy statements—usually through the agency of a special issuing organization. In addition, some stockholder relations programs include special letters and bulletins from the president and other interim aids and promotional devices. Public relations should see to it that all *new* aspects of company activity which are colorful or informative are passed on to the stockholder. For example:

1. The election of new officers or changes in management should be passed on to stockholders, along with pictures and biographical data. This is frequently done by a letter and an accompanying four-page pamphlet.
2. Stockholders should be informed of new products or new developments which might make for widespread publicity.
3. It is advisable to advise stockholders *in advance* of any important special event, such as a fair, an important broadcast or telecast, or a special contest.
4. It is also important to keep stockholders informed about various human interest activities of the company, such as the feting of an employee who has been with the company for twenty-five years.
5. Some large companies maintain excellent stockholder relations by sending occasional informative newsletters from the president as well as samples or pictures of new products.
6. Finally, all new stockholders should receive a note of welcome from the company president.

## THE ANNUAL REPORT

In the preparation of the annual report, which is intended primarily for stockholders, public relations functions as an adjunct to the financial and legal departments. The public relations director's job is to supervise the format and printing, to write copy about plans and projects, to fill the reader in on important achievements, and to select appropriate illustrations for inclusion. A report which enhances the stockholder relations with the company will be built, if possible, around some basic theme or keynote for the year. It will embrace more than mere optimistic phrasings by including at least one important *news item,* such as the divulging of a big expansion program. And it will be illustrated by colorful, attractive, and informative pictures and captions to enlarge upon the copy.

A recurrent problem in some companies is whether to speak only in terms of optimism or to include a frank statement of problems by stating, simply, that any organization, however successful, faces problems and decisions. A candid but skillful account of such problems makes for better stockholder relations than an attempt to omit or gloss over them. A large company recently found that it would have to sell one of its subsidiaries because it constituted a constant financial burden. Originally, the explanatory copy in the report read, "Your Company decided to discontinue this division because, despite our efforts, it was not making a profit." The final version, as approved by management and the public relations director read, "Your company decided to discontinue the operation of this subsidiary, with resulting economies."

The basic contribution of the public relations department to the annual report lies in making sure that those elements that bring better stockholder relations are included. While the report will contain several pages of balance sheets, the main body of copy, which is the president's letter, should explain the company's earnings and general financial situation in clear language. The report should also describe the company's outlook for the future and should make mention of any specific plans or projects which are contemplated. It should discuss any special governmental, legislative, or tax problems. It might include a strong endorsement of the caliber of men who head the executive staff. And it might contain some important human interest angle, such as an account of what is being done to cement relations with employers, customers, and the community.

Still another aspect of stockholder relations which falls within the purview of the public relations director is the annual stockholders' meeting. This can be smooth sailing, or it can create a stormy and controversial period for everyone concerned, particularly if the press is in attendance. There are, among stockholders, always potential complainers and cranks who come for the express purpose of heckling and irritating management. On occasion, when an issue is controversial, some stockholders come to make their opinion vociferous. And some simply attend to be better informed. The public relations man must insist that, whatever the problem and from whomever it is expressed, the president himself must undertake to answer it. The answering of questions at a stockholders' meeting is the job of the top executive.

The meeting can be purely academic, or it can be accomplished in an atmosphere which is brisk, businesslike, and pleasant for everyone concerned. Preparations for handling the meeting are a legitimate function of public relations, i.e., displays of products, copies of the report, brochures, and, if feasible, a buffet luncheon or tea for those attending, *including the press*. Proper and cordial handling of the press at the meeting can be extremely helpful in creating the atmosphere and tone for a good, solid story.

Stockholders, therefore, are important not only because they buy shares, but because they influence public opinion. Indeed, many companies boast more stockholders than management and employees put together. Good stockholder relations result in a favorable press and in the formation of a favorable climate of opinion.

## THE COMMUNITY

There are two other special areas of public opinion formation which are related and which are of inestimable value to a business enterprise. One area concerns the developing of a loyal and enthusiastic employee group. The other involves the creating and maintaining of good will with the community. A manifestation of good will by each is important in itself, but each also complements and implements the formation of opinion in the other. A company which can develop the support and good will of both has built a firm foundation of constructive public relations. But a crack in either foundation constitutes a potential danger because these publics interact one upon the other. A company which has negative employee relations usually does not enjoy the support of the community.

It is not hard to discern why the employee and the community are powerful handmaidens in helping to build or destroy company prestige. For no amount of pressure publicity or exploitation will avail if the employee public is dissatisfied, for this attitude puts honest public relations on the defensive and forces it to resort to flamboyant press agentry. At the same time, a company which has not earned the respect of the community which it serves will lose, sooner or later, the aura of good will which it may enjoy with the employees and with other related publics.

Large business enterprises which employ many people and which are located importantly within a given geographical area should include a community relations program among their public relations objectives and activities. At one time, particularly at the turn of the century, community relations did not mean what it means today. The plant-city operation of an earlier economic period was a kind of feudal kingdom of its own in which the head of the company established what was virtually a separate city within a city, with its own company stores, school, and other agencies. Fortunately, this kind of benevolent despotism has yielded to a more enlightened and responsible management attitude, but in too many cases no constructive program of community relations has replaced it. Community relations program does not mean the building of a community only for the hired help. It means the application of socially constructive concepts on the part of the company which will contribute to the social, economic, and cultural growth of the community at large and which will, as a result, enlist the support, coöperation, and good will of all community agencies.

Such a program can be accomplished by applying the practice of sound public relations on the community level, by developing constructive policies in the public interest.

Invariably, the first task is internal, i.e., to convince management that the road to community support must be paved with more than good intentions. It must rest on a foundation of constructive projects and deeds in the interest of the community itself. Management must develop a pro-community attitude.

Management, at the same time, must be cautioned against flaunting its so-called good deeds. The community leaders do not take kindly to benevolent despotism. Contributions and support of various community projects need not be flaunted.

But, once management has accomplished something worthwhile in the way of supporting or establishing significant community projects, the public relations department can tell the community about them in a dignified manner—by stories in the press, special events, promotional aids, and paid advertising.

Those public relations men who have analyzed the need for community support can readily understand why the company must plan so carefully in the area of its community relations. Studies of community reaction to the business enterprise reveal that most groups are initially suspicious of big business; that they fear the iron fist in the velvet glove; and that they tend to be resentful of overt patronizing or of flamboyantly publicized efforts, such as large contributions to the Community Chest. The basic problem, therefore, is to develop a sound program of genuine community *service* and then to enlist the support of the mass media, such as press, radio, and television, in helping to tell the story. It should be remembered, incidentally, that the press and other local media are part of the community and that they, too, must be convinced of good intent, buttressed by solid achievement. Because the mass media are the most important avenues to good community relations, the public relations program must be scrupulously mindful of truth. Facts must be presented in a manner which will dispel suspicious and false impressions and replace them with an impression of candor and truth. This means, essentially, that management, once again, may have to be convinced of the necessity of airing certain unpleasant data to the press and public. It means, further, that when the company is in error, management must admit the error *publicly* and take steps to correct it.

Management is not always easy to convince. Frequently, it will challenge this kind of philosophy as wishful thinking or false idealism that has no place in the pragmatism of the business world. By careful research, however, public relations should be able to marshall sufficient facts to convince management that pragmatism, in business, means facing community issues squarely and meeting them honestly. This can be accomplished, as a rule, by a scientifically conducted opinion measurement or survey, the results of which are presented and interpreted to management. If the research shows that certain negative factors do exist in the community relations area, public relations is expected to implement this situation by asking for specific changes in company policy. And, if management agrees to necessary changes, public relations should then advise the community about them by a successful publicity program in the mass media. The information may be conveyed:

1. By factual, human interest stories to the press, radio, and television.
2. By preparing and distributing brochures or other aids in which the company policies are made clear.
3. By a personal exchange of visits with community leaders.
4. By open house days at the company, lectures, films, and other special aids and events which tell the company-community story.
5. By arranging for speeches, slides, and motion pictures to be presented, outside the plant, at schools and other community agencies.

Management should know, of course, that these steps are not valuable *only* when surveys show a negative public opinion. They are even more valuable in maintaining and strengthening a favorable climate of community opinion. Indeed, the public relations director who functions on the policy-making level is in a unique position to develop a continuous program of sound community relations so that the moment of crisis will be avoided. For example, constructive public relations can show management how to consider the community relations aspects *before* it undertakes a new project by asking simply, "Will this act be in the interest of the community as well as of the company?" Management, too, should be aware that employees are a guide to good community relations; it should be made aware of the necessity of a forward-looking attitude toward industrial relations problems, for these affect community opinion. Public relations should point out to management that the community is not a faceless and homogeneous mass but rather a number of social groups—or publics—whose total opinion becomes expressed as community opinion. Such groups include the schools, the PTA, the religious organizations, the housewives, and the professional groups. Finally, the principle, noted earlier, of psychological and geographic areas applies with particular emphasis to community public relations. Management must take into consideration, in all of its actions, the size of the town, the political climate, the economic status, and the basic social and cultural requirements.

The most important philosophy that public relations can inculcate in management is that the establishment of sound community relations is *not* accomplished by statements and contributions from the executive echelon alone but by every person within the company who represents it in any capacity whatsoever. When management has been convinced of the need and worth of a sound program, the public relations department can utilize the mass media to tell a continuing story of good, solid community relations. A management that truly operates in the public interest can earn formidable support through such devices as the following:

1. *Publicity:* By making all releases truthful and informative and by refusing to whitewash negative news when it occurs, such as an imminent strike or other problem.
2. *Institutional advertising:* By paid advertisements which point out the contribution of the company to the community.
3. *House organs:* By including a community relations aspect to all company-issued publications, e.g., Red Cross, Community Chest, PTA, etc.
4. *Annual reports:* By making copies available to community leaders.
5. *Special events:* By arranging for exhibits, displays, theatrical events.
6. *Educational activities:* By issuing films for schools and by

arranging significant scholarships, such as the Westinghouse Science Scholarship, among secondary schools.

7. *Civic activities:* By coöperating with civic and religious leaders on various community projects.

The development of sound community relations requires, therefore, that the public relations director have the basic support of company management in building a constructive program *within the company*. Once the need for directing the efforts of management into community-minded channels has been accomplished, public relations is in a unique position to enlist the support of the mass media in telling the story to the community. The area of community relations is, like that of employee relations, an aspect of *human* relations. It concerns every discrete public whose opinions fuse into an organic whole which becomes an expression of community—or public—opinion. A sound community relations program will emphasize the cardinal principles of all good public relations. It will render a service *to* the community by instituting projects in the interest *of* the community. It will communicate the importance of these projects to the community by utilizing the support of the mass media toward the end of achieving an expression of good will, and a favorable climate of opinion, within the community.

## THE CUSTOMER

The customer, like the stockholder, the employee, and the community leader, is a public. This is, however, a less clearly defined or delimited public. Customers *may* be a closely knit unit for a specific small establishment. But, in large organizations, they are a large, heterogeneous public. A large establishment, such as R. H. Macy and Company, has an employee and stockholder public, each of which is clearly demarcated. But it also boasts of a vast receiving audience of customers.

As important to the economic growth of the country as the industrial giants are such retail agencies as Macy's, Gimbel's, and others in New York as well as similar establishments in large metropolitan centers throughout the country. The function of retailing is sufficiently important to be taught as a special curriculum in many colleges which have set up schools of retailing. The difference between the manufacturing company and the retail establishment, from a public relations viewpoint, is that the latter is more directly concerned with the customer or consumer than is the former. And, in the area of retailing, there are many valuable possibilities for the application of human relations and public relations techniques.

In the area of retailing, even more than in the industrial or manufacturing enterprise, public relations does not develop in a vacuum. It exists from the moment an establishment attracts customers to its doors. The large retail department stores, with or without a public relations department, enjoy customer relations because public opinion exists about them (as in the case of such stores as Macy's or Gimbel's) both within and beyond the bounds of their geographical location. A public relations (or customer relations) program operates to dissipate negative public opinion and to develop and solidify a constructive and positive one. In other words, what the establishment does in the way of winning good will among its customers determines whether it will enjoy good or bad public relations.

In general, it may be said that if the executive or operating heads approach their jobs with a public relations attitude, the department heads, managers, and sales staff will also practice sound customer relations. Retail establishments have more than an institutional objective to their public relations. They have a necessary and practical end in view. For the point is not merely to attract potential customers but to attract them so successfully that their visit will become a habit and, ultimately, a necessity, because the establishment is a *good place at which to buy*. This difference in objective between the more remote manufacturer and the retailer is evident in other fields beyond the department store. General Electric, for example, manufactures products, but thousands of retail stores sell them to the consumer or customer. This is the last step in the economic process of production and distribution, and it is the chief source from which the customer's dollar flows. It embraces direct selling or hard-sell on the part of the public relations department, through advertising, promotion, and publicity, but it includes institutional aspects and special events as well, such as the Macy Thanksgiving Day Parade.

Good customer relations eventuate out of indirect or peripheral activities as well as direct ones. If the employee relations program is sound, the customer will learn implicitly that the employees *are* an integral part of the establishment. The quality and integrity of the advertising copy are equally important. An announced sale should really be what the term implies, not a come-on to buy other goods alone. The publicity media—press, radio, and television—can be enlisted to tell the story by means of coverage of special events, such as a fashion week, by having executives participate in forums, and by skillful feature planting in newspapers and magazines. Ultimately, however, successful relations with customers depend upon how courteously they are handled within the establishment in terms of service and satisfaction. From a successful internal program, the establishment can take steps toward establishing its institutional importance to the community by getting across the idea, through advertising and promotion, that it is making an important and worth-while contribution to the growth and prestige of the community.

The consumer or customer public relations program involves

a combination of direct selling and merchandising along with indirect or institutional advertising and promotion. Macy's accomplishes both by combining its symbol of "It's smart to be thrifty" with direct selling of its specific products. This is accomplished basically through newspaper advertising, although hard-sell can be accomplished also by means of spot announcements on the air and by including merchandising data in mailings with statements and bills. Most stores include these envelope promotions, but a few which have a cash policy do not find it feasible.

The retail establishment's public relations department can find many opportunities for publicity through the press conference, publicity release, or special event. Promotion tie-ins are frequently undertaken with motion picture companies, book publishers, air lines, and other relevant agencies. For example, an author will appear in the store's book section to autograph copies of his new book. The interview can be used when the executive head has an important story to give the business or financial editor. Publicity releases concerning changes in policy or special merchandising plans are of interest both to press and community. Special events, such as fashion shows, toy shows, parades, concerts, etc., almost always secure a formidable amount of feature and picture publicity. The press usually welcomes legitimate publicity about a retail establishment because, apart from the fact that the store is an advertiser, its activities are always of interest to the community.

In the area of customer relations, certain standard public relations practices are as important as they are in the industrial and manufacturing areas. Opinion measurement should be undertaken from time to time to determine reasons for satisfaction or complaint on the part of the customer. Complaint areas should be ameliorated by suggesting constructive changes in policy.

And these should be communicated to the customer, as always, by means of appropriate advertising, publicity, and promotion. The public relations director must remember that this is an age of standardization in which prices *and* quality do not vary very much from product to product. It is, therefore, of great importance that public relations concentrate on the development of an attitude and of activities so specifically aimed toward the public interest that the *one* establishment which it represents will stand out above all others as the best place to do business.

# CHAPTER 24

## Government and Politics

Public relations in government, or by government agencies, is to be distinguished from political public relations, but there is nevertheless an analogy. The former involves those techniques which government officials and agencies employ to keep the public informed and to disseminate information about federal, state, and local activities of various departments. The latter involves the planning of public relations and publicity designed to help aspirants to achieve government or civic office. Since both activities involve a communication link between officials or those who aspire to be officials and the public by means of mass media, they fall within the same general public relations area.

### OBLIGATIONS AND RESPONSIBILITIES

The government, sometimes positively, sometimes negatively, is involved both directly and obliquely with public relations, public opinion, and mass communication. The fact of inextricable linkage is always present in the activities of government officials and their agencies. But the government also faces problems in determining the extent of its operations. What are its obligations, its restrictions, and its limitations? There is, in *any* governmental operation, always an implicit danger of an official arrogating to himself or his office the prerogative of a censoring, restricting, or suppressing force. For, like all management, the government and its agencies are *people* who react with the identical emotional and directive bias of all other people. Censorship, implicit or explicit, can both restrict and control the news that should be disseminated by mass media; and the battle against censorship, from official agencies, semiofficial groups, and special interest publics is one that appears to have no terminal point because of the human equation involved. Censorship of the news increases or decreases depending on social, political, and economic events. It is greater in crisis, but it is always a potential danger to the free flow of information.

Censorship on the part of civic agencies becomes a public relations problem when the public is prevented from receiving the news because the mass media cannot gain access to it. And the purpose of such censorship, subtly or directly applied, is to prevent public opinion formation from becoming established, or from changing, in a given area. Basically, "freedom of the press" and other mass media means free access to sources of information and freedom to print the news, provided it is not printed in terms of libel or pornography and that it is not detrimental to the general welfare or security of the country and its citizens.

Who, however, is to determine what is detrimental to the general welfare—the issuing or censoring agency or the press? The basic problem in government public relations vis-à-vis the press and the public is simply whether there is *any* realm of discourse in which an official agency has the prerogative of exercising restrictive power over the news. Should not a free and responsible press and other media jointly decide what is and is not potentially dangerous or harmful? There has always been criticism, since the early days of the Republic, of civic information and publicity specialists who, it has been alleged, do not aid the flow of news. The press complains, on occasion, that "public servant" publicists classify information when there is, in reality, nothing secret about it. But this depends upon point of view as well as personalities involved. It may be said, however, that the greatest safeguards of a free and responsible press —and a free flow of news—are the vigilance and integrity not only of those who operate the media, but also of those who represent official agencies. These, plus an alert and informed public, can go far to guarantee the kind of informational flow which will engender democratic discussion and opinion formation.

The government (city, state, federal) does not regulate the content of mass media, nor does it exercise control over their independence. The only official agency is the Federal Communications Commission whose function is to allocate the broadcast frequencies to assure "clear" broadcasting and, at the same time, to see to it that stations operate in the "public interest, convenience, and necessity." The fact is that, as a matter of historical, social, and technical development, the mass media have outgrown much of the legal data relating to questions of freedom and libel. Communications media so completely engulf our environment today, and they are still developing so rapidly, that today's regulation may be an anachronism tomorrow. It is difficult, in contemporary journalism, to hang a libel suit on even some of the more disreputable writers whom a distinguished newspaper editor has termed the "flotsam and jetsam of contemporary journalism."

Because administrations, officials, and agency heads change

from time to time—and because social and economic conditions also are in flux—there will always be the problem, even in a democratic society, of attempts to *control* the content of mass media. And since changes in government mean changes in personalities, the human equation is such that eternal vigilance —by government officials, press, and public—is essential to the continuing freedom of the media of mass communication.

On the other hand, the government has been, and can be, a source of aid to the media. It can encourage them to further their pursuit of objective news coverage in the interest of promoting the general welfare and keeping the public adequately informed. Government can also, when conditions demand, be a helpful "regulatory" symbol without becoming either restrictive or autocratic. The government, through the FCC, for example, reserved 252 original channels for the exclusive use of educational institutions, against the strong objections of many commercial broadcasting interests. The government has prevented the development of monopoly in some areas by implementing antitrust laws, as in the consent decree divorcing the *distribution* of motion pictures from exhibition. The government also can aid in the growth of the mass media by encouraging communications study and research through the Department of Education and through related agencies. It is conceivable that funds may one day be appropriated for experimental research and for the training of communications experts in the colleges, universities, and technical schools of the country, as is now being done in the physical sciences.

But probably the greatest service to be rendered by government is the development of the attitudes and the means which will facilitate the flow of official news and information to the public by means of the mass media, both directly by press conferences, releases, and participation in radio and TV forums and indirectly by the publication and distribution of pamphlets, brochures, and other informational material. In times of national stress or crisis, the mass media must be expected to coöperate and understand the need for restrictive devices. But, other things being equal, the access to official news is the democratic right of press and public alike.

Civic agencies have shown a greater sensitivity to public opinion, and consequently to public relations, since World War II. This is due to the circumstance of a critical national situation in which public opinion and consent had to be mobilized not only in a military sense but in the social and economic spheres as well. Government entered into a close proximity, from a public relations viewpoint, with business and with those who were responsible for the operation of the mass media. Problems of censorship required the enlisting of aid from the press. The need for the dissemination of communication content regarding bond drives, and explanatory data concerning our international aims, required the coöperation of business and industry as well as mass communication. World War II, indeed, marked the beginning of a period in which the government depended upon the support of business to help tell its story, and particularly upon such media as the press, radio, television, motion pictures, and national magazines. In recent years, in fact, some of the mass media have been criticized from various quarters for a liaison with civic and political agencies which is thought to be too close for comfort.

The first move, however, was not from government, but from business itself—and it was inspired by public relations. During the war years, many companies had no consumer products to market, owing to the demands of the war effort. But canny public relations counsel devised a method of institutional advertising whereby brand names and national companies would be kept before the public. This type of advertising and promotion aimed to create a favorable public opinion toward the company as an *institution* against the day when consumer products would be available again. And, within this frame of reference, business was eager to sponsor government messages, particularly patriotic motifs which were "contributed as a public service." It should be noted, parenthetically but significantly, that business did not desist in its institutional efforts after the war. An unusually productive and booming economy, plus high taxes, allowed sufficient money to continue the institutional or public relations type of advertising and promotion. Companies proudly tied in their public relations with government programs, with the Citizens Committee for Better Schools, with the Red Cross, the National Safety Council, and other nationwide public interest projects. Many companies which used the media of radio and television for hard-sell commercial advertising also saw fit to insert such closing messages as "This is your announcer, John Jones, saying good night for the Miracle Manufacturing Company and reminding you that this is Boy Scout Week. Have you made your contribution to your local Boy Scout movement?"

The interest of business in government promotion was a welcome step so far as officials were concerned. The power, reach, and penetration of mass media are such that now, as never before, government must be aware of their impact on public opinion. The government agency, however, cannot engage in flamboyant promotion. Government leaders, themselves not averse to normal publicity, are quick to investigate any unusual spending or effort, as are other groups in the special interest area—civic, economic, religious, political, and educational. Still, there is need for sympathetic understanding of the government official's problem. Has a government agency not as legitimate a right to have its story told to the public as any business effort? Is the public not entitled to information about the work of its representatives and their respective departments? How much knowledge does the public have of the myriad functions of the Department of Health, Education, and Welfare? Or, of the Interior? Or, of the Justice or Agriculture Department? Certainly much of the material available from the Superintendent of Documents, Government Printing Office in Washington, D.C., is poorly executed from an art and production viewpoint, and it is questionable whether it can win friends and influence people.

The government agency, of course, has access to mass media. The official has the privilege of calling a press conference, of issuing releases, of making speeches, of distributing reports, of appearing on radio and television and in the newsreels. Some officials take realistic advantage of these media. Some, however, appear to believe that the media are available to them when convenient but that they have the prerogative of refusing to see the press when it might prove inconvenient or embarrassing. The safety valve is, of course, the power of the mass media to bring such special situations to the attention of the public. This, in itself, can be an object lesson in public relations in a democracy.

From the standpoint of utilization of mass media, there is some degree of competition among the various government agencies. In the course of any one day, for example, the Armed Forces may want a story on recruitment needs; the health agencies may ask for space on the polio vaccine; the Interior Department may have a special conservation item; the Justice Department may release the story of an important antitrust case. Since there may not be a genuine publicity liaison between these agencies, important announcements frequently may compete with one another for coverage by the mass media.

Generally, the devices or outlets used in government publicity, apart from the formal release or press conference, are 16-mm films, radio and television, and various informational documents in the form of brochures or pamphlets. Commercial radio and television, in fact, constantly promote and publicize government agencies by using, with permission, backgrounds and characters from various departments. The only public relations outlet which is specifically out of the pale of the government is the paid advertisement. Government pamphlets and films can be reproduced and distributed by many of the giant corporations. But the government does not have the funds to undertake the kind of promotion and distribution undertaken by private business.

Because of these factors, the liaison between government and business has proved to be fruitful, in a public relations sense, for both. Business has produced films and brochures with the "coöperation of" a given department. When the subject is germane, business has tied in with government on specific promotions. For example, a motion picture company which had produced a film about a great American issued a poster to thousands of schools and libraries, relating the subject matter of the picture with the Treasury Department Bond Drive.

The public relations objectives of government are quite simple. Government cannot function for long without the consent of the governed—and to achieve and maintain the consent of the public, the government needs the support of mass media. Paradoxically, however, some government officials call upon mass media at their convenience but thwart the efforts of reporters to get at the core of a good story. Here, again, emotive factors operate, and the problem is frequently one of human relations among the personalities involved. A politically favorable press may go along with restrictive devices, but an opposition press is likely to raise a storm of protest. In the long run, the government cannot disregard the power of the media of communication, for they are the only direct avenues to public opinion.

## THE ARENA OF POLITICS

Publicity, promotion, and advertising, as tools of a public relations campaign, go into high gear during the political seasons. More and more, in recent years, political parties have looked to the advertising and public relations specialist to help mold a favorable climate of opinion. And this is not always a spark to the democratic process, for it cannot be denied that advertising and promotion can be as obscure as they can be clear in purpose and intent. The political campaign is illustrative of the attractive as well as the more mischievous facets of public relations as a propaganda technique. How much respect for fact, for example, has gone into the basic establishment of policy and into the promulgation of that policy in speech writing, television campaigning, billboards, and news releases? In the arena of politics, the newspaper writer is apt to be restricted, pro or con, by the policy of his publisher. The political publicist, too, is dealing with at least an implicitly biased press. For, no matter how great its respect for truth, the newspaper itself campaigns for a chosen candidate. It is one of the fortunate aspects of democracy, however, that the majority of the press and the other media does make great effort to give an impartial presentation of both sides in its news coverage, although the editorial page and other columns may be vibrantly partisan.

An important question for political publicists is that of the degree of depth and penetration. How much political publicity, so far as the public is concerned, is literally useless? How seriously does the public respond to the plethora of stimuli disseminated by mass media? And which of the media are more, and which less, effective in moving the voter to action? Political publicity is subject to many extraneous influences. International events, the health of an official, the fluctuations of the stock market can render the most carefully wrought public relations campaign completely ineffectual.

Political publicists engage all media. But surveys have revealed that the reader of politics in the newspaper tends to listen to politics on the air, while the person who does not read political news will not watch it or listen to it on the air. However, the political publicist will still concentrate on *all* the media, simply because no opportunity can be neglected in the relatively short haul of a political campaign. But the publicist who is wise in the ways of public opinion will not concentrate on the black or white areas, i.e., those whose votes are decided upon a priori. He will, so far as possible, centralize his campaign in the gray area, among those publics where there is a possibility of flexibility and opinion change. In terms of mass media, both the press and radio and TV are probably the most immediate and powerful for a political campaign, with the broadcast media offering the unique power of directness and immediacy of impact.

Political publicity, in essence, proposes to change the political convictions and orientations of various publics. It tries to lead the predispositions and opinions of the public *away* from one viewpoint and *toward* another. And for this purpose, the press is not so important as the broadcast media. No other agency can approach the effectiveness of a "fireside chat" or a "talk to the nation" as can radio or television. For these media offer a sense of immediacy, a feeling of participation, an implicit agreement that the personality is *in* the living room making issues come alive with a vital importance. In addition, the broadcast media stimulate public discussion which is the catalyst of opinion formation and change.

In addition to the press and the broadcast media, national magazines have become important because some have taken on an implicit political bias in both their news and their editorial content. With millions of readers, they are a potent factor in political publicity for they can, and do, help make up the minds of a good part of these millions on political issues and candidates.

One final area, however, should not be overlooked. Significantly, and despite the power and reach of mass media, the political candidate has taken to the road. Even the most sophisticated of public relations has been fearful of omitting the whistle-stop campaign, the direct meeting with the people. And this, in an age when public relations techniques and mass media are thought to be all-pervading, is a welcome paradox, for it indicates that, in a democracy, the individual still manages to stand out, however dimly, in the concept of the mass.

# CHAPTER 25

## *Public Relations in Education*

There are two aspects to the utilization of public relations and publicity in the area of education. One concerns the objectives and techniques of educational publicity as they are accomplished by academic or semiacademic institutions. The other revolves around the educational publicity programs of business institutions, such as scholarships, institutional promotions, and the use of audio-visual aids.

### THE EDUCATIONAL INSTITUTION

Educational institutions have become acutely aware, in recent years, of the need for, and importance of, intelligent public relations and publicity. Courses in communications and in public relations are growing rapidly in colleges and professional schools throughout the country. Some institutions offer graduate credit and degrees in specialized areas of communications research. In addition such events as the White House Conference on Education have made the press and the public, as well as the educator, aware of the importance of education in our national life; and professional organizations such as the National Education Association have worked vigorously to inform the public of major problems, issues, and objectives in American education.

The basic objectives of an educational public relations program, on the part of a college or university, are largely identical with the purposes of any general public relations campaign: to keep the public informed, to build a solid foundation for favorable opinion formation, and to create active consent. The difference is not one of kind but of degree. Educational public relations, in other words, operates in a specific area or realm of discourse. It attempts to influence those publics which are relevant or germane to this particular area. The public relations director of an educational institution is concerned with creating a favorable climate of opinion among the following publics:

1. *The alumni:* The good will of this group is important for many reasons—endowments and contributions, recruitment of students and faculty, word-of-mouth recommendation of the institution, interest in its objectives. Publications such as the *Alumni News* are printed for more than their informational value. They are powerful organs of opinion formation.

2. *The faculty:* An institution which has a fine reputation, both in terms of scholarly achievement and in terms of its central administration, can attract a strong and creative faculty. And the public relations man, both as publicist and as educator, can serve as an effective communications link between administration policies and faculty, and between faculty and the world outside.

3. *The student body:* Educational institutions strive to attract a productive student body—in the classroom as well as in other related areas of university life. Good public relations, by creating favorable public opinion, can attract a superior student body.

4. *The local community:* A major function of the public relations director is to relate the college to the community, to see that its resources are utilized by the students and faculty, and,

even more importantly, to offer the resources of the institution for use by the community.

5. *The national community:* It is part of the educational public relations man's function not only to relate the institution to the immediate community, but also to take steps to establish its reputation on the broader national level as an institution of true national prestige and achievement.

6. *The world community:* Finally, in larger institutions, the public relations director can relate the organization to the world educational community by establishing its reputation throughout the civilized world.

Intelligent and dignified public relations can reach and influence each of these areas by employing the techniques of publicity and promotion. But the major problem confronting most educational public relations men is not one of technique or of skill but of lack of policy and inertia on the management level which, in educational circles, is usually known as the central administration. School and college officials, while they profess to want and to welcome publicity, are nevertheless timid about taking steps to receive it. There is trepidation, too, among the faculty that perhaps an interview on the occasion of publication of a new volume would be considered egotistical and undignified. The coöperative institutional educator, from a publicity viewpoint, is in the minority; while the professional educators, i.e., those who represent the national associations, seem to take greater pride in talking with the press and getting their names into print.

Apart from the paradox of having to deal with educational officials who would welcome sound publicity if they did not fear it, many educational institutions also face the problem of a genuine dearth of trained public relations personnel. Both college publicists and many college administrators frequently fail to understand what coöperation with the press can accomplish in the way of affirming a solid block of favorable public opinion. Educators, too, frequently look upon the press as an intruder on academic privacy and show no genuine desire to learn how the press functions and what it can do in the way of positive publicity. And, even when educators do decide to deal with the press, their lack of knowledge of its needs is manifested in poorly conceived and written publicity releases which lack the professional touch of the trained publicist. All of this is unfortunate, for editors welcome good education stories and pictures, and the inevitable result of a better liaison between the educator and the mass media would be stronger liaison between the educational institutions and the other community agencies. The public and its institutions, business and otherwise, can only support education when they understand its problems and objectives.

W. Emerson Reck, vice-president of Wittenberg College and former president of the American College Public Relations Association offers this definition of educational public relations: "Public relations is the continued process of keying policies, services and actions to the best interests of those individuals and groups whose confidence and good will an individual or institution covets; and secondly, it is the interpretation of these policies, services and actions to assure complete understanding and appreciation."

According to this concept, then, the function of the educational public relations expert is to guide the administrator toward an attitude by which the policies and actions of the institution are keyed to the interests of students, alumni, faculty, and the larger relevant publics; as a *result* of which these groups are contacted, by means of mass media, to enlist their understanding and active support. National organizations such as the National Education Association must acquaint legislators and the public with specific educational problems. Specific institutions, on the other hand, must work continuously to add to their individual prestige, stature, and reputation.

Public relations in education functions, as it does in other areas, to set up sound policies and then to inform the public about them. The educational publicist's particular objective is to keep the public informed about the functioning of the schools and colleges of the nation. He must devise the means of convincing particular groups that the educational process is important in a democratic society. He must establish a method of bringing the educator into closer harmony with parents and with business and community leaders. He must be prepared with facts and information which will help to dispel false ideas and will clear up areas of misinformation about the nature and function of education.

In a more specific area, educational public relations works to interpret the policies of the institution to the public, but, as in many other management situations, the public relations director has no real opportunity to help in the establishment of policy. In a general way, the administrator expects public relations to add stature and prestige to the institution, to find ways of interesting superior students, to inform the public through the mass media of important research achievements, to interest individuals in its endowment needs, and to help attract the best teachers and scholars.

Obviously these objectives are sound, but they cannot be accomplished in a vacuum. They must be promulgated by individuals who know both public relations techniques *and* educational problems. Until schools and colleges see fit to add educational public relations to their training of administrators, the problem of telling the story of education to the community will be an acute one. The educational public relations director should be familiar with educational problems, and the administrator should have some knowledge of the importance of public relations. The best college publicity directors are trained as both journalists and teachers. They are able to make the objectives of the institution vocal and articulate through both public speaking and publicity writing.

Obviously a college public relations department cannot stand the economic pressure of a large industrial concern. But, at a minimum, an educational institution of any size and importance should have a departmental administrator who is responsible to the president and who helps to formulate policy. It should have writers, so-called "leg" men, at least one photographer, a radio and television expert, and at least one person trained in the technique of writing and preparing brochures and speeches.

On an internal or administrative level, the educational public relations director should be able to see all statements so that he can determine their probable impact. He should supervise all public copy, from a commencement address to a sports event. And he should develop avenues of liaison not only with outside agencies, such as the press, but with students, faculty, and alumni. An educational publicist can frequently be more helpful in publicizing a new book by a faculty member than the publisher—and the results can be excellent in terms of prestige for the institution through newspaper interviews and features, radio and TV forums, and related events. The basic essential, however, is that the public relations man have a hand in formulating policies and in carrying them out without interference from either the trustees, president, or faculty.

Given a vote of confidence and at least a relatively free hand, the educational publicist can devise techniques to reach and influence at least the following ten important publics:

1. The alumni.
2. The faculty.
3. The student body.
4. The potential student.
5. The board of trustees or directors.
6. The community leaders.
7. Civic officials.
8. Educational and trade associations.
9. Industry leaders.
10. Potential endowment contributors.

The techniques employed are those of publicity via the mass media and promotion by means of direct mail. There are invariably news and feature stories in the activities of administrators, faculty, and students. There are speeches to be made and reprinted for mailing to leaders. There are alumni publications, luncheons, and special days. There are research projects to be announced. In addition to the press and to feature possibilities in the magazines, radio and TV offer a productive area for educational publicity. Stations use educational news or programming under their license from the Federal Communications Commission. And, in recent years, many institutions have established their own studios or work in coöperation with municipal or other commercial broadcasting companies. The field of educational public relations offers a challenge and a tremendous opportunity.

## AUDIO-VISUAL AIDS

Audio-visual devices, such as 16-mm films, slides, displays, exhibits, posters, radio, and television have a specific use and are frequently of great value in public relations and in opinion formation. They are used differently, but with equal effectiveness, both by educational institutions and by business.

Internally, audio-visual aids have value in industrial training and personnel programs, particularly in employee indoctrination in the public relations objectives of the company. Motion pictures are of considerable value in this area. In addition to films, it is also valuable to show employees advance copies or proofs of advertisements and promotions. Externally, audio-visual aids are valuable in selling, as in a film or display or slide presentation of the importance of a product; in dealer promotion; and in institutional and educational public relations, such as a film prepared by The Curtis Publishing Company entitled "Magazine Magic" which told the story of the entire process of the making of a magazine and was distributed to schools throughout the country.

Apart from their usefulness in business training and sales programs, audio-visual aids are employed most successfully among special publics. For example, schools, colleges, and libraries welcome audio-visual aids, such as posters, if they are not too commercial in nature. Other outlets are the Parent-Teacher Associations, the various local women's clubs, civic groups, and, when the material is relevant, religious groups. Still other outlets are farm organizations and professional groups. The use of radio can also be applied to promotion with professional groups. A recent network broadcast mentioned a national scientific assembly, and the professional group responded by a story and picture in the journal as well as a direct mailing to all member doctors and scientists, urging them to listen to the broadcast.

Many national organizations, such as Elks, Lions, Kiwanis, and other groups are important outlets for audio-visual promotional material. For, in one group may be found educators, business leaders, and civic and political figures representative of the community. To these groups, it is advisable to combine a film showing with an informal dinner or discussion. For example, a representative of a national magazine addressed such an organization meeting and found opportunity to show a film indicating the advertising scope and impact of the publication.

Annual meetings of organizations are also outlets for audio-visual aids, but in this area hard-sell is best avoided. If, for example, the head of a broadcasting network is to address a convention of doctors or educators, the audio-visual material may be used to substantiate or elaborate upon the speech by highlighting how broadcasting networks contribute to the medical or general education of the public.

Basically, however, the educator is the most feasible target. Teachers welcome audio-visual aids if they are not overtly promotional. They will use posters, films, and slides which are educationally or informationally significant and which supplement the teaching and learning process. Scientific displays, art material, background material about selected motion pictures, and current events data are all important and useful provided that they are educational in content and that the message is of an institutional and noncommercial nature.

The choice of which audio-visual aid, or aids, to use depends upon the requirements of the receiving audience. The choice is wide—films, displays, slides, exhibits, recordings, posters, brochures, etc. One aid may accomplish what another will not, but some are more expensive than others. Ten thousand posters may cost $700, while a thirty-minute color film can run anywhere from $25,000 to $100,000.

Audio-visual promotion to schools may not yield immediate returns, except in trade publicity, but such promotion is of inestimable value in building institutional prestige, in developing future buyers and adherents, and in delineating the long-term public relations objectives of a company.

Part VI

# Propaganda
# and Ethics

*Relationship among public relations, public opinion, and propaganda—Need for an ethics or system of value judgments in public relations—Public relations' contribution to democracy*

# CHAPTER 26

## *Public Relations and Propaganda*

Propaganda has gone by many names, many guises. It has proved to be amenable to many formal definitions. Considered from the vantage point of public relations and the techniques of influencing public opinion, it remains to determine not whether propaganda can be defined in classic terms but whether its purposes and objectives can be described in terms of function.

There has always been propaganda, for leaders and groups have always espoused a cause and taken steps to *propagate* it among others. But the perfection of the mass media has given propaganda technicians new avenues; and the growth of public relations and its techniques has frequently been identified so closely with traditional concepts of propaganda that *all* public relations has been termed propaganda, although all propaganda has not necessarily been equated with public relations. It is not easy to delimit the nature and function of propaganda by definition. It is still difficult, although social scientists have made considerable progress, to devise an accurate scientific method for studying propaganda in action or even to determine whether the phrase "art of propaganda" is scientific fact or mere rhetoric. To

349

some extent propaganda can be made amenable to study by the techniques available to the social scientist. To some extent, hypotheses can be set up and verified on the basis of empirical evidence. Some social scientists have described propaganda as an act—or series of acts—with the two-pronged objective of influencing thought and opinion and of guiding or directing behavior into channels desirable to the propagandist. The desire to guide or direct behavior is undertaken with peculiar zeal and fervor, for the propagandist is dedicated to the promulgation of some specific objective.

## WHAT IS PROPAGANDA?

Is propaganda different, as an art of persuasion, from the techniques of advertising and public relations? To state that it is not would be to do a disservice to ethical public relations, because the stimulus-response syndrome to the term propaganda is almost always a negative one. Propaganda has been identified with Hitler and Goebbels, with the political infiltration tactics of the Russians, and with international ideological conflicts such as democracy versus fascism and communism. In the political sphere, propaganda is both negative and positive in action. Negative aspects include the hue and cry of the totalitarian state for peace, even while it creates international mischief, as in the Middle East. Positive aspects include the efforts of the United States to disseminate vital data about freedom through the medium of radio, as well as the publicized intent of the United States to work through the machinery of the United Nations. However, are *both* of these activities propaganda, or is there only a negative side to this technique? Does propaganda, by its historical function, work only toward nefarious ends, or is there a technique of propaganda toward ends which are constructive, such as the dissemination of information about democracy? Should there be a term other than propaganda for this effort?

The popular stereotype of the propagandist is certainly not a healthy one. The portrait is one of Machiavellianism, of a sly and subterranean influence working to subvert public opinion toward some socially harmful end. Derived from the Latin verb *propagare*, the term at one time meant the spreading of religious belief. In a contemporary context, the term does not only resist definition in the world of things, but it has strong emotive and directive aspects. We know that it is involved deeply in the process of opinion formation, that it can be a tool of public relations, and that it involves the communication of ideas for the purpose of influencing opinion. To decide, however, that propaganda is invariably a negative social force is not a tenable conclusion unless certain other functional aspects are considered. Does propaganda always work with deliberation toward some preconceived objective? Does it always involve the problem of ends versus means to the extent that the desired end justifies *any* successful means, whether it be socially deleterious or not? Is the motivation always obscured, or can it be overt? Is propaganda always an effort to distort meanings, or can it also deal with substantial and verifiable facts and information?

Propaganda, as an effort directed toward the influencing of opinion, employs the media of communication in order to disseminate its message, on behalf of an individual or cause, as widely as possible. Its purpose is not only to influence opinion but to instigate some overt and desired action. Its grist is public opinion, for this phenomenon is the power that generates power. In the pluralistic universe of a democracy, public opinion is least static, because there are many groups, many opinions. Communication content can operate to influence opinion. Paradoxically, however, propaganda techniques are utilized mightily by totalitarian countries in which opinion does not eventuate out of implicit controversy but is constantly under autocratic control. The democracy offers public opinion a system of checks and balances. Negative propaganda fortunately has not been able to change basic institutions. Propaganda functions also to combat propaganda.

Two functional aspects of propaganda have been described by the social scientist. The end of propaganda techniques is invariably *predetermined;* and the effort to channel public opinion is an *organized* one. Furthermore, the success of a propaganda effort involves more than the mere exposure of a group to the message via mass media. It depends upon the *reaction* of the group to the content, for individuals react to opinion-making stimuli in terms of their prior educational, economic, social, and religious training, orientation, and conditioning. The public's opinions do not always predict its ultimate behavior, for individuals will venture an opinion and act to the contrary. Individuals and groups react to propositions in terms of their general attitude toward the basis underlying the proposition. For example, the reaction of an individual toward the issue of federal aid to education is conditioned by his basic attitude toward education in general. The attitude toward Arab-Israeli relations is conditioned by the basic attitude toward Jews and/or Arabs. The effect of propaganda, therefore, depends upon the orientation and value judgments which individuals bring to the proposed idea or issue. But even when opinion is overtly expressed, it may not predict ultimate action. Actual behavior may differ completely from expressed opinion.

In spite of these psychological reservations, however, there are other individual and group tendencies which provide an area in which propaganda techniques can function. Individuals tend to follow the lead of other individuals who are held in esteem. This follow-the-leader tendency is utilized constantly in promotion campaigns when testimonials from famous personalities as to the quality of a product are displayed to persuade others to climb on the band wagon. The symbols of prestige, esteem, and authority are set for others to recognize and emulate. Secondly, most individuals also tend to conform to the general pattern of group behavior, because digression is considered anomalous or different. Third, self-interest (or selfish interest) and need for ego gratification are significant in opinion formation. Fourth, individuals are subjected to many stimuli and propelled in many directions. The ultimate choice depends upon prior conditioning, social orientation, and ability to learn, among other factors.

One of the difficulties in working toward a functional definition of propaganda and of determining its use, appropriateness, and effectiveness in public relations is the confusion of ends and means. Propaganda is not an end. It is a means to an end. And it is not always as diabolically efficient as its adherents and detractors like to believe. The speed of social, political, and economic events and changes frequently results in some objective being achieved without—or in spite of—the benefit of propaganda. It is not as influential or as accurate in hitting its goal as the historical aura which has grown around it would indicate. Propaganda can contain the kernel of its own limitations. For propaganda works consciously to mobilize (or immobilize) opinion in one direction or toward one goal. But other influences operate toward the creation of opinion besides the mass media, which happen to be the avenues of both propaganda *and* public relations techniques. The school, home, and religious institutions, as we have noted, tend to provide an important orientation. What an individual tends to think at a given time may be conditioned strongly by the immediate social

environment, particularly if there is a crisis. Neither public relations, nor propaganda, nor the media of communication are
entirely responsible for opinion formation. Responsibility also
inheres in educational and religious institutions, and in the
home.

Studies in propaganda techniques distinguish between what
has been termed the theory or policy behind the propaganda effort and the practical methods undertaken to achieve a desired
objective in opinion formation. The policies behind a propaganda campaign include the total effort, the overall or organic
aims of the campaign, while propaganda in practice involves
the specific techniques which are applied to the mass media in
order to reach and influence public opinion and action. Propaganda aims at achieving some carefully preconceived goal or end,
and it is accomplished, in practice, by the dissemination of the
message to the particular publics involved.

Whether propaganda and public relations are analogous or
similar techniques depends upon their purpose and function. It
may certainly be reiterated that, while propaganda uses public
relations techniques, many public relations efforts would not
conform to a definition of propaganda, either as a dedicated effort to lead the public into some particular channel or as a socially harmful and deliberate attempt to *mislead* and falsify in
the interest of promoting some special interest rather than the
general welfare. For the criterion of judgment of any public relations effort is determined in terms of whether the effort might
prove to be a socially deleterious one to any particular group.

Both propaganda and public relations, since they are concerned with public opinion, must take into consideration the
needs, hopes, fears, and aspirations of the public. Totalitarian
propaganda provides an outlet for hate, fear, and aggression.
From the standpoint of value judgments, determining factors of

the so-called destructiveness or constructiveness of propaganda would appear to be the end desired, the means undertaken, and the kind of outlet provided. How propaganda is practiced will depend upon the ultimate objective. If the objective is political change, the technique will be to provide dissatisfaction and irritation with the status quo. If the objective is to maintain status quo, the technique will be to create inertia about or satisfaction with prevailing conditions. In either technique, the propagandist will make use of accepted stereotypes and institutions such as the American flag or other symbols which are acceptable to the public in terms of its needs, interests, and aspirations—health, educational goals, money, sex drives, religious convictions. Thus, familiar phrases and symbols which have become part of the folkways are employed partly because of their meaning and partly because of their meaninglessness.

Such phrases as "The facts speak for themselves" or "Let's look at the record" are familiar in advertising and promotional copy. Are they used out of a sense of conviction that the truth will prevail under *any* circumstances? Students of public relations know that, unfortunately, they are not. They know that, in the area of propaganda practice, lies can frequently create consent as quickly, if not more quickly, than unvarnished truth. The reason is not hard to find. It is simply that, all too frequently, the public does not want the truth. A distortion is more in tune with their dreams and aspirations. Truth is sometimes unpleasantly rude and practical. And this knowledge offers a temptation for public relations which is difficult to resist but which must, under conditions of integrity, be resisted if the propagation of an untruth proves socially harmful. Some groups might prefer to believe that radioactive fall-out is not biologically harmful; if it were proved to be harmful, however, ethical public relations must resist the temptation to propagate a dangerous illusion. Much depends on the theme and the desired end. Of course, it must be remembered that each individual within a public or group accepts or rejects the message in terms of his own value judgments and orientation. That is why a bald telling of the facts will not always be successful in practice. Apart from ethical considerations, however, facts are useful in public relations because, in the long run, they are less troublesome and more valid. They tend to solidify the base of operations for the future, both with mass media and the public.

Dissemination of facts, or telling the story, is not always a profitable or strategic technique. Situations may arise in which prudent public relations decrees a moratorium on statements, releases, and press conferences. The technique may be an *act* rather than a statement, such as a charitable gift, a sit-down strike, or a dignified silence. In other situations, the public relations technique may call for graphic physical proximity, such as a picture of a management executive and a trade union leader at a luncheon, an educational exchange or scholarship program, a conference of scientists, artists, and editors to discuss some major social problem. Bringing diverse groups together physically through a special event can accomplish more, in some situations, than an exchange of letters or indirect statements through releases to the press. News photos that tell a story are truly "worth a thousand words" in a release. Other techniques, in addition to pictures, are vital links to opinion formation. The use of a clean, simple advertising copy line, with sufficient "white space" is more apt to be read than a closely knit and involved message. And, if the message is presented in terms of recognizable and accepted symbols, it is more apt to elicit an affirmative reaction from the receiving audience. In the event that the story is to be told in terms of release copy, two aspects are important. One is repetition of the content as frequently and in as many media as possible; the other, linked to the first, is an appropriate and newsworthy variation of the content so that it has greater chance of being used in more than one medium and more than once in the same medium. In publicity or advertising copy which espouses a special interest or point of view, emotive content is usually more successful than cognitive or directive content, for people are moved to action more readily on an emotional basis than on any other. The best publicity copy will give the facts an emotional over-tone and will also lend a factual aspect to an emotionally charged circumstance or event.

## PROPAGANDA AND MASS MEDIA

What is the relationship between propaganda techniques and the mass media, particularly an institution such as the press? Since the rise to prominence of informational and propaganda agencies during and after World War II, readers of newspapers and radio listeners have been on the alert to call specific communication content propaganda. What should not be forgotten, however, is that what is propaganda to one group may be fact to another. Certainly, those who espouse a cause with fervor and those who are dedicated to a public relations campaign in favor of such a cause hesitate to admit that they practice propaganda techniques in the popular semantic aspect of the term. But, we have indicated that propaganda, as a purely negative semantic symbol, is what it is when the ends desired are antisocial or injurious to a particular individual or group. A socially desirable end, for example, may be reached by socially unacceptable means, but an *undesirable* end may not call forth undesirable means. Propaganda, as a purely negative term, depends upon a point of view or a frame of reference. Is the fact that all political parties enlist the aid of propaganda techniques in a campaign indicative of the unsavory aspects of propaganda? Does the government in its efforts to effect a cohesion of the free world and to combat communist propaganda practice *constructive* propaganda? Why cannot good as well as bad causes employ propaganda as a public relations technique? Probably because propaganda, in its literary and historical contexts, has been viewed as the propagation of seeds of untruth, designed to make the worse appear the better reason, as Plato pointed out. Traditionally, the popular conception of propaganda has been as a sophisticated philosophy which decrees that any means justifies a strongly desired end.

Because of sporadic campaigns to expose the "propaganda experts," the publics are conscious of the shabbier aspects of the technique. Philosophers wrestle with the problem of propaganda analysis while attempting, at the same time, to discover a definition of truth. And the mass media themselves have not helped to clarify the definition and function of propaganda, because there is still a minority group of editors who view *any* public relations effort with suspicion. Probably this attitude stems from the conception of propaganda as a planned effort to create or change a climate of opinion in order to achieve a preconceived end. In other words, the purpose of propaganda is not truth in terms of the dissemination of fact or information; rather it is a conscious effort to influence public opinion toward a special, or minority, point of view. Further, the propagandist is not supposed to consider the *consequences* of the act but only the successful termination of it. What is confusing, however, is that this conception implies that the *end* of propaganda, as well as the means, is always injurious. There has been no realistic or valid acceptance of propaganda as a *constructive* effort to influence public opinion toward *desirable* ends. If a distinction can be drawn, it would seem to inhere, first, in the integrity of the press and, secondly, in a social group sufficiently oriented and enlightened to make the distinction on the basis of cognitive analyses rather than emotion.

To some readers, even among the so-called "intellectual elite," the mass media are basically organs for the spreading of propaganda because they are prejudiced, by the policies of the owners, toward a point of view which may be inimical to the popular interest. To deny that many newspapers have strong convictions about business, labor, or politics which they try to pass on to the reader would be to deny the obvious. But it is also true that the American press has a traditional attitude of fair play and a respect for facts; and it is equally true that the growth of educational services has given rise to an increasingly informed and critical public.

Public education and the opinion-forming process are powerful levers in a democracy. That is why, despite popular polls and the strong support of the mass media, favored political parties and candidates have lost the election to the underdog more than once in our political history. Even with their element of bias, the mass media are still astonishingly free and independent institutions when viewed in relation to the control exercised in most other countries. Mass media are not the culpable agents for the spreading of harmful concepts. The great danger lurks in the rabble-rousing message delivered under the symbolic protection of the American flag, in the privately circulated newsletters, and in the other smear literature disseminated under the guise of exposé or information.

Actually, what is propaganda to one group may be gospel truth to another, depending upon social, economic, and political motivation. Most Republicans found the medical statements about President Eisenhower's health, in 1955–1956, statements of heartening truth; most Democrats found them pure propaganda, designed to offer false assurance to the public. Propaganda, in this garb, depends upon who is dispensing it, and to whom. But the mass media, it must be emphasized, are not the only influence on public opinion. Other operational influences include the school, the home, the religious organization, and the professional and social alignments. But these agencies help to clarify issues and make necessary distinctions between the truth and great lie. Training in logic and semantics offers a tool for analysis of communications content; and the integrity of such institutions as the press helps to keep content responsible and, in the main, truthful.

Since almost every business or social organization has a publicity message which it hopes to pass on to the receiving audience via the mass media, it behooves those who operate the media to separate the wheat from the chaff. The newspaper editor, for example, can set up certain operating criteria. Is the item newsworthy, i.e., does it contain some element of human interest, will it arrest the attention of the reader, does it cohere with the important events of the day, is it socially beneficial, harmful, or neutral? The *news* value is the ultimate determinant. Editors who cavalierly reject releases merely *because* they may plug some individual or idea are not using good editorial or news judgment. On the other hand, there are minority groups who would like to see the press omit a speech by a foreign government leader simply because it is propaganda. An editor who conforms to this point of view is not using good judgment of what is news, nor is he fulfilling his responsibility to keep the public informed.

The editors and other purveyors of communication content have other criteria of judgment. They must consider the reputation of the publicist as a careful and legitimate source of news. They must recognize that most public relations has a legitimate objective. And they must realize that publicity content, unless either socially harmful or lacking in news interest, should be weighed only in terms of one final determinant—in the judgment of the editor is the item fit to print? The owners of mass media can resist the strictures of special pleaders and of the advocates of official regulation if they discipline their personnel to an appreciation of the democratic process. The editor has an obligation to print what is newsworthy, but he is not obliged to yield to pressures to print a special interest message or point of view. Indeed, the mass media themselves exercise a healthy investigative function. A publicity story is frequently an invitation to assign a reporter to dig for more facts, to ask for access to data, and to request statements of policy. Only lazy and irresponsible editors rely on the press agent to write copy and answer questions for them. Even with the invaluable assistance of publicists, there is no substitute for honest reporting and editing.

The mass media, of course, report items which many consider to be propaganda. But the media are agencies, or instruments. While they must exercise a sense of care and responsibility, other agencies must also accept a social obligation—the business enterprise and its management, the educational world, the home and religious group, and, finally, the public relations man himself and his staff. Each day, the press is faced with many more items than it can possibly use. It accepts or rejects publicity on the basis of newsworthiness, timeliness, human interest, personalities, and drama. Even a flamboyant press agent's stunt will find its way into print if it makes news. Some editors, unfortunately, believe that events which are contrived as special events should not be printed. But a news item should be tested not only by its publicity source, but also by its news interest to the receiving audience. The wise choice of what is "fit to print" must be determined by the training, experience, and judgment of the editor; and the editor who is both wise and mature will select the copy on the basis of its news value, but he will not reject a newsworthy item from a publicist because of its source. The best publicists are, in fact, a kind of news service or news bureau to busy editors. The majority of newspapers, after all, have taken to rely on the news bureaus and news services for much of their content. Some of these are great timesavers, such as membership in the Associated Press, United Press, or International News Service. They secure news not obtainable as readily or as easily, but they should be no substitute for vigorous reporting and editing, and in the best papers they are not. On the other hand, some special service agencies can be a source of genuine news or a medium for useless publicity or propaganda. At their best, agencies add color and depth to the news. Here, again, what is printed depends on the training and experience of the editor. He must evaluate the material and *assign a reporter* to look for additional facts if he feels that something vital has been omitted.

## SPECIAL INTEREST PUBLICS

The real sources of discomfort to the scrupulous editor are the multifarious special groups which disseminate the classic garden variety of propaganda, the publics which promote a cause with zeal and fervor regardless of its social consequences. Ethical considerations are unimportant. The objective must be achieved regardless of its worth and regardless of the means employed. These publics—the political ax-grinders, the militant minorities, the lunatic fringe group—insist that their story be told prominently and insist, also, that failure to use it is a sign of obvious discrimination. As the social climate changes, or as situations producing tension arise, these groups multiply on the seeds of discontent, and they employ every conceivable device to get their communication content disseminated to other publics—news releases, newsletters, direct-mail folders, newspapers, fact forums, and what not. If they are backed by powerful and wealthy interests, the job of stripping fact from fiction becomes more difficult because of the enormity of the effort. Devices other than the news release are used not only to reach the constituency, but also to influence the mass media.

Special interest publics or organizations are doctrinaire. They are fighting for position in the social atmosphere, striving for the acceptance of their idea. The idea may be socially efficacious or it may be harmful. But value judgment is nonexistent. The successful promulgation of the concept is what is important and not its consequences. In times of social upheaval, special interest groups multiply, particularly in the economic and political spheres. And, because they are minority groups, they accuse the mass media of discriminating against them. On the other hand, there are vigilante groups which excoriate the press for printing content from special interest groups; but failure to print at least *newsworthy* data would bring the accusation of suppression of the news. The editor's obligation is twofold: to present *both* sides of a controversy, if the content makes news, and to reject both equally if the content has no news value.

Special interest groups go by many guises. Usually they are allegedly nonprofit organizations. They are, usually, tax free. Their purpose may be fund raising, political or religious persuasion, or legislative pressure. In many cases, the objective is not only highly legitimate but also praiseworthy. Unfortunately, however, the activities of the many unscrupulous minority organizations have given the phrase "special interest" a selfish and negative connotation.

Special interest groups are skillful in public relations and promotional techniques. They work vigorously in the art of applying political pressure by means of wires, letters, phone calls, and direct contact. They enlist the support of peripheral groups. They work directly with the mass media by means of publicity releases and paid ads. They tie in promotionally with other pressure groups for their mutual advantage. An estimated sum of more than one hundred million dollars is disbursed annually by the sum total of these special publics. There are known to be anywhere from 2,500 to 4,000 such organizations, each dedicated to espousing some special interest in the fields of health and medicine, politics, business, education, religion, and international affairs. Some, as we have indicated, have laudable social objectives. But most are known to predicate their activity on a selfish motivation of benefit only to the special group and not to the general welfare.

Paradoxically, government by democracy gives rise to these special, undemocratic special interest publics. In a pluralistic universe, there is room for many voices to demand a hearing. But they tend, fortunately, to cancel each other out. Because democracy instigates public opinion formation by creating an atmosphere in which opinions are free to form, grow, and proliferate, there will always be implicit controversy, and, therefore, special interest groups will spring up. And, even when the morality of the issue is cloudy, special interest groups, by *raising* certain problems, may ultimately strengthen the democratic process. Public education and a free press combine to form a formidable combination in the interest of a healthy analysis of, and attitude toward, communication content. On occasion, for example, editors have scored various government officials for refusing to hold press conferences. The press has brought to public attention the inertia of government information specialists in making data available. For news can be restricted, as well as disseminated, in favor of a special interest. And the unhealthiest omen for a democratic society is the arrogation of the power to restrict or censor news on the part of officials, except when it can be shown that the public welfare or national interest is involved. In these instances, a free press is the safety valve of the democratic process. A responsible and discerning editor, publisher, or broadcaster is, in the last analysis, an enlightened guardian of the integrity of the media of mass communication.

The behavior and content of each of the mass media are, to a great extent, the product of the sum total of our social institutions. All of the mass media are, at least implicitly and potentially, instruments for the dissemination of propaganda. For many special groups try to influence the attitude and content of the mass media so that the media will, in turn, help to influence public opinion toward a point of view. The mass media, however, do not *control* public opinion, nor do they exert as strong an influence as many have claimed. The press, and other avenues of mass communication, not only help to influence opinion, but they also *reflect* public opinion. Some social scientists have even declared that both public relations *and* the press do not change opinion so much as they tend to solidify it. Public relations techniques can be successful in changing or influencing opinion when at least two psychological conditions are satisfied: (1) when the climate of opinion is flexible and malleable, and (2) when the content disseminated not only coheres in some way with the needs, goals, and aspirations of the individual, but also tends to satisfy at least some of these needs.

How may the public be made aware of the implications, positive and negative, of content which is slanted toward a preconceived and socially harmful end? First, by free and responsible mass media themselves. Second, by democratic education. For the educational process can reveal how propaganda techniques are applied. It can reveal the cracks in the foundation of a campaign which uses such devices as name-calling without proof; of calling up emotional symbols which have no direct relevance to the issue; of the use of accepted names and personalities to render implied or direct endorsement; of the suggestion that one conform because "everybody is doing it"; and of the spurious objectives of the special pleader who joins a "public" not because of a common social bond, but for the purposes of creating discord and breaking existing ties with the group.

These efforts can be discerned. The mass media can help expose them. The schools can help. A healthy attitude of empiricism places the burden of proof on the persuader, not the persuaded. It demands that statements be substantiated by fact. It recognizes broad generalizations based on unfounded data. And it realizes, finally, that in the area of public opinion there is seldom a final and categorical answer, that opinions are subject to change and reëvaluation as new evidence is accumulated and presented. The mass media, again, are the agencies that must stand ready to channel these new data.

# CHAPTER 27

## *Ethical Considerations*

The creed of competition has become more than an accepted and inevitable aspect of a healthy economy. It has become something of a fetish which extols competition, not only within various industries, but also as an aspect or problem in labor-management relations that can never be resolved. In other words, there are those who speak of an economic jungle in which the Darwinian principle of survival of the fittest prevails. Such an attitude, carried to extreme, does not contribute to the growth of social and economic rapport. Competition, normally a healthy sign, deteriorates into unhealthy factionalism. An analogous situation exists in the sphere of international relations and in domestic politics. Political leaders of respective parties, and diplomats from different nations, meet not in an atmosphere of trust, but in one of mutual suspicion.

Obviously, society functions best when optimum conditions can prevail. And rapport can be brought about, under optimum conditions, specifically through the communication arts. Intelligent, forthright, and ethical public relations can contribute to the development of an atmosphere in which facts replace fictions, in which individuals and groups can at least relegate, if they will not relinquish, their competitiveness and suspicion in the best interest of all concerned. In the last analysis it is fundamentally through the perfection and use of the instrumentality of communication that people can share significant experiences, that the tributary stream of human events can be merged into the main stream of human understanding and knowledge. Communication media are the connective tissue of the social environment. And the techniques of public relations, intelligently applied, can also serve as a potent instrument in strengthening the matrix of communication into a socially beneficial whole.

The techniques of public relations can also be both negative and positive. Public relations as such is neither good nor bad. Its value lies in how it is used and by whom. And the language of public relations—in advertising, publicity, and promotion—is both directive and emotive. Its thrust is forward into the future. It urges an action and promises some tangible future result if the action is taken. The public is asked to buy a particular product because it is "the finest." Now if the product is, in reality, the finest, the exhortation poses no problem. But, if the public, acting as a result of public relations techniques, does buy the product only to discover that it is *not* as fine as touted, an informed public opinion will become operative. People will conclude, by test and subsequent word of mouth, that it is not the finest. Advertising and promotional directives will be ignored. And, ultimately, the group will abandon the product for another. Public opinion in action is sufficiently formidable for public relations to insist upon truth, if not in the interest of the public, at least in the interest of the employer or client! Ethical public relations, therefore, does not erect false standards or symbols around which the public will rally.

## THE MASS MEDIA

Communication, in a public relations sense, always has a purpose. It is specific rather than general in tone and content. While the basis of contemporary civilization is communication, public relations employs the *media* of communication in a teleological sense. It has an end in view. It strives to influence public opinion, to create consent, and to generate action. Public relations uses the media to influence opinion by calling symbols into play for the purpose of persuasion and the creation of good will. Whether the techniques employed are ethical, in the classic sense of their social rightness or wrongness, depends upon the nature of the desired end or goal, the means taken to achieve it, and the use or abuse of the media involved. For communication has many uses. It may be employed purely on an emotional level. It may be purely categorical or directive in content. Or, it may strive for pure cognition. Literally, however, few public relations techniques—advertising, publicity, or promotion—are always pure, unadulterated information. Public relations works purposefully. A public relations message, however honest and factual, still has the legitimate prerogative of surrounding the content in an atmosphere which will create consent. Emotive content strives to induce a visceral reaction or motivation. Directive content points toward a specific action, such as "Buy a box tomorrow!" Cognitive content, seldom used in a literal sense, strives for the presentation of facts and figures from which a conclusion can be drawn and a decision made.

It has been said that the mere delineation of these content areas only serves to frame more clearly the picture of public relations as a technique of manipulating public opinion. Again, much depends upon who is doing the "manipulating" and toward what end. Totalitarian states manipulate opinion by coercion in one direction. And, while it is true that some advertising techniques in a free and competitive society are employed with small sense of responsibility, it is also true that competitive forces, the power of the press, the efforts of such organizations as the National Better Business Bureau and the Advertising Council, and public opinion itself all act and interact as a healthy lever. From a public relations viewpoint, the ethical problem is one of responsibility to society. How, for example, can the need to sell and promote a product or an idea be reconciled with the ethical considerations which arise when linguistic symbols are used to influence the behavior of social groups? Public relations itself has attempted to set up standards and criteria through its own professional organizations with its own canons of behavior. The press and other media have helped by resisting many of the blandishments of advertising and publicity. Business has contributed through the Better Business Bureau. And the public itself is operative through consumer research organizations. All of these, plus the schools, contribute to a healthy orientation of public opinion and create a demand for self-containment in the public interest. These safeguards, it appears, are the only feasible ones in a democratic society; for government regulation is fraught with even greater dangers because it centralizes authority in individuals who are themselves elected on the basis of what is intrinsically a public opinion campaign and who could conceivably use their authority to perpetuate their own cycle.

More than an awareness of publicity techniques is required, however. There must also be an awareness of the limitations and the possibilities of the mass media. The communication arts have made it possible for peoples to speak to peoples with speed and precision. They can be used cohesively or divisively. Mass media have made it possible also for the public to receive more information more quickly and efficiently than ever before. They are truly "mass" media, for they reach overwhelmingly large numbers of people. Significantly, the media can also be employed with some degree of precision, owing to the perfection of techniques for measuring opinion. And, most important, the *potential* influence of the mass media on public opinion is tremendous. If, for example, all of the agencies—press, radio, television, magazines, motion pictures, newsreels—were to join forces toward the accomplishment of a single objective who is there who can calculate the good or evil which would result, depending upon the nature of the objective?

But the mass media, while powerful, have their limitations. They are the avenues of opinion formation and they also raise important issues. On the other hand, the media are obligated to report various issues which accrue from the interaction of social, political, and economic forces. A discerning public should reveal as much interest in what the media do *not* say as in what they do say. There is a tendency, brought on by the omnipresence of the media, to attribute perhaps too much influence to these instrumentalities. It has been claimed that the content of the media has become increasingly directive, that exposure to certain of the media leave the receiving audience in a state of uncritical acceptance and surrender. But social science has not determined the ultimate effect of exposure. Mere size and magnitude, while formidable, do not necessarily mean impact, depth, and lasting penetration. The basic problem revolves not around the number exposed but around the quality and degree of exposure. There is no ultimate device for predicting behavior. An individual may be exposed to several political speeches by candidate "A" and vote for candidate "B" in the privacy of the polling booth.

Beyond their limitations, the mass media are powerful, and

public relations techniques, working through these instrumentalities, can influence opinion under certain circumstances. When the mass media accept and disseminate publicity they lend an aura of importance and credibility to individuals, products, institutions, and ideas. They add prestige or publicity values. The publicity message, as carried by the media, also tends to make public certain issues, facts, and concepts. Under optimum conditions, publicity exposure may force a decision and resulting action, as in cases of social, economic, or political reform. Publicity in the mass media also presents alternatives and, albeit implicitly, suggests questions. It should not be forgotten that public relations and mass communication are as important for what they do not say as for what they say. Inertia which results from *lack of information* is an important factor in public opinion formation.

## THE QUESTION OF CONTROL

Since the effect of mass communication can be the creation of dissidence as well as cohesion, the question of regulation and control arises. But control, or regulation, of mass media suggests certain basic questions. Obviously control, if exercised at all, is exercised in the public interest. Is the public interest best served by vesting responsibility solely in the hands of private business? Is it served by government ownership of some, if not all, of the media? Should the media be privately owned and operated but under state and/or federal supervision?

It has been suggested that the healthiest control in a democratic society is self-regulation, i.e., a free and responsible press, an adherence to the canons of journalism, standards and criteria of professional ethics in public relations, and a public which is alert and informed as the result of training and education. But responsibility raises still further questions. What are the limitations, if any, to freedom of the press? When does freedom border on license? Who will determine responsibly what news is fit to print or broadcast or, more significantly, *not* fit to print or broadcast?

These questions bring up ethical considerations and value judgments which are not easily resolved. The mass media have been accused of being monopolistic and, occasionally, of placing restrictive obstacles in the face of coverage of the news. But the media are, paradoxically, fiercely competitive. On the face of it, society, through its duly elected government representatives, has the right to prohibit the dissemination of content which will create discontent and foment social discord. The question arises, however, as to what is dangerous about any given content—and to whom? Will officials determine the social efficacy or harm of content on the basis of whether it is helpful or harmful to *them* or to the general welfare? For this is the basic criterion of ethics in public relations and mass communication. In this country, as elsewhere, there will always be minorities who will attempt to strangle the spirit of inquiry and the freedom to communicate information which is inimical to their own special interest. To these groups, the purpose of the mass media and of public relations is not to enlighten and inform but to preserve a status quo. But the founding fathers, in their wisdom, foresaw these potential dangers and provided two safeguards: the First Amendment which enjoins the passing of any law to restrict freedom of speech or of the press, and the Fourteenth Amendment which prohibits any state from depriving any person "of life, liberty or property without due process of law." The forced closing of the great Argentine newspaper *La Prensa* was clearly a violation of both of these principles.

There are those who have made an ostensibly formidable

case for a degree of control or regulation on the basis of monopoly. It is affirmed, for example, that one cannot establish a newspaper or radio station without the expenditure of millions of dollars. Furthermore, it has been demonstrated that there is interlocking of ownership, as in the case of a newspaper operating a local radio station. There are also many areas of the country in which the public has access to only one newspaper, with no opposition voice to be heard. There is a tendency for newspapers to consolidate and for chain ownership to occur. And, in broadcasting, there are only a few major networks which are said to control radio and television communication because of their station links throughout the country over the limited number of available very-high-frequency channels.

In principle, however, the conviction is universal that the communication media must be in the vanguard of our free institutions. "Free," however, is a relative and not an absolute term. The media are not free in the literal sense. Public opinion is an implicitly restrictive influence, and public opinion has on occasion formed around ideas and concepts which are inimical to free inquiry. There are times, such as in war or similar crisis, when the public interest demands a voluntary censorship which is, basically, a curtailment of freedom. What must be watched vigorously is the danger that censorship will hang on tenaciously when the public interest is no longer served by it. The implicit irony is always that the free institutions for which a democracy fights will be lost in the process of fighting to preserve them. There are always problems of control and of "enlightened" regulation of mass media. These are more prominent in times of international tension and crisis. In the long run, however, the media have enjoyed a unique and healthy freedom of operation, restricted only by the need to preserve the integrity and privacy of the individual and the equally important need to prevent them from indulging in slander, libel, obscenity, or incitement to riot. The restrictions, if they may be termed that, have been in the public interest and welfare. What public relations and mass media *can* do is to help encourage an airing of all relevant facts without the fear that the printing of them will traduce anyone. Forthright dissemination of news and information strengthens and enhances the attractiveness of democratic institutions. A free and responsible medium will not hesitate to present conflicting points of view and will stoutly defend its prerogative of responsibility in determining what to print, film, or broadcast.

## WHAT PUBLIC RELATIONS CAN CONTRIBUTE

One important contribution which public relations can make in a democratic society is the dramatization of a need for dynamic social institutions. Sociological studies show that groups, or publics, develop behavior patterns which tend to organize around some established norm. The tendency to accept common and familiar stereotypes offers an easy road to relaxation. The conventional portrait of the gangster, the tycoon, the clerk, the doctor in motion pictures is not questioned in terms of its accuracy or validity. Inertia and habit patterns accept these stereotypes uncritically. What public relations techniques can accomplish is the demolition of these atavistic patterns by showing that a more dynamic behavior is, in the long run, healthier for everyone concerned. Public relations, by showing that these attitudes and patterns are lazy, can be a constructive social influence. In fact, public relations directors of business institutions have done a most constructive job of reorienting management attitudes and policies in employee relations, labor-management relations, and personnel policies. Many of our institutions ulti-

mately lose their power for good and become moribund because they resist change. Dynamic public relations can show
the way to new environmental adaptations on the part of business, educational, and social institutions. When, for example,
some business groups fulminated against the so-called welfare
state and against government interference, public relations convinced management that criticism without constructive action
would bring no feasible solution. As a consequence, business
set about to devise employee programs, insurance and pension
plans, recreational outlets, and other constructive efforts.

On the other hand, public relations can contribute also toward the preservation of moribund institutions. It can obscure
the need for change by substituting slogans for facts, such as
"Get the government out of business" or "Unions are open
sesame to graft." Facts are obscured and clouded in a welter
of spurious issues, designed to sidetrack the main problems. Indeed, the press and other media can also contribute toward the
perpetuation of atavistic institutions. Newspapers, for example,
can accept handouts and releases uncritically from special interest groups. The mass media may be tempted to favor certain interests with which they may have a common economic
viewpoint. The press, and other media, in an evident desire
to be totally objective may lose sight of the fact that publishing
evaluative data is also in the realm of dispensing relevant facts.
In the fine press coverage accorded the 1956 White House
Conference on Education, the press presented excellent factual
coverage of what transpired. It gave short shrift, however, to
a serious study of the implications of federal aid to education
versus state aid. What, for example, would federal aid accomplish specifically? *How* would it interfere—if it would—with
states' rights? How willing and able were the individual states,
cities, and communities to develop their own educational programs?

In areas such as this, and in many others, forthright publicity and an equally forthright and coöperative press can take a "Let's air the facts and find out" attitude. Such an attitude of healthy empiricism grows out of many roots: responsible public relations and a free and responsible press; a careful regard for public opinion on the part of all enterprises, management and otherwise, whose activities impinge on the public; and a sufficiently alert and interested public opinion which is capable of rejecting the false and of demanding an honest account. The role of public opinion cannot be discounted as a factor in establishing ethical public relations. Those who are exposed to the mass media can be interested, for example, in their content. They can come to understand that words which represent reality are not identical with what they represent or stand for. Despite the perfection of advertising copy, the public can discern that such copy often leaves more unsaid than said. The public can distinguish between content which is emotive, directive, or cognitive and, at the same time, can come to appreciate that verbal symbols have meaning only when analyzed in terms of their context, not in isolated phrases.

On the other hand, public relations, as a two-way street, can perform important internal and external functions. Internally, the public relations director can steer management in a healthy direction in its relations with press, employees, and other publics. He can act as a safety valve against cliché or stereotyped thinking. He can prevent management from going off the deep end in times of crisis by voicing statements which it will later regret. And he can work towards educating management to appreciate the need for a dynamic and functioning institution, not an anachronistic and static one.

Externally, in its contact with the public by means of mass media, public relations should not overlook the fact that the *ultimate* referent of *mass* communication is the individual. Further, public relations must continue to work toward a system of self-regulation and self-discipline by means of the development of a dynamic code of ethical practice. Finally, if public relations is to be more than press agentry, it must be predicated on a respect for our social and cultural institutions as well as on a regard for the dignity of those human beings who make up its public.

# Part VII

# Concepts
# and Campaigns

*Ten concepts, examples, or case studies in various fields—magazine publishing, transportation, trade association, business institution, educational organization, educational foundation, the arts, family service, human relations, business ethics*

# CHAPTER 28

## Concepts and Campaigns

We have indicated that public relations, and its component parts of publicity, promotion and advertising, are not reducible to any hard and fast definition. Experts in the field almost uniformly agree that public relations is concerned with building good will or with establishing a policy of good deeds in the public interest which, once accomplished, should be talked about to the public by means of the media of communication.

As a philosophy of management and a communication technique, public relations is best defined not by any verbal declaration of what it is, but by what it does—in other words in terms of its *function*. Good public relations, even though it is understandably prejudiced in favor of that which it represents, functions to create an internal atmosphere of solid achievement which may be communicated to the public by means of mass media. It functions to *inform* in the interest of creating a favorable climate of opinion for an institution, individual, product, or idea.

Various organizations approach the area of public relations in different ways, depending upon the nature of the institution, the objectives, and the public—or publics—involved. Following are a number of representative examples of public relations concepts, illustrating various approaches to the problem in the fields of business, human relations, and education.

## MAGAZINE PUBLISHING: THE CURTIS PUBLISHING COMPANY

The Curtis Publishing Company publications include such world-famous national magazines as the *Saturday Evening Post, Ladies' Home Journal, Jack and Jill,* and *Holiday.* E. Huber Ulrich, vice-president and director of public relations for The Curtis Publishing Company, describes this institution's public relations policy below:

### Public Relations Concept

My own personal concept of public relations is that it is nothing more complex than the making—and keeping—of friends. We want the world outside of this Company to know that our magazines are interesting to read, and are strong, vigorous vehicles for the conveyance of advertising. Moreover, we want our customers to know that our corporate motives are good, and that our operations contribute to a higher standard of living for all of our citizens. Now this concept, I suppose, would have certain built-in limitations for some companies, but when you consider the nature of the magazine publishing business it appears that the range of our public relations interests is without horizon. Our customers are our readers who are engaged in every type of enterprise and who represent every social, educational, and economic level. They are our advertisers, who mine, process, or manufacture this nation's industrial product. So for all practical purposes, we must say that all persons over certain age limits are either our customers or potential customers. (Even this limitation can't be relied on too much: there are hundreds of thousands of juvenile readers of *Jack and Jill,* our children's magazine. Each issue of *Jack and Jill* is transcribed into Braille for the benefit of blind children.)

In thinking of such a broad market in terms of public relations, we find that we must operate on a broad basis and use many tools and methods. Our Public Relations Department is set up, therefore, with a view to functioning in any area of communication into which we seem led by the best interests of our Company. The Department is constituted as follows, with each constituent having a definite function but subject to call to help out on other projects when needed:

*News Bureau.* This unit, manned mostly by former newspapermen, plans and writes news releases about our magazines, releases all Company announcements to the press and radio, and serves as the Company contact for queries from the press. The News Bureau also handles special writing projects, prepares articles for trade publications, maintains biographical files, writes speeches, and in general serves as the writing arm of the Department.

*Community Relations Bureau.* As implicit in the title, this unit represents the Company in its dealings with its home community, with the service clubs, civic groups, women's clubs, schools and with various fund and blood donor drives. In addition, it helps entertain distinguished visitors from all parts of the world.

*Motion Picture and Speakers Bureau.* The Company film, "Modern Magazine Magic," is handled by this unit, although bookings are made through Modern Talking Picture Service. When requested, speakers accompany the film. Traveling art exhibitions, made up of original art from our magazines are booked and routed by this unit. It also conducts plant tours for special groups and assists in entertaining visitors.

*Educational Bureau.* All requests from schools and colleges for reprint material from Curtis publications are handled by this unit, which also sends, throughout the school year, regular mailings of certain selected reprints for classroom use. A group of six top educators are retained as consultants to guide us in this work.

*Special Services.* This unit handles presentations, exhibits, and displays required by the Departments, designs layouts, prepares booklets, handles production, and performs all intradepartmental art functions.

*Washington Office.* Also manned by former newspapermen, the Washington Office handles the Company's liaisance with the Federal Government, issues special newsletters, operates as a Company listening-post, and is a service office for all departments.

*Travel Bureau.* Although more of a service unit than a strict public relations function, this bureau obtains hotel and transportation accommodations for Company executives, as well as for authors, illustrators, and photographers on assignment for our magazines.

As of now, this Department is fully capable of carrying out the public relations functions of the Company, and I believe it is doing so in a creditable way. If some new function should be given us, and there were no way to integrate it practically into our present organization, we would create a new unit. In this way I believe we can remain fluid and avoid the crippling effects of rigidity.

How does the staff carry out its day-to-day functioning? Since to give an example of each of the seven units would require considerable space, I shall mention only one—the News Bureau. Each Friday morning the News Bureau holds a publicity meeting for the *Saturday Evening Post.* Working a full month ahead of publication date, the entire staff of the News Bureau, together with representatives from the Advertising and Circulation Departments, gather and discuss every article, editorial, and often works of fiction, in the issue under consideration. All suggestions for publicity or news stories are taken down. This program is later edited by the Chief of the News Bureau, who removes any proposals that appear of doubtful value or of questionable taste. The final program is then turned over to writers and production people who prepare the releases, clear them with editorial and advertising executives, and see that they are mailed in time to synchronize with the appearance of the magazine. Similar meetings are held on other publications.

Quite often there are speeches or special events which occur irregularly. These are handled by the director of public relations, or by those of his associates who are best qualified to handle these specific assignments.

The public relations value of "Modern Magazine Magic" is enormous. Only a very small fraction of our readers will ever be able to visit our plant or our editorial rooms, but there is no reason why we should not go to them. This is done by means of the film, which is a 16 mm movie in full color and sound, prepared in a non-technical manner for all age groups. The Curtis Publishing Company is the world's largest and only completely integrated publisher of magazines, and "Modern Magazine Magic" shows the complete Curtis operation—from the growing of pulpwood in our own forests to the delivery of the magazines to our readers. It shows—step by step— what it takes to produce an average of 1,400,000 Curtis magazines every working day. About 100,000 audiences, totaling more than 10,-000,000 people, have seen this and our earlier film. These figures certainly attest to the public relations value of our motion picture.

## TRANSPORTATION: THE NEW YORK CENTRAL RAILROAD COMPANY

The New York Central Railroad Company has prepared a special brochure entitled "How to Meet the Press," designed to assist its officials and employees in this important area. The material was prepared with the aid of suggestions from newspaper editors, reporters, radio and television newsgatherers and public relations men. Some of the significant concepts are included here, and they illustrate many important facets of intelligent press relations.

### How to Meet the Press

The telephone rings. It's a newspaper reporter. Like all reporters he has some questions. Train No. ninety-blank is reported to have left the rails. Or there's a rumor that we're planning a big improvement program at South Bend or Syracuse.

What should you answer?

Occasionally it might be far more than a $64 question. It could be worth many thousands to the New York Central. The stakes are high in the never-ending struggle for favorable public opinion.

On a broad front, almost everything the public says about railroads in general has direct effect on us, for informed public opinion is the basis of national and state legislation and policies.

As an individual railroad, the Central is equally concerned with public opinion. The basic commodity we sell is service. The amount of that service, the security of our jobs—they all depend on what the public thinks and says about us and the courteous and efficient service which we provide.

Our mutual concern, therefore, is to deserve favorable public relations and, deserving them, to help foster recognition of them. So whether you're an old hand at talking with newsmen or have yet to answer your first query, you might like a little coaching. There are many niceties involved, but the essentials are to give the full facts clearly, accurately and as quickly as circumstances permit.

The policies explained and expressed here represent what New York Central Public Relations Department representatives have been practicing for years. A number of executives have been following them. Because of the pressure of other duties and because of routine turnovers in personnel, however, not all Central people in positions of responsibility have had the opportunity to become familiar with these helpful policies and practices.

You and your fellow officials are our principal contacts with the newspapers, radio and television stations at the many System points where we do not have full-time public relations representatives. To employees of these news organizations, as well as to the public at large, you are the New York Central.

## WHY NEWSPAPERS, RADIO AND TV ARE IMPORTANT

Because virtually all adults in this country are newspaper readers, most experienced public relations men consider newspapers the chief means of reaching the public. In addition, most of the news presented by radio or television stations originates either with newspapers or with the newsgathering agencies maintained by or for newspapers. Thus, in all probability your dealings as a source of information about the Central will be chiefly with newspaper people.

Although they generally do not carry on extensive newsgathering operations, radio and television stations are of great importance in the *presentation* of news.

Because both TV and radio are vital factors in broadcasting news and entertainment to most American homes, they have become increasingly influential in helping mould the opinions of the public— your next-door neighbor multiplied thousands or millions of times.

## HOW REPORTERS AND NEWSPAPERS WORK

Newspaper practices and mechanics vary greatly, in rough ratio to the size of the city, the newspaper's circulation and its frequency of publication. The New York *Times* and the Norwalk (Ohio) *Reflector-Herald* are as dissimilar as the New York Central and the Dardanelle and Russellville Railroad—yet each has its place and its importance to its customers.

Because of this, any generalized picture of newspaper operations is subject to some distortion-by-omission, but within this limitation a brief summary may be helpful.

News originates, of course, with reporters. Someone remarked that "all generalities are untrue, including this one." But it's still correct to note that the reporter who bustles around with a bottle in one hand and a pencil in the other lives today only in the movies. Like wooden coaches and knee-length bathing suits, he passed out long ago.

Most of the time he's in a hurry, for there's always an edition to make, just as we have schedules to keep. Generally he's quick-witted, conscientious and extremely interested in his job—which is to get the facts which are the basis of all reputable news or feature stories.

Frequently reporters are called "leg men" (because of the walking they do outside the office to collect news) or "beat men" (because they are assigned to "cover" specific "beats" or news centers such as the police station, city hall and the court house).

On smaller newspapers, and sometimes on the largest ones, reporters shuttle back to their offices to write their stories. On metropolitan papers, however, a beat man usually telephones his facts to an office "rewrite man," who actually writes the story. Between such duties, a rewrite man frequently develops other stories through direct telephone calls to other sources of information, such as hospitals and the weather bureau.

The story or "copy" usually flows to the city editor for editing. He may write the headline, send the story to the composing room where it is "set" into type on one of a battery of linotypes. On the larger papers, however, the close editing and headline-writing are done on the "copy-desk" after the city editor has reviewed the story.

You'll find that on most newspapers, the publisher is the man who formulates the broad policies. The editor carries out those policies, with a particular eye to the editorial page. Next in line may be the managing editor or executive editor, who is in charge of the general reportorial and news setup of the paper. Under these executives—if the newspaper is large enough—are such people as the city editor, telegraph (or wire) editor, state editor, financial or business editor, labor editor, picture editor, sports editor and the society editor.

## A LOOK AT THE WIRE SERVICES

While the newspapers are functioning, the wire services also are busily at work. These are principally the Associated Press, the United Press and International News Service. All operate nationally and internationally. They are keenly competitive, measure their "scoops" or "beats" over their rivals by minutes. Aside from local and area news, they provide the bulk of the stories in the average daily newspaper.

The wire services have bureaus in principal cities. Sometimes there are several such offices in a state, sometimes only one. In Ohio, for example, AP has bureaus at Cleveland, Columbus and Cincinnati; in Indiana, only at Indianapolis. In all other cities of a state the wire services rely on "correspondents" or "stringers"—usually men who are on the payroll of a newspaper, and who are paid by the wire services on a wordage-used or "string" basis. To speed their stories to the wire services, they use telegraph or long distance telephone.

In Washington, New York, Chicago and a few other large cities, and in state capitals the wire services maintain comparatively extensive reportorial staffs. Otherwise they rely largely on individual newspapers for the bulk of their news. In broad concept the wire services function as mediums for the *exchange* of news which originates from newspapers.

Through a variety of special wires feeding teletypes operating at fifty to sixty words a minute, the wire service news flows into every daily newspaper of any consequence in this country. Some newspapers have only one wire service, others have two or all three. But even those metropolitan newspapers with but one wire service may receive stories on several teletypes, operating simultaneously. Most of the smaller daily newspapers receive their out-of-town news over a single wire. This usually is filed from a central point within the state, and consists of a blend of the news filed on the national-international, financial, state and sports wires tapped by the metropolitan papers. From this central point, and through a device called a teletypesetter, it often is automatically set into lines of type, ready for publication.

## THE ROLE OF RADIO AND TV

The wire services sell their news to radio and television stations as well as to newspapers. A few stations receive the regular newspaper wires, and in their "news rooms" rewrite or rephrase these newspaper-type stories for the ear. Most news received by radio and television stations, however, comes over a special teletype circuit, which is called a "radio wire" to distinguish it from the wires serving newspapers.

The news on "radio wires" already has been rewritten for the ear by the wire services themselves. The stations' news room employees assemble, tailor, rewrite or rephrase the wire service stories to meet individual station needs.

Occasionally—but only occasionally—the radio or television news room writer may use the telephone or his legs to develop a local or area story. Most of the time he relies on the wire service, and whatever additional interesting news he can obtain from the local newspaper.

At the same time, both radio and television have become increasingly energetic in presenting comments on the news, forums, and on-the-scene reports (in some cases by film), so that they have a considerable role in shaping public opinion as well as in disseminating news.

## PICTURES ARE NEWS, TOO

Important newsreel and "still" pictures are distributed nationally to newspapers and some television stations in a manner similar to news itself. Since the mid-1930's still pictures have been transmitted regularly by wire, just like news. And like feature stories with no urgent "today" time element, pictures also are distributed by mail.

Except for disasters, you'll seldom see a syndicate photographer. In case you do, the AP has lensmen operating under its own banner and that of Wide World, a subsidiary. United Press Newspictures serves as the UP's picture affiliate, while INS' picture-sister is International News Photos (INP).

The picture syndicates have relatively few photographers of their own except in the largest news centers. Just as wire services buy news from editors or reporters on individual newspapers, picture syndicates buy photographs from cameramen on individual newspapers.

In addition to using still photographs furnished by the syndicates, television has brought the movie camera into additional use for coverage of news events. In a matter of hours, a national TV network can show such a newsreel in millions of living rooms.

### GREEN AND RED BOARDS

*It's vital to keep cool* if you are approached for information on a controversial matter. It doesn't pay to show irritation, even if you feel it. The best course is to explain the company's position thoroughly, fairly, clearly, and without anger, regardless of the situation.

*Sometimes you won't know the answer.* That happens to all of us. The wise official will say so, frankly, and be as helpful as he can. He may call on another department or on division headquarters for aid. If it is a system-wide or headquarters matter involving company-wide policies which a local representative would not feel qualified to discuss, he may relay the inquiry to the Public Relations Department, which will try to dig out the facts as quickly as possible.

When the material does become available, it's important to *inform the reporter at once.* It could be too late—but *he* likes to be the judge, and you've made a friend for next time.

*Reporters and their bosses don't like red tape, evasive answers or standoff treatment.* If they get it, what might have been a favorable story may never be written. In extreme cases an unfavorable story may appear on page one under a large headline, whereas under normal circumstances it probably would have appeared "inside" unless it concerned outstanding news.

Most newsmen are frank to declare that *the more unnecessary* ob-

*stacles placed in their way, the harder they will work to get their story,* for getting it becomes a point of honor. Almost always they'll manage to print something on it, though such stories are bound to contain a high ration of inaccuracies if the actual facts are denied to reporters by the very persons who are in a position to know the facts.

*There's no reason why you can't be quoted by name* on most stories, if you like. You won't want to overdo it, and there may be occasional controversial matters where it would be to your advantage to be referred to anonymously as a "company spokesman." You're the judge, and all reporters will honor *specific requests* not to quote you by name, if that's your preference.

*On telephone inquiries* concerning controversial or otherwise difficult subjects, it sometimes pays to promise to call back in a few minutes—and to use those minutes in developing an unmistakably clear reply. This may avoid misunderstandings, for while you know what you're talking about, not everyone understands the railroad terms and situations which are so natural to us.

*The more difficult the story, the better it is to talk to the reporter in person,* rather than over the telephone. If there isn't time to do this, you might wish to write out a short statement and read it to him to avoid mistakes. But if you've had the opportunity to size up the reporter as intelligent and careful, the telephone should be adequate for most contacts.

*If you are going to participate in a press conference,* it's a good idea to prepare a written statement on the essentials of the announcement you wish to make, especially if it's complicated. You should have plenty of copies. After reporters have read the statement, you can expect plenty of questions. It's a lot easier to anticipate as many as you can in advance, and to figure out the best answers. All of us have had the experience of making the perfect answer—an hour too late.

Naturally *there is never any reason or excuse for coloring or stretching the facts.* A good reporter quickly recognizes a roundhouse curve, and such tactics will spoil an entire case. Trite as it sounds, honesty is the best policy.

To stay on the right track with reporters and editors, *don't attempt to work through a daily newspaper's business office or advertising department on an editorial department matter.* Stories called "B. O. (for

business office) Musts" happen occasionally, but editors and reporters are quick to resent the use of this infrequent back door route,
and may find occasion to remember it in subtle but effective ways.
They are equally resentful of threats or scolding.

As a general rule newspapermen object to such questions as
"When will this appear?" or "Will you send me a clipping?" or "Will
you give us a break on this story?" or any similar suggestion that special favors are being solicited. *You're much more apt to receive a good
break if you don't ask for it.*

*Few reporters are interested in showing a copy of their story before
it appears.* The reasons include the necessity for speed and a frequent
lack of appreciation that they must report *both* sides of any controversial matter, whether they agree with the other side or not. If the
reporter had interviewed only one person, it might have been the
person on the other side and your case might not have appeared at
all.

On ticklish stories, however, newsmen sometimes will read back
the essentials over the telephone, and on feature or technical stories
with no urgency they may ask you to check their copy as a precaution
against errors of fact. If you do receive this high compliment, *it's wise
to confine suggestions to what you believe are clarifications of the
facts,* and not to attempt other revisions which are considered the
sole province of the editor. *It's not out of order to suggest such a
checkback procedure* if you make it plain your interest is in accuracy
rather than in attempting to act as an editor.

If the headline point of a story turns out to be something different
than you thought it would be, don't be surprised. It happens frequently, though it may be the exception rather than the rule.

Despite all precautions, *sometimes there will be errors in newspaper stories.* Responsible editors and reporters recognize that they
occur too frequently, tend to lessen public confidence in newspapers
and make many businessmen relatively unapproachable for stories
due to fear of misquotation. Regrettable as this is, it's wise to expect
some errors and to be philosophical about them. Everyone makes
some mistakes, and it probably doesn't matter to anyone except us
whether the noon train arrived 23 minutes late in that heavy storm
or was only 13 minutes late.

*If the mistake is really important,* it is entirely in order to mention it courteously to the reporter at the earliest opportunity. If he thinks it's serious enough he probably will make a correction in a separate little story or in a subsequent story dealing with a similar subject. Complaining to the reporter's superior seldom produces anything except ill will for the future, without helping the present. Few newspapers relish making corrections—an understandable human trait which emphasizes the desirability of being unmistakably clear in the first place.

*You shouldn't thank an editor or reporter for printing a story* unless you know him well enough that he will not misunderstand your motive. "We editors often go through a lot of ritual to convince ourselves of our own integrity," says one. "The editor likes to feel that he printed your story because it was news and not because it would make you happy." It is, however, a gracious gesture to compliment a newsman on expert handling of a story. Everyone appreciates a good word on a job well done, and newspapermen are no exception.

## YOU CAN'T HIDE ACCIDENTS

Despite safety devices and other extensive precautions, there are bound to be some accidents on railroads, just as with all other forms of transportation. As one veteran railroader expresses it, "There's a hazard every time a wheel turns."

*Railroads probably have made more newspaper enemies as a result of obstructionism at wreck scenes than in any other way.* This is principally because some railroads—though the number is decreasing—persist in the historic practice of attempting to block newsgatherers and photographers from the scene of any mishap.

The theory is that stories of wrecks are harmful to the railroad. In actual practice, however, *no amount of obstructionism ever succeeded in stopping a story about any important wreck.*

In the first place, newspapers can and do obtain news and details of disasters from police, hospitals and other secondary sources. In the second place, they can observe damage and rescue efforts and take their notes and pictures from any point just off the right-of-way, as long as that point isn't company property. It seldom is. Photographers also use airplanes on most important wrecks, and obtain surprisingly clear close-up pictures from the air.

One railroad threw a cordon of company police around a wreck scene. *That didn't stop a single picture,* though it was wartime, which prevented the newspaper from chartering a plane. One photographer, for example, found an elevation just off company property, and used a telescopic lens. Irritated at the railroad's tactics, the newspaper spread the picture the width of the page; otherwise it would have printed in only three columns.

Innumerable examples could be related of such fruitless obstructionism. Because of such incidents, one wire service started to keep a running score of all accidents on a particular railroad. Most of them were minor, involving few or no personal injuries. The story of each accident, however, carried the sentence "This is the _____th accident on the _____ Railroad in the last ____ weeks." The number rose to eight in less than three months, and each story created the public impression in many newspapers that the railroad was a carelessly-operated, rundown line not equipped to provide safe, reliable public service. The railroad had no recourse, for the wire service was reporting only facts.

One highly respected newspaper editor in a city served by several competitive railroads recently declared "The next time a railroad tries to make a mystery of a wreck, I'm going to assign two reporters to the story full-time for a week." In the normal course of events the story would die a natural death in one or two days. The editor meant what he said—yet he is a friend of the railroads, as a youth worked for one, and frequently demonstrates his friendship in the editorial columns.

Unpleasant though wrecks are, they are news of top public interest, and attempts to hide them can create only antagonisms. All of which spells out that with accidents or anything else, it's beneficial to everyone concerned to give an inquiring reporter all the facts you can, as accurately, as clearly and as quickly as possible, and not force him to rely on inaccurate and sometimes irresponsible sources of information.

## FULL ACCESS FOR NEWS GATHERERS

There's bound to be confusion at the scene of any major wreck, since they occur so infrequently on the Central that only a few of our employees have had any experience in handling them. A number of telephone calls also can be expected from wire services, newspapers, radio and TV stations, anxious for all the details they can obtain before their own representatives reach the scene.

Whenever and wherever an accident occurs, it is company policy to permit full access to all newsmen and newspaper and television photographers, and to count on their good sense to avoid impeding any rescue efforts. All carry some means of identification and will be glad to produce it upon request.

The wise course is to *keep your head and to make all facts available to newsmen promptly and fully,* whether you're at the wreck or at the dispatcher's office. The facts include the names of casualties and the extent of injuries, if you have them or can get them. When reporters can obtain their information from you or some other responsible official in a position to speak with authority, their stories are less apt to be based on exaggerations voiced by the excited persons who collect at the scene of all public disasters. On the contrary, they probably will be as accurate as possible within the understandable limitations of human error.

Naturally there is no reason to telephone a newspaper every time a freight car leaves a track. Accidents generally are news only when someone is injured seriously, the number of cars involved is large, tracks are blocked, or where there is some other unusual factor which makes them interesting to newspapers and the public.

But you will be doing both the company and the newspapers a favor if you *advise your newspaper sources promptly on any major wreck involving serious personal injury or loss of life,* and if you provide all the facts you can as quickly and as accurately as you can.

This will help minimize wild rumors. The facts are seldom as bad.

## CONFIDENTIAL MATTERS

The New York Central has nothing to hide. Every business—including the newspaper business—has a few confidential matters of a policy or competitive nature which cannot be disclosed at the moment. Newspapermen are aware of this.

If you are asked for information about a matter which really is confidential, it's best to tell the reporter so. Try to tell him why—that anything on the subject now might disclose company plans to competitors prematurely, that it would be likely to jeopardize current business negotiations, or whatever the reason may be.

*But be certain it's justifiable!* Obviously there is nothing confidential, for example, about train delays in a winter snowstorm, or a new radio system in a freight yard.

A matter which is confidential today may not be confidential tomorrow, next week or next month. *If you expect to be able to give the reporter the answer to his question later,* the smart thing is to say so. When the time arrives, it's good business to make certain that you do, and that you don't volunteer the information to the reporter's competitor. His competitors want news, too, but they recognize (reluctantly, sometimes) that an alert inquirer has earned the right to collect the fruits of his work, and that next time the shoe may be on the other foot.

In unusual cases *you may receive inquiries from two newspapers* before you are in a position to provide any information on a subject. In such situations it's cricket to call both newspapers and explain to each that both have made an inquiry, and that you are giving the requested information to both. This avoids unpleasant suspicions that you might be playing favorites, and establishes you as a man of your word.

Occasionally it is desirable to give *background information* so that the reporter will be able to evaluate and interpret the facts you are presenting. Regardless of all that has been said and written on the subject, the term "off the record" is not universally understood. Some newsmen interpret this to mean the information may be published if it is not attributed to the source. Others interpret it to mean the information cannot be published at all. If you encounter such a situation, it is wise to specify whether what you say is "not for publication" or whether "it should not be attributed to us if it is published." This may avoid embarrassing misunderstandings.

### "RUNNING EXTRA"

We have no desire to become "publicity hounds"—as newsmen term story-seeking *pests*. You have your own primary job. Even so, there will be occasions when a small amount of time spent in doubling as a reporter for the Central will benefit both you and your local newspaper contacts.

Every newspaper and wire service has its own slants on what is news. It would be most helpful and practical to *visit the city editor and ask for advice.* They'll be glad to see you and to outline the ways in which you can be of assistance.

A near-essential is to volunteer your home telephone number, so that you can be reached in emergency. *Important news seldom waits.* Your afternoon newspaper, for example, may not go to press until the next afternoon, but the wire services, morning newspapers and radio and TV stations won't sit if the story really is important. The facts you supply to representatives of your local newspapers in a real emergency at night may appear almost immediately on radio and television news broadcasts, and in the morning newspapers.

It is desirable to make occasional return visits to newspaper offices, but *don't wear out your welcome!* Once every few months should be often enough. The best time to visit editors and writers on an afternoon newspaper is early afternoon or mid-afternoon, after the edition-making rush is out of the way. The best time to visit news department workers on a morning newspaper is late afternoon or early evening, before the real rush gets under way. The better newspapermen know and respect you, the more apt they are to get in touch with you when they hear of news concerning the Central. That will give you a chance to be sure they're on the right track, or to switch them there if they aren't.

## THE UNUSUAL IN STORIES

It doesn't happen every day, but every now and then railroad employees perform some unusual service which produces a *top-notch human interest story.* Here are two examples:

Both heating boilers broke down at an eastern hospital. There was no other means of heating the institution, and it was sharp winter. There was a siding outside the hospital boiler room, and a railroad arranged to send a locomotive quickly. The engine provided emergency heat for the hospital until repair parts could be obtained for the institution's boilers. Needless to say, the story of this unusual courtesy appeared prominently in many newspapers and produced considerable public appreciation for the railroad involved.

A passenger found a half-frozen kitten on the observation platform of a "name train" in the northwest. Kitty was taken to the dining car, fed warm milk and revived. The crew arranged to return her to the town where she had blundered onto the train. It was feared some child there was heartbroken. The Associated Press picked up the story from the newspaper which originated it, and it was printed on page one of newspapers all over the nation. There were dozens of letters commending the railroad for its humanity.

When you hear of similar human interest stories, *your newspaper friends will appreciate being informed of them.* And if all the details aren't at your fingertips, the reporter probably will be glad to dig them out.

## OTHER STORIES TO WATCH FOR

In addition to the unusual story situations already outlined, there are other types of stories which will occur more frequently. Here is a quick checklist which might be useful:

1. New construction or improved facilities, including stations, bridges, shops, yards, etc.
2. Important purchases made locally.
3. Large tax payments. In many communities the railroad is the principal taxpayer.
4. Schedule changes; unusual freight or passenger movements such as shipment of the first carload of a local crop, or a chartered train.
5. Public addresses by Central people, and public talks to groups of Central people. Most local newspapers welcome a one-page summary, especially if it includes direct quotations on the "headline points."
6. Visits of top-ranking railway officers, or of important non-railroad people we may know about (except for *confidential* business trips).
7. Promotions, transfers, retirements, new jobs created, new men or women on these jobs.

8. Awards of gold passes; safety and valor awards; citations for meritorious conduct.
9. Family service records, father-and-son teams, etc., particularly when the story can be timed to an anniversary.
10. Behind-the-scenes railroading, including servicing of locomotives, and cars, operation of signal towers, lost-and-found departments, etc.
11. Perfect Shipping Month drives, and similar campaigns to improve service.

There will be other items, but these will suggest what we have in mind. On many occasions the reporter will be glad to develop such stories with your help. If he thinks there are *picture possibilities,* he may bring a photographer, too.

While there can be no strict formula for dealing with *all* members of any group, you'll experience few difficulties if your good manners and common sense are on the job, and if you remember the four C's: be Clear, Conscientious, Courteous and Complete.

## TRADE ASSOCIATION: AMERICAN GAS ASSOCIATION

The American Gas Association carries on a continuing program of public relations, both with its member companies and along general institutional lines. Through regional public relations workshops, through promotion, through stories issued from the Public Information Bureau, through informative brochures on such subjects as community relations, the story of the association and its members is told. In its publication *PR and You,* the AGA tells the story of how the member companies can work to win good will through organized public relations.

### PR and You

#### THOUGHT STARTERS

*PR and You* is a digest of successful public relations thinking and experience in the gas industry. It is addressed to the newcomer and the veteran practitioner; to the division manager and supervisor as well as top management. It is a thought starter and a guide—not a gospel.

Prime objective of this volume is to help *you* strengthen PR *action* at the gas company level.

## PR—WAY OF LIFE

"Public relations" said an anonymous wit, "is the art of *not* treating the public like relations!"

The president of a large Canadian utility expressed it another way:

"You can avoid publicity. You can avoid advertising, but relations with the public you cannot avoid. The only question is whether they are going to be good, bad or indifferent."

Through trial and error, management has developed the cornerstone of modern PR practice: People like to buy from, work for, invest in, and deal with companies that operate in the public interest, companies that are good corporate citizens.

PR is the continuing and active interpretation of *good public service*. It is a way of life—not a campaign that can be started and then dropped.

PR means *doing* and *telling*. It has been aptly described as:

*"essentially right living by a definite plan
and getting credit for it"*

## GOOD WILL STORAGE

You can lay five miles of pipeline for a quarter of a million dollars, but if you don't translate this into what the pipeline will mean to the public, you've failed PR-wise.

A New York State gas company determined that PR is advanced or retarded every time its employees come into contact with a customer—roughly 10,000 times a day! This astonishing figure takes into account only activities of sales people, servicemen, special crews, collection and branch office personnel. It doesn't even begin to reflect personal dealings with customers over the telephone.

A California gas company concluded that "Diplomacy, good manners, simple kindness, a desire to be helpful, are PR weapons as potent as all the high-powered battery of media devised by the experts.

"But such weapons are two-edged. A brusque word from a telephone order clerk; a meter-reader's foot in the flower bed; a temporary cutoff of gas supply without advance notice; a serviceman's muddy tracks on the kitchen linoleum; a tedious, sloppily written letter or a disregarded complaint can undo the good will laboriously built up by hundreds of man- and woman-hours of devoted service.

"The result is that employees must be impressed again and again with the supreme importance of maintaining and increasing our *reservoir of good will* with the customer and the community."

## LITTLE THINGS COUNT

Public understanding and good will are won through planning and patience, courtesy and consideration—a mosaic of little things that count. Some of these "little things that influence PR" are suggested by a large utility service organization:

1. Is the employee's need for recognition satisfied?
2. Do employees feel that management is on their team?
3. Are stockholders encouraged to participate in company affairs?
4. Is there a friendly welcome for new stockholders?
5. Do collection policies retain business friendships?
6. How does the night man answer telephone calls?
7. Do maintenance crews stress public safety and convenience?
8. Is employment policy fair and sound? Do rejected job applicants retain a favorable opinion of the company?
9. Are news releases distributed impartially?
10. Is top management readily available for interviewing?
11. Are educational and recreational facilities offered for employees and community groups?
12. Does the company have a working interest in school and church affairs?

## WHERE DO YOU START?

Eight basic steps are required to set up an *organized* PR program:

1. Assign over-all PR responsibility to a qualified executive.
2. Select competent staff or counsel to execute your program.
3. Determine your company's major PR problems and their relative importance.

4. Prepare a written program with specific objectives and policies.
5. Stimulate all employees to become active members of the PR team.
6. Initiate action to communicate the company's story to its various publics.
7. Draw up a practical plan to handle emergencies.
8. Develop yardsticks to measure the program's effectiveness and to keep it on target.

## WHAT ARE YOUR PROBLEMS?

A good PR program enlightens, doesn't mislead the public. To keep others informed, management itself must know what its public, customers and employees think of the company. PR cannot operate in a vacuum.

An objective opinion survey to *pinpoint problem areas* is essential before specific PR targets can be plotted.

One utility learned from a survey that half of its customers had no idea rates were regulated. Institutional advertising on regulation was then started, resulting in a significant increase in customers who felt that rates were reasonable or low.

Another company conducted an employee opinion poll to help create an atmosphere in which employees like to work efficiently. More than 20,000 comments were received and are being used to help shape company policies and practices.

Employees of another company went directly to the public in a grass roots, cracker barrel approach. Publishers and editors, doctors and merchants, bankers, municipal officials, educators and clergymen, were asked to say frankly what they thought of the company and its operations.

With information from these personal interviews, the company put its PR house in order.

## TECHNIQUES THAT SELL

Experience shows that the amount of money spent on PR is not a true index of effectiveness. Success or failure depends largely upon the *quality of the planning and the techniques* employed.

Communication techniques range from personal contact to mass appeal. Personal contact is established when an employee addresses a civic club or discusses company problems with regulatory officials.

Mass appeals are made through the press, motion pictures, radio and TV. They may be addressed to the general public or to specific audiences such as customers' service clubs, clergymen's organizations and organized labor.

In each case, the audience and its interest will determine the techniques and media used. Employee meetings and bulletin board notices help to maintain good customer relations. Candid "here are the facts" talks are especially effective before civic groups. A sound-color film can do a dramatic job of explaining the average gas bill.

The modern gas industry story should be told through:
1. Newspapers and magazines
2. Radio and TV
3. Films
4. Word of mouth
5. General and special purpose literature—pamphlets, billboards, signs and stickers
6. Community thought leaders
7. Salesmen, home service and other direct contact employees
8. School and educational groups

## PR IN ACTION

Here is one utility's program that is paying substantial dividends in good will. Similar programs can be tailored to meet the needs of even the smallest gas company.

A. *Employee relations with the public*
1. Customer relations training program for employees
2. Employees' magazine
3. Employee handbook
4. PR bulletins to supervisory personnel
5. Suggestion boxes
6. Merit award certificates to employees for outstanding accomplishments and long service
7. Encouragement of employee group-sponsored activities
8. Plant tours by employees

B. *Customer Relations*
   1. PR advertising
   2. Customer relations training program
   3. Basic theme line or slogan
   4. News stories
   5. Open house
   6. Letter of welcome to new customers
   7. Better handling of complaints
   8. General housekeeping
C. *Community relations*
   1. Cooperation with civic leaders in community planning
   2. Community boosting programs
   3. Home service contacts with adult and youth groups
   4. Travelog and other material for talks by company personnel before service clubs and other civic groups
   5. Displays and exhibits at local community level
   6. Tie-in with local industrial development activities
   7. Reports to municipalities
   8. Financial contributions
   9. Active participation in charitable and other civic activities by key personnel
D. *Press relations*
   1. Background, biographical and photographic material about company and personnel for use in news stories
   2. Personal contacts with the press
   3. Press releases of general public interest
   4. Conducted tours of company property
   5. Annual reports and financial statements to the press
   6. Central news clipping file
   7. Press conferences
E. *Investor relations*
   1. Quarterly and annual reports
   2. Talks to securities analysts
   3. Stockholder meetings
F. *School relations*
   1. A.G.A. educational service bureau materials made available to all high schools and colleges in territory

2. School loan plan for new gas equipment—follow-up by home service and service departments
3. Plant visits by students and teachers
4. Talks before student bodies

## PR CHECK LIST

How far has your company traveled on the road to good PR? Is its program dynamic? Well-rounded? Flexible? Supported by the chief executive?

Check this list of PR policies that are building good will for "Utopia Gas Company." How many are true of your company?

1. PR is specifically assigned to a qualified executive.
2. PR staff has competent, experienced personnel.
3. Company president has studied the PR program and issued a statement of policy in writing.
4. Major company policies are stated simply and clearly to avoid misunderstandings.
5. Company's immediate and long-range PR problems have been determined through survey or other means.
6. Definite program of PR action has been drawn up by company executives to meet specific targets.
7. PR department (or director) services not only top management but also other important departments.
8. PR thinking permeates all echelons of management.
9. PR personnel work closely with safety engineers to prevent accidents to employees and public.
10. Home service, customer relations, sales and other personnel keep PR personnel well posted on public attitudes.
11. Employees are well briefed on the program, its objectives, its progress and importance of their contributions.
12. Regular reports on company progress and needs are made to customers, employees, opinion leaders and public.
13. Rates, storage and other phases of company activities are explained at every opportunity.
14. Employees are thoroughly trained to give courteous and prompt handling to complaints.

15. Open house is held whenever occasion arises, such as new building, renovated offices and others.
16. Close cooperation is practiced with other companies and organizations in programs to benefit the community.
17. Gas company employees have good relations with the schools.
18. Civic activities are sponsored and well supported (churches, schools, Scouts, community chest and others).
19. Employees are encouraged to be active in service clubs, women's clubs and other community organizations.
20. Stockholders and securities analysts are kept well informed on company achievements and programs.
21. Company executives maintain personal contact with opinion leaders in community.
22. Adequate plans are ready to handle natural or enemy inflicted disaster.
23. Employee achievement in PR is honored by awards, recognition or other means.
24. Employee morale is high. Cashiers know what the meter readers are doing.
25. Public is shown at every opportunity the many steps gas industry and local gas company are taking to protect their health and safety.
26. Company officers are required to make regular calls on established or prospective customers.
27. Managers and supervisors hold company seminars to discuss PR procedures in theory and actual practice.
28. Management considers PR a way of living, not a short-term program.
29. PR committees have been set up in local plants with the guidance of the central PR department.
30. Management anticipates problems and situations—continually considers possible effects of proposed policies and actions.
31. Employees participate actively in economic education program utilizing modern picture-story technique.

## BUSINESS INSTITUTION: THE INSTITUTE OF LIFE INSURANCE

The Institute of Life Insurance, which is the central source of information about life insurance, has a coördinated public relations program, involving both press information and institutional or public service advertising. The story has been told by means of advertising designed to combat inflation; through reprints of articles and speeches, e.g., "Importance of Public Understanding" by Holgar J. Johnson, president of the Institute; through promotional reprints of advertisements, such as those on inflation; through information data on the Institute—what it is, what it does, how it operates.

## Public Relations Objectives

The Institute of Life Insurance is the public relations organization of the life insurance business, supported by 167 legal reserve companies. As the central source of information for the public—particularly writers, editors, publishers, commentators and authors—it is the point of contact for the entire life insurance business with the press, radio, television and other media in the field of communications.

In cooperation with the life insurance companies of the country, the Institute gathers industry-wide facts and statistics about the business and its operations. These are made available in the form of press releases, booklets, displays, charts, film strips, motion pictures and other material to various groups.

For example, the Institute works with teachers and school administrators to expand the teaching of life insurance in schools and colleges. It assists women through their clubs and organizations to obtain information about life insurance. It helps community librarians to select worthwhile life insurance books for their bookshelves.

Working with life underwriter associations and other life insurance organizations, the Institute stimulates activities that contribute to a better public understanding and appreciation of life insurance.

In addition to preparing and distributing life insurance information to the American people, the Institute continuously studies public opinion concerning the performance of the life insurance business and interprets its finding to the companies, helping them to serve better the interests of their policyholders and the public.

Dudley B. Martin, Director of Press Relations, has described
the work of this division in a talk before the Annual Management Conference of the General Agents and Managers Conference of the National Association of Life Underwriters:

Our job in the Press Division of the Institute is to spread an understanding of life insurance among the thousands of editors, reporters, feature writers and commentators throughout the country. That
way, we reach their millions and millions of readers, listeners,
and viewers—prospects and clients, and friends of prospects and
clients.

We do this by issuing monthly several printed news bulletins and
scores and scores of special releases to the press in the course of a
year. These cover the developments in the business and touch on the
social and economic significance these have in the life of the nation.

To tell you that in a year we distribute some 300 news stories to
publications all over the country would not be the full story of our
work. We receive inquiries—written, telephoned, and by personal
call—every day from writers who are in various stages (the earlier
the better) of thinking or writing about life insurance or something
it will fit into.

By this continuous process of presenting the life insurance news
—and feature material, too—we are creating an atmosphere into
which life insurance agents may move and may find that people
know at least what they are talking about.

In addition to the news materials we distribute, opportunities are
given us to *suggest* stories. This is especially the case among those
editors and writers who wouldn't dream of printing a "handout,"
as such, but who love to swap ideas, and who often will take the
thread and write their own story.

By following closely the developments of the day and the wants
of the press, we can *associate* life insurance with other desirable
things, tangible and intangible, and persuade the various communications media to include our service as one of the building blocks in
the articles and programs they are constructing.

Let me refer briefly now to our relations with the magazines. Here, too, is a most important aspect of our work, the job of *humanizing* life insurance among their hundreds of millions of readers.

The various magazines' editorial formulae present a challenge to all persons and businesses who hope to be included in their columns. You find here a delicate business of *having* to popularize and yet not going off base; maintaining this balance is part of the fun we have.

Before closing, I'd like to make a little request. It is this:

You men out in the field are acutely sensitive to any unfavorable mentions of the business. Naturally. But what we would ask is, when you see something in a magazine about, or allied to, life insurance and you *like* it, that you drop a note to the editor and tell him so. He likes to hear that he's appreciated—and, besides, your pat on the back will help us all to build an editorial climate strengthening our efforts to tell the story of life insurance.

Under the heading "You and Public Relations," Holgar J. Johnson, president of the Institute told the members of the General Agents and Managers Conference:

You have now had the opportunity to hear how the Institute came into being, how it developed, and what it is doing today, especially as to how it affects you and your business. But that is not the entire story.

There remains something else to be said, to be sure that we do not leave you with a false impression, both as to the Institute and its place in the scheme of things, and your own responsibilities.

It is this: the Institute can *not* do the whole public relations job for the entire life insurance business. It does have the responsibility of giving *leadership* in the public relations area to all elements of the business and implementing the public relations program at the institutional level.

No one can bestow good public relations upon more than 1,000 life insurance companies, nor more than 200,000 fieldmen. But if we can point the way, devise sound philosophies, methods and procedures, and bring to your attention the best public relations ideas of your contemporaries, we feel that the Institute will have made a permanent contribution to a greater public understanding of our business.

How, then, does this affect the agency head and his agents in the field of public relations? Because of their direct public contact, they are the people who play a most important role.

Because you *are* on the firing line, you have a heavy responsibility in this area, even though it may not be so strongly fixed in your consciousness as the selling and servicing of our product—for that is in essence part of the public relations activity. As in every other business, the ability of life insurance to survive as a fundamental of American life lies in creating and maintaining the good will of our customers and prospects. We at the Institute can advance and nurture that good will to a reasonable degree, but you are the people who create it.

So I believe, assuming that you wish to have public good will, that good business judgment *demands* certain things of all agency heads and their associates:

*First,* to develop in themselves a consciousness of what constitutes good public relations. This implies not only being good citizens, but treating every single business situation they face in the light of this question: "Is this act acceptable, understandable, and plausible to the public that will feel the impact of it?"

*Second,* to inculcate into the minds of everyone they work with this same consciousness, because no person can succeed to the optimum in our business unless he has conscious understanding of and desire to create good public relations.

*Third,* all this requires that we treat good public relations as just as vital a part of the marketing process as prospecting or training or supervision.

*Fourth,* to develop a *program* for good public relations. I would suggest a simple, four-step program that guides the Institute in its work and which can be adapted by every agency and agent in America. Its just this:

Step One:      Find out who your publics *really* are.
Step Two:      Find out *what* these publics think about you.
Step Three:    Decide what you *want* each of them to think about you.

Step Four:   Put down on paper your program, and do the things that will achieve these ends.

If you follow these four steps, you will have an integrated public relations program in the work pattern of your agency, and you will have made a significant move forward.

*Fifth,* we must realize that *all* elements of the life insurance business must act as a team to achieve the best possible public relations. There can be no weak link in the chain of public relations. When any one of us overlooks an assignment, that failure rubs off a bit on all the rest of us.

And here is where we, at the Institute, act as a catalyst. When you have problems of an institutional nature where you think we can be helpful, feel free to come to us. When you face a local situation that demands delicate handling, don't feel that you're alone, because we may have help or be able to advise you where to get it. And when you have done well in solving a public relations situation, let us know about it, because we may be able to impart *your* knowledge to someone else who needs it badly.

And that, I believe, is the story of the Institute. It is our responsibility to be a central source of information for the business, both with the public and the business; to lead in interpreting to the public what the business is doing and thinking, and *why;* to interpret to you and the business what the *public* is thinking, and to suggest ways of fitting action most closely to that thinking; and to exercise a position of leadership in all the public relations aspects of our business. That, we believe, constitutes our mission.

## EDUCATIONAL ORGANIZATION: NATIONAL EDUCATION ASSOCIATION

The National Education Association is probably the largest professional organization in the United States. From a broad public relations viewpoint, the function of the NEA is to further the cause of education and raise its standards, both professionally and economically, by keeping the public informed of the status, needs, and aims of the teachers and educators of America. In the following exposition, Roy K. Wilson, director of the division of press and radio relations for the NEA, describes the public relations program of the Association.

## National Education Association: A Brief Summary of Its Public Relations Program

Public relations play an essential role in achieving both of the major objectives of the National Education Association, a voluntary organization of more than 700,000 teachers, administrators, and other workers in education which seeks (1) to elevate the character and advance the interests of the profession of teaching and (2) to promote the cause of popular education in the United States.

An important instrument of the NEA for reaching the public is the Division of Press and Radio Relations. That Division conducts a continuous program of communication, to both the public and members of the teaching profession, about the services and activities of the NEA, its departments, committees, and commissions, and about the achievements, programs, needs, and problems of America's schools.

To insure the steady flow of information about the NEA, the Division maintains day-by-day contacts with the men and women who write for press associations, newspapers, national magazines, radio, television, and motion pictures. Liaison is also maintained with the public relations representatives of many organizations. The communications media, in turn, inform the people across America about the interests, policies, problems, and performance of the organized teaching profession, and about current developments and issues in the schools themselves.

For example, when the NEA Research Division issued its study on the *Status of the American School Teacher,* the Division of Press and Radio Relations scheduled a news conference between NEA representatives and members of the press. Not every development rates a news conference, but the Division regularly and consistently prepares releases on pertinent happenings and distributes them to writers, and radio and television newscasters all over the nation.

State and National education journals, with a combined circulation of more than 1 million, receive the same news releases as the daily press. They also get a steady flow of information about the NEA through the monthly *News Report from NEA Headquarters,* prepared in the Division.

Writers and public relations representatives who are planning projects to interpret education often come to the Division for help. For example, *Look* magazine recently called on the Division for background material for an article, "What Is a School?" Professional journals, also, come to the Division quite frequently for information when they are planning articles about the NEA, or about schools or teachers.

Publicizing special NEA projects and events, such as the recent Centennial Observance, or the NEA's current legislative program at any given time, is part of the Division's responsibility.

Division members also attend some 20 national conventions held annually by the NEA and its departments. There they help to publicize the *conference* proceedings, and help writers and broadcasters report the most timely news. For example, several staff members operate a "convention press service" for the annual meetings of the American Association of School Administrators, now attended by over 20,000 educators and school board members.

## RADIO AND TELEVISION

During a recent school year, the NEA joined forces with an established television show, cooperating with the producers of *Youth Wants to Know,* a network production. A division member, specifically assigned to radio and television relations, recruits the young panelists who take part in the show and helps with other program arrangements.

The Division also arranges for the appearance of NEA representatives on television network programs. For example, NEA President Martha A. Shull appeared on Dave Garroway's program "Today" to discuss the "Status of the American School Teacher." Dr. Sam Lambert, director of research for NEA, appeared on the Arlene Francis "Home Show," to explain the problem of teacher shortage.

Four national radio networks broadcast the address given by President Eisenhower at the Centennial Birthday Party. "Martha Rountree's Press Conference," a television network production, originated from the NEA Centennial Convention in Philadelphia.

A special kit was prepared for 3600 radio and television stations, including spot announcements and program material on the NEA Centennial and on the need for more fully-qualified teachers. These announcements have been seen and heard by millions of persons during recent months.

## AMERICAN EDUCATION WEEK

Stimulating the observance of American Education Week is also a responsibility of the Division of Press and Radio Relations. This observance is set for the week each November that includes Veterans Day. National sponsors are the NEA, American Legion, U.S. Office of Education, and National Congress of Parents and Teachers. During AEW about 20 million people visit schools to see them in action. Millions more are reached through the press, radio, and television coverage arranged by NEA, and through exhibits, meetings, and literature. AEW for next year will be observed November 10 through 16, using as a general theme the NEA Centennial slogan, "An Educated People Moves Freedom Forward."

## MOTION PICTURES

In cooperation with the state education associations, the NEA produces each year a public relations motion picture film to interpret a current educational problem. "Not by Chance," which portrays the professional education of teachers, was completed this summer as the seventh of the series. The films are planned by a committee composed of representatives of the NEA Staff and state education association staffs, under the chairmanship of the NEA assistant executive secretary for Information Services. Coordination of the film program, including the promotion and sale of prints, is a responsibility of the Division of Press and Radio Relations.

Millions of American citizens each year see these NEA-sponsored films on the television screen. For example, "A Desk for Billie," the hour-long Centennial motion picture which was released at an NEA Convention in Portland was premiered over 216 TV Stations. This film recently was selected by *Scholastic Magazine* as one of the ten best films in education for the year. It also won a Golden Reel Award in a recent competition of the American Film Assembly.

Now available for use in the public relations film series, in addition to "Not by Chance" and "A Desk for Billie," are: "Mike Makes His Mark," "Freedom to Learn," "Skippy and the Three R's," "What Greater Gift," and "Secure the Blessings."

Most of these films are available for loan through state education associations or film libraries throughout the United States. Many local education associations and school systems make use of them at meetings of community organizations, service clubs, and church groups, as well as before school groups.

### INSTITUTES FOR EDUCATION WRITERS

Institutes to improve school news reporting have been conducted jointly by the Division of Press and Radio Relations and the Education Writers Association since 1950. More than 1,000 newsmen, school administrators, school board members, and PTA leaders have attended the meetings held since 1950 in Washington, New York, Chicago, St. Louis, Louisville, and Cincinnati.

### COOPERATION WITH THE MAGAZINE PUBLISHERS ASSOCIATION

For four years a joint committee of the NEA and the Magazine Publishers Association has arranged an annual conference for 100 leading educators and 100 representatives of the magazine industry. Conference programs have centered around educator-editor cooperation and their common interests.

### NEA CENTENNIAL

The NEA celebrated its Centennial year in 1957. The long list of special activities was climaxed with the Centennial Convention in Philadelphia, June 30 through July 5. Just 100 years ago, 43 educators met in Philadelphia to found the organized teaching profession in America.

On the official Centennial birthday date, April 4, 1957, more than 2500 of the 6000 local education associations affiliated with NEA celebrated the event with birthday parties and dinners attended by several hundred thousand teachers and other citizens in communities across America. The national Centennial Birthday Party, in Washington, D.C., was attended by about 1400 persons, including the President of the United States who made a major address on education on that occasion.

The U.S. Post Office issued a special commemorative stamp, honoring the teachers of America and the NEA Centennial, putting it on sale July 1 in Philadelphia.

Edgar B. Wesley has written a special Centennial history of the NEA entitled, *NEA: The First Hundred Years*. It was published by Harper & Brothers. Author Wesley, who at the University of Minnesota and elsewhere taught teachers of history for the past 40 years, looks upon his 419-page work as the story of what 100 years of the NEA has brought to American education.

Several agencies and groups have given special Centennial "salutes" to the NEA. A special Centennial film, "A Desk for Billie," has been seen by millions, first on a nationwide television premiere in the fall of 1956, and then to thousands of groups across the country.

## FOUNDATION: THE FORD FOUNDATION

The Ford Foundation has issued a prospectus which includes salient information about the activities and organization of the Foundation and the independent, nonprofit corporations it has established. The Foundation's programs, which are described here, include the following: Problems of the Schools; College Teacher Salaries; Medical Education; College Scholarships; Libraries; Liberal Adult Education; Educational Television; Recruiting College Teachers; Public Affairs; Urban and Regional Problems, Economics and Business Administration; Natural Resources in the United States; The Study of Human Behavior; Mental Health Research; Problems of Youth and the Aged; Hospitals; Foreign and International Affairs; International Legal Studies; Person-to-Person Contacts; Grants in Europe; Overseas Development; New Programs; Fellowships.

It should be noted that the prospectus explains the Foundation at the time of its publication. However, the objectives and operations are flexible so as to allow for necessary changes and growth in new directions.

## A Prospectus

*The Ford Foundation* is a private, nonprofit corporation established in 1936 by Henry and Edsel Ford. Its purpose is to serve the public welfare. It seeks to strengthen American society by identifying problems of national importance and underwriting efforts toward their solution, principally through educational means.

Except in a limited way, the Foundation itself does not engage in direct operations. Its primary business as a philanthropy is to make grants of funds to other nonprofit organizations.

Thus far it has given more than a billion dollars to some 6,000 institutions and organizations in all forty-eight states, in three territories, and fifty-four foreign countries.

Most of the Foundation's grants have gone to American institutions. Of the total amount it has allocated for all purposes, about two-thirds has been for the support of education.

### PROBLEMS OF THE SCHOOLS

Many of the Foundation's programs are concerned with problems of the American educational system—how more and better teachers can be trained, for instance; how better use can be made of those now available. For work on such problems, in addition to larger sums granted directly, the Foundation has given $57.4 million in the past six years to The Fund for the Advancement of Education, an independent organization it established in 1951. At the beginning of this year the Foundation and the Fund brought their activities into close coordination, as a step toward a joint decision to consolidate.

### COLLEGE TEACHER SALARIES

A total of $260 million was appropriated in 1955 and 1956 to help raise the salaries of college and university faculty members.

These funds were distributed to all the nation's 630 four-year, regionally-accredited, privately-controlled colleges and universities. Each institution received an endowment approximately equal to its 1954 instructional payroll for the liberal arts and sciences; 126 received more than half again as much in recognition of efforts already made to improve the compensation of their teachers. Apportionment of salary increases is at the discretion of each institution.

## MEDICAL EDUCATION

The nation's forty-four privately-supported medical schools received endowment grants totaling $90 million to strengthen their instruction. While helping to maintain the standards of medical training, these grants assisted higher education as a whole by easing the strain which the high cost of medical education places on university budgets. An additional $10 million was appropriated in 1956 for the National Fund for Medical Education to match on a sliding scale its annual income earmarked for distribution to all the accredited medical schools in the United States, public and private.

## COLLEGE SCHOLARSHIPS

The National Merit Scholarship Corporation, established by the Foundation in 1955 in cooperation with the Carnegie Corporation, helps worthy high school students to get a college education. The organization conducts an annual nation-wide competition among high school seniors and, with merit as the sole basis for selection, awards the winners four-year scholarships to colleges of their choice. Of the $20 million grant the Foundation made to the National Merit Scholarship Corporation, $8 million is being used to match contributions from business firms and other donors interested in establishing scholarships. In its first year of operation the Corporation awarded Merit Scholarships, averaging $630 per year, to 556 students. They attended 160 different colleges. An additional sum is given to each college to help it meet the actual cost of the student's education.

## LIBRARIES

The Council on Library Resources was created in 1956 and financed by an appropriation of $5 million to work on problems affecting the usefulness of libraries. It is seeking to develop and demonstrate mechanical devices and new techniques and methods that will improve library organization and service. Also, it is experimenting with ways to improve interlibrary cooperation, particularly as an aid to research.

## LIBERAL ADULT EDUCATION

The means and opportunities for learning for adult men and women have been supported mainly through grants to The Fund for Adult Education, which has received $47.4 million since its establishment by the Foundation in 1951. The Fund is supporting the development, testing, and introduction of both formal and informal programs of liberal adult education, especially in institutions of higher learning. It also has programs of research and training to establish higher and more professional standards within the field and to create a wider interest in it.

## EDUCATIONAL TELEVISION

A total of $19.1 million has been given to support educational television. Of this sum, $8 million was appropriated in 1956. The Foundation set aside $1.5 million of these funds to help pay for releasing college faculty members from their regular duties so that they can work on educational telecasts. Over $6 million is being used to support the Educational Radio and Television Center at Ann Arbor, Mich., which develops and produces programs, exchanges kinescopes, and acquires films. The remaining $11.1 million of the total support to educational television was spent by The Fund for Adult Education prior to its withdrawal from the field, mostly to help construct some seventeen educational stations.

Between 1952 and 1957, the Foundation's TV-Radio Workshop, producer of the experimental program, "Omnibus," undertook to demonstrate that educational television could compete successfully for both audience and sponsorship over a commercial network. This venture is now being carried on under private ownership.

## RECRUITING COLLEGE TEACHERS

To reduce the mounting shortage of college teachers, the Foundation has given $25 million for a nationwide recruitment and fellowship program aimed at attracting able college students into the academic profession. The funds will permit expansion of the National Woodrow Wilson Fellowship Program, at Ann Arbor, Mich.

Over a five-year period, the objective will be to provide 1,000 fellowships a year, averaging $2,200 each, for a first year of graduate study. Graduate schools will receive a stipend of $2,000 for each Woodrow Wilson fellow enrolled, three-fourths of which must be used for aid to graduate students (not only Woodrow Wilson Fellows) beyond the first year. The rest is for general strengthening of graduate programs.

The recruitment program is to be based on a corps of 100 or more faculty members working part time on approximately 1,000 campuses to stimulate faculty cooperation. Nominations for Woodrow Wilson Fellowships will be made by local faculty members, and selection will be made by a national committee comprising active university and college teachers.

## PUBLIC AFFAIRS

A variety of scholarly, educational, and civic activities receiving Foundation assistance are aimed at helping to strengthen self-government in a free, democratic society. Support has been given to programs both among adult and school groups working to further citizen understanding of democratic ideals, processes, and institutions and to encourage a more active citizen participation in public affairs. To aid in the development of leadership on a wide front, grants have been made to improve public service training and to assist the work of such organizations as the National 4-H Club Foundation.

Other activities to receive support are concerned with ways to increase understanding of the legislative process on both the state and national level. And to help achieve a better knowledge of the whole science and art of representative government, grants have been made to a number of universities and other organizations for research and training in such areas as American government, governmental affairs, and the problems of public service. Finally, grants to improve the training of law teachers and to enrich legal research in the field of law and society are helping to strengthen the contribution of the legal profession to public life.

## URBAN AND REGIONAL PROBLEMS

Six universities are conducting research on the many problems arising from the growth of cities into huge urban complexes. Metropolitan areas currently being studied under recent grants are Boston, St. Louis, New York, and the "Piedmont Crescent" of North Carolina. Work on such problems as conflicting jurisdictions, taxation, and land, water, and power use, for instance, may contribute to better planning in metropolitan regions generally.

## ECONOMICS AND BUSINESS ADMINISTRATION

Nearly $16 million has been given for teaching and research in economics and business administration, and to improve basic public knowledge of economic affairs. These funds have gone mainly to university graduate departments of economics and schools of business and, in a few instances, to national research institutes, such as the Brookings Institution and the National Bureau of Economic Research. Teaching is being aided through fellowships and faculty additions; research, through the support of general departmental or institutional programs and through financing individual scholars by means of small grants. Examples of the many studies undertaken are: consumer behavior, manpower, income distribution, the business cycle, and economic growth and stability.

## NATURAL RESOURCES IN THE UNITED STATES

Research and education on the development, conservation, and use of natural resources is being conducted and supported by Resources for the Future, Inc., an independent organization which has received grants totaling more than $4 million since its establishment in 1952. Its program includes studies of water resources, energy and minerals, land use and management, regional problems, and the relation of resources to the national economy.

## THE STUDY OF HUMAN BEHAVIOR

Advancement of the sciences relating to human behavior, such as sociology, psychology, and anthropology, has included over $15 million in grants for training and research at fifty-five colleges, universities, and other institutions. These funds have helped build up teaching—largely through faculty additions and fellowships. Foundation activity in this field will be discontinued gradually during 1957.

Of the total amount given, some $5.3 million has gone to the Center for Advanced Study in the Behavioral Sciences, at Stanford, Calif., which was established by the Foundation in 1952. The purpose of the Center is to provide opportunities for senior scholars and a number of younger men to do concentrated work on their individual specialties while at the same time associating with one another on common problems and interests.

## MENTAL HEALTH RESEARCH

Basic research and research training in mental health are being supported by an appropriation of $15 million. Grants from this fund are assisting twenty-one research programs in the United States and five abroad. Grantee institutions include hospitals, medical schools, research institutes, and biological and social science departments of colleges and universities.

Research training is being assisted through a grant of some $3.6 million to the Foundation's Fund for Research in Psychiatry, of New Haven, Conn., which, in turn, is making grants for fellowships, the expansion of research faculties, and other training aid to scholars and scientists.

## PROBLEMS OF YOUTH AND THE AGED

The National Probation and Parole Association is being assisted in a program to strengthen community means and facilities for the treatment of juvenile offenders.

Funds have been appropriated for the general support of the National Committee on the Aging, of the National Social Welfare Assembly. The funds are being used by the Committee chiefly to establish and maintain an information and consultation service on behalf of organizations and community groups that are engaged in helping older people.

## HOSPITALS

Approximately 3,500 voluntary, nonprofit hospitals in the United States, Alaska, Hawaii, and Puerto Rico have received a total of $200 million to help improve and expand their services to their local communities. The grants ranged from $10,000 to $250,000. Some of the ways in which the recipient hospitals have chosen to use their grants include the improvement or addition of: buildings, isotope laboratories and radiotherapy facilities, research laboratories, new departments for children or elderly patients, training programs, and specialized personnel.

## FOREIGN AND INTERNATIONAL AFFAIRS

Several colleges, universities, and other educational organizations have received help for training and research in foreign area studies and international relations. The Foundation has given particular attention to increasing knowledge of Asia, the Near East, Africa, the Soviet Union, and Eastern Europe. It has awarded more than 750 fellowships for studies concerning these areas. Several fellowships are also awarded each year to help teachers in international relations broaden their backgrounds. Besides this assistance, aimed at improving scholarly and professional knowledge, grants have been made to organizations advancing public education on foreign countries and international issues. Among these are the Council on Foreign Relations and the Foreign Policy Association.

## INTERNATIONAL LEGAL STUDIES

Grants to expand the international legal studies of American law schools are helping to meet the need for more people trained to handle the growing number of transactions between the United States and other countries. In the past three years, thirteen law schools have received Foundation assistance under this program.

## PERSON-TO-PERSON CONTACTS

Foreign students studying in the United States are being assisted through grants to organizations which help the student get the most out of his experience here. Grants also are being made to expand the opportunities for mature citizens from abroad—teachers, scholars, technicians, businessmen, journalists—to visit this country. Two of the exchange-of-persons organizations being assisted are: the Eisenhower Exchange Fellowships, Inc., and the Institute of International Education.

## GRANTS IN EUROPE

A few organizations in Europe are receiving support for education and research aimed at improving international understanding, particularly between European countries. Also, through grants to European agencies, aid is being given to Hungarian refugee scholars and to some 500 Hungarian refugee students entering European educational institutions. An exchange of scholars, students, and other professional specialists between Poland and the United States and Europe is being undertaken to establish or renew educational, scientific, and cultural relationships.

## OVERSEAS DEVELOPMENT

Since 1950, nearly $60 million has been given for a wide variety of activities in India, Pakistan, Burma, Indonesia, Nepal, and eight countries in the Near East. The Foundation is seeking to help these people help themselves in overcoming the challenging social and economic tasks they face. It is doing so chiefly by support for the improvement of formal education—from the village school to the university; by helping enlarge the means for technical and agricultural vocational training; and by assisting adult education programs aimed at raising the general standard of living, particularly in rural communities.

## NEW PROGRAMS

The Foundation has recently given support to the humanities and the arts. An appropriation of $1.7 million provides help to a group of some thirty college and university presses for the publication of scholarly books in the humanities and social sciences. A grant of $2.6 million to the American Council of Learned Societies is supporting fellowships, research, and other activities to strengthen humanistic scholarship.

Development of programs in the natural sciences and engineering is under consideration.

## FELLOWSHIPS

Fellowships have been awarded in significant numbers in all fields in which the Foundation is interested. These have been provided largely through grants to graduate departments and professional schools of universities, and grants to research institutions and other educational organizations.

But for special purposes in certain fields—namely, foreign area studies, international relations, economics and business administration—in the absence of other means, the Foundation awards fellowships directly.

Foreign area training fellowships are open on a competitive basis to college seniors about to enter graduate school, to graduate students, and to persons of demonstrated ability in professions for training related to Asia, the Near East, the Soviet Union, Eastern Europe, and Africa.

International relations training fellowships are open to college and university faculty members for further training in international relations, other social sciences, and the humanities, or for study of one of the foreign areas mentioned above. The normal requirement is the Ph.D. degree or the equivalent.

For further information concerning these programs, write to:

> The Secretary
> The Ford Foundation
> 477 Madison Avenue
> New York 22, N.Y.

The Foundation awards two types of fellowships in economics and business administration: predoctoral fellowships to outstanding candidates for the Master of Business Administration degree, or those who have recently acquired it, and doctoral dissertation fellowships to graduate students who have completed all other requirements for the doctor's degree except the thesis.

Candidates for these fellowships are nominated by the college under a quota arrangement with the Foundation. The Foundation makes its selection with the aid of screening committees. Those interested in applying should *not* write the Foundation but should check with the appropriate office of their college or university.

## HOW TO APPLY FOR A GRANT

Applications for grants may be made by sending a written outline of a proposal to:

> The Secretary
> The Ford Foundation
> 477 Madison Avenue
> New York 22, N.Y.

The letter should include a statement of:
1. The objective of the proposal
2. The methods by which it is to be accomplished
3. The period of time it is expected to take
4. The funds required and an estimated budget in some detail
5. The qualifications of the organizations or individuals involved, and the organizations' eligibility for tax-exemption privileges
6. Whether similar projects have been undertaken previously
7. Whether support has been, or is being, requested of other foundations

Applications are generally declined unless they fall clearly within programs currently in operation. Each year, the Foundation's income is exhausted through favorable action on only a small percentage of applications.

Please note that, as a tax-exempt organization, The Ford Foundation can give its funds for only educational, scientific, and charitable purposes. It does not support charitable projects limited to local purposes or effects, nor does it ordinarily make grants for general operating expenses or construction.

Additional information is contained in the Foundation's annual reports, its quarterly grant announcements, and its occasional special publications. These are free, on request to the Foundation's Office of Reports.

## THE ARTS: METROPOLITAN MUSEUM OF ART

As more leisure time becomes available, increasing numbers of people are turning to cultural interests and pursuits. The fine orchestral programs available on radio, for example, have accomplished a great deal in the way of music education. Similarly, the art museums of the country are proving a constantly growing attraction to the public. Here, Lillian Green, supervisor of publicity of the world-famous Metropolitan Museum of Art, discusses the public relations activities of the Museum.

### Public Relations Activities at the Metropolitan Museum of Art

A public relations program in an art museum has several objectives: to acquaint the public with the museum's collections and its activities; to ensure continued support through maintaining and increasing membership; and to give news to the press of special events, major acquisitions and other museum activities.

The public information desk in the Metropolitan Museum's entrance hall is open seven days a week during gallery hours, answering innumerable questions from visitors, giving directions and distributing illustrated floor plans, handling telephone inquiries about the Museum's collections, programs and services and acting as reception center and clearing house for the many callers who come on business to the various curatorial and service offices.

Like most privately endowed institutions operated for the public good, the Metropolitan Museum derives considerable support from its members (currently some 13,000) who pay annually $10.00 to $100.00 or make single donations of $500.00 to $50,000.00 or more. An active program is planned for the members and their friends, including subscription series of concerts and lectures also available to the public at slightly higher rates, previews of special exhibitions, and other interesting activities. They receive the monthly illustrated *Bulletin,* and other announcements. Membership is maintained and increased through direct mail solicitation and by personal contacts made through the membership office, which is open every day (five days a week during the summer), and which serves as a center for members coming to the Museum.

By means of news releases on all major exhibitions and other events of current interest, the Museum's publicity office provides news for publication in newspapers and magazines. Press views are arranged in advance of each opening, when curators are on hand to talk to reporters, photographs are available, and *Bulletin* articles or other authoritative statements are distributed to supplement the brief outline provided by the news release.

Among the devices frequently used to publicize major exhibitions are on-the-spot news coverage of arrival of loan collections; car cards in buses and subways; posters for display in libraries, schools, art galleries, restaurants, and hotels; transcribed radio announcements; and guest-appearances of curators or newsreel coverage on television.

News of current exhibitions, concerts, and lectures also goes regularly to the press, the public, and the Museum's members through a *Calendar of Events* leaflet, issued monthly from October through May, which is distributed free of charge upon request.

A good proportion of the publicity staff's time goes into assisting various representatives—from newspapers, press associations, magazines, book publishers, advertising agencies, and photographic studios—to get the material they need from the Museum for stories and layouts that they have already planned. The stories that they originate are the extra bonus for a museum—the kind of publicity that can't be bought.

"Public relations wasn't a profession in 1870," wrote Floyd D. Rodgers, Jr., former Manager of Public Relations at the Metropolitan Museum, "it wasn't even a gleam in anybody's eye. Yet it's doubtful that any of the experts in the field today could have asked for a more enlightened charter upon which to build a program than that drawn up by the founders of the Metropolitan Museum of Art and enacted as a New York State law on April 13, 1870. The charter was obtained:

"For the purpose of establishing and maintaining . . . a museum and library of art, of encouraging and developing the study of the fine arts, and the application of arts to manufacture and

practical life, of advancing the general knowledge of kindred subjects, and, to that end, of furnishing popular instruction."

## FAMILY SERVICE: COMMUNITY SERVICE SOCIETY

The Community Service Society of New York is the biggest
organization of its kind in the country. It is concerned with
multifarious social service problems, but one of its paramount
interests is the bettering of family life and relationships. The
basic problem for this organization is, of course, the need for
financial support in order to accomplish its work. In the following, William A. Platt, director of public information, describes a typical recent publicity and public relations program
of the Society.

### Public Relations and Publicity Program Outline

The program outlined below is in keeping with certain broad objectives related to particular audiences in the community. In each
case the media for reaching these groups are indicated.

In addition to the broad objectives, there are a number of specific
considerations that must be kept in mind in the over-all interpretation of the Society's role. These include:

1. The non-sectarian and "open door" character of the agency.
2. How the private or voluntary agency differs from the public
   or tax-supported program.
3. What the CSS does not do, as well as what it does do.
4. Confidentiality of service.
5. Fee service for those who can pay.
6. Respect for the integrity of the individual.
7. CSS belief in the importance of the family.
8. Professional expertness of staff, its special training and com-
   petencies.
9. What casework is and how it differs from role of psychology
   and psychiatry.
10. CSS research or self-examination process.
11. CSS role in social action.

12. Historic, pioneering achievements of the Society.
13. CSS a citizen movement.
14. How CSS relates to The Greater New York Fund.
15. CSS part of a network of community services.
16. Professional leadership of the Society.

| *Audience* | *Objective* |
|---|---|
| I. Prospective Clients | To inform prospective clients about available CSS services. |

   A. Media

      1. Literature describing CSS program and services; specially prepared literature for use by referral groups.

      2. Talks before selected groups as warranted by current client volume in a particular district.

      3. Press, radio, television and other mass media as warranted.

| *Audience* | *Objective* |
|---|---|
| II. Present Clients · | To encourage and maintain clients' conviction about CSS as a community institution and for purposes of morale; to help clarify CSS services; to assist clients to refer their friends and associates intelligently. |

   A. Media

      1. District office waiting rooms

         A. Bulletin boards

            a. Selected press clippings (possibly enlargements) on CSS activities.

            b. Photos depicting CSS activities such as Senior Citizens Week, National Family Week, Nutrition Week, etc.

         B. Waiting room tables

            a. Descriptive CSS literature.

b. Educational materials such as "About Home-making"—guide series.

c. Scrapbooks on camps, Ward Manor, other CSS activities in hands of caseworkers.

| *Audience* | *Objective* |
|---|---|
| III. Allied Social and Health Agencies | To encourage appropriate use of CSS services; to facilitate participation in matters of common concern, including improvement of social conditions; to give information so that personnel of other agencies can interpret CSS with conviction when appropriate or necessary. |

A. Media

1. Professional journals such as *Journal of Social Case-work, Public Health Nursing Journal* (to inform readers of CSS activities, point of view, researches; to sustain professional reputation of CSS and its staff).

2. Professional news letters such as *Better Times, Channels, Highlights, Community,* etc. (to inform lay and professional readers of these publications about CSS activities).

3. Meetings (organizations and their committees).
   a. Welfare Council.
   b. Family Service Association of America.
   c. Health agencies (Public Health Association, New York Tuberculosis and Health Association, County Medical Societies).
   d. National, state and regional social work conferences.

4. Annual Report.

5. Descriptive CSS literature.

6. Reports and studies.

| Audience | Objective |
|---|---|

IV. "General Public" and      To secure social action.
Special Groups
A. Media
    1. Letters to key people on housing matters, court proposals, etc.
      a. Legislators.
      b. Community leaders.
      c. Special groups such as Bar Associations, dental and medical societies, etc.
    2. Reports on matters such as court studies, Housing Committee action, etc.
    3. Reports on research studies.
    4. Meetings.
      a. Appearances before legislative bodies (Board of Estimate, City Council, etc.).
      b. Civic, social, health, legal, religious and educational groups.
    5. Press.
      a. Reports on CSS position on social action matters.
      b. Editorial endorsements on CSS position on social action questions.
      c. Letters to the Editor when appropriate.
    6. Radio, magazines, television.

| Audience | Objective |
|---|---|

V. CSS Staff                   To build and maintain staff morale, to encourage and train them as interpreters of CSS program.

A. Media for dissemination of information
    1. "What's Going On."
    2. General staff meetings.
    3. Exhibits (agency bulletin boards).
    4. Come-and-see tours.
    5. Orientation materials for new staff.
    6. Official memoranda.

B. Training conferences (group and individual) for becoming interpreters of CSS
 1. On interpreting CSS in daily associations.
 2. On case material for *Times* Hundred Neediest Appeal.
 3. On case material for use in Bulletins.
 4. On use of visual aids.
 5. Solicitor training for Family Fund Appeal.
 6. On appearing before community groups, radio, television.
 7. On being interviewed by press, magazines, etc.

|              *Audience*       |              *Objective*                  |
| VI. CSS Alumni | To maintain professional relationships, to recruit promising staff through former staff members, to create feeling of status among present staff. |

A. Media
 1. "What's Going On."
 2. Annual Report.
 3. Individualized letters.
 5. Get-togethers at national conferences.

|              *Audience*       |              *Objective*                  |
| VII. Prospective Contributors | To insure financial support of CSS through fostering an understanding of its services. |

A. Campaign period
 1. Campaign name: CSS Family Fund.
 2. Campaign theme: You help troubled families when you give to the CSS Family Fund.
  *Note:* The name and the theme of the CSS campaign were adopted a year ago. One of the publicity objectives of this and future appeals will be to establish firmly the identity of the campaign by its formal name and theme.

Campaign publicity will be geared to three major audiences: campaign workers, present contributors and prospective contributors.

The media for reaching these groups fall into a pattern recognized in most campaigns. It should be pointed out, however, that the CSS Family Fund appeal is not a "saturation" type campaign. Because of its narrower base, CSS campaign publicity will not seek to take advantage of such media as taxi bumper strips, mass window displays, flags, banners, lapel buttons, restaurant menus, or such devices as a Mayoral Proclamation, CSS Week, changing the street name of Times Square for a month, etc.

Although the plan outlined herein is geared to the campaign period, October through December, it is certain that it will be supplemented by the normal flow of publicity on the CSS program and activities. In many instances, however, the stories will be of a kind that may easily justify mention of the CSS Family Fund.

B. Media
  1. Newspapers (dailies).
      a. Leadership appointments (with photos).
      b. Campaign events (kick-off meeting, progress reports).
      c. Feature stories (interviews with staff, campaign leaders).
      d. Picture layouts (CSS services).
      e. Editorials (endorsements).
      f. New York *Times* Hundred Neediest stories.
      g. *Daily Mirror* "Most Helpless Children" stories.
  2. Neighborhood weeklies.
      a. Local slant on CSS activities by districts.

    b. Campaign leadership (West Side, Harlem, Queens, Uptown, Bronx, etc.).

    c. Canned editorials.

    d. Picture layouts on neighborhood CSS services.

3. Trade and professional publications.

    a. Announcements of Business & Professional leadership appointments, with photos.

4. Magazines (local).

    a. *New Yorker* magazine, *Cue* magazine, etc.

5. Radio (local).

    a. Spot announcements and station breaks.

    b. Guest appearances and interviews on established shows, panels, etc.

    c. CSS "sponsorship" of disc jockey programs with CSS features replacing commercials.

6. Television (local).

    a. Spot announcements (telops) and station breaks.

    b. Guest appearances on established shows, panels, etc.

    c. Appearances on network shows where possible.

7. Car cards.

    a. Subway trains.

    b. Commuter trains.

    c. Ferry lines.

    d. Buses.

8. Commuter time tables.

    a. Free advertising space with copy and art supplied by CSS.

9. Posters.

    a. Subway station platforms.

    b. Commuter station platforms.

    c. Terminals (Penn. Station, etc.).

    d. Apartment house lobbies.

    e. Neighborhood windows.

10. Basic facts leaflet telling the CSS case and spelling out goals of campaign.

11. Letters explaining CSS activities and outlining campaign message.
12. Editorial reprints—for use as enclosures in follow-up appeal letters.
13. CSS sponsored meetings.

| *Audience* | *Objective* |
|---|---|
| VIII. Campaign Workers | To inform campaign workers about CSS program and to stimulate their interest and activity in the fund appeal |

A. Media
1. Kick-off meeting and subsequent progress report sessions.
2. Come-and-see tours taking in "observable" features of CSS activities, program, plant, etc.
3. Annual Report and other descriptive CSS literature.
4. Orientation meetings in small or large groups featuring:
   a. Speakers—CSS staff and campaign leaders, guest celebrities.
   b. Exhibits—CSS program, campaign aids.
   c. Flip charts—the financial story.
   d. Films and film strips—documentaries on CSS history, program.
5. Basic facts leaflet telling the CSS case and spelling out goals of campaign.
6. Personal interviews between CSS fund-raising staff and campaign workers.
7. Individualized letters to campaign workers explaining CSS program and need for their support.
8. Campaign newspaper (8 issues), with photos for worker stimulation.
9. Editorial reprints from major metropolitan newspapers for campaign worker backing and orientation.
10. Announcements with photos of campaign leaders and their activities, sent to their professional or trade publications.

*Note:* In addition to the media listed above, the mass media (newspapers, radio, television, car cards, etc.) will also be expected to reach the campaign worker audience.

| *Audience* | *Objective* |
|---|---|
| IX. Present Contributors | To cultivate present contributors and stimulate their renewed or increased giving; to enable them to interpret CSS to others. |

A. Media
 1. CSS Bulletin—a bi-weekly which tells in warm and human terms the story of how CSS helps families, based on real experiences from the agency's files.
 2. Annual Report.
 3. Special reports to foundations and other contributors on disposition of their gifts.
 4. Individualized letters for renewed or increased gifts; personalized acknowledgments.
 5. Women's Council meetings—an educational and cultivation device.
 6. Background letter from CSS Board Chairman.
 7. Year-end appeal letter.
 8. Camp appeal letter and leaflet to selected givers.
 9. Personal visits or telephone communication.
    *Note:* Here again, this audience of present contributors is reached also through the mass media.

| *Audience* | *Objective* |
|---|---|
| X. Service Volunteers (Present) | To maintain and increase their enthusiasm and to educate them about CSS so that they become better interpreters. |

A. Media
 1. Meetings.
    a. Women's Council.

      b. Workroom luncheon sessions.

      c. Opportunity shop volunteer teas.

      d. Annual meeting for all service volunteers.

  2. Come-and-see tours.

  3. Orientation interviews.

  4. Handbook and other CSS literature.

  5. Recognition of efforts.

      a. Citations and corsages.

      b. Pins.

      c. Press publicity.

      d. CSS house organ.

| *Audience* | *Objective* |
|---|---|
| XI. Administrative Volunteers (Present) | To maintain and increase their interest, stimulate leadership qualities, and educate volunteers about CSS so that they become better interpreters. |

A. Media

  1. Orientation meetings and interviews.

  2. Come-and-see tours.

  3. Women's Council meetings (for women).

  4. Annual meeting of the Society.

  5. Meetings of district committee chairmen and directors.

  6. Programs of committee and trustee meetings; their projects.

| *Audience* | *Objective* |
|---|---|
| XII. Prospective Service Volunteers (Women) | To recruit. |

  A. Media

    1. Women's Council meetings.

    2. Enlistment by present volunteers and staff.

    3. Press, radio, television, exhibits (as volunteer opportunities in CSS develop).

    4. Central Volunteer Bureau, Junior League, colleges, etc.

    5. Distribution of recruitment pamphlet.

## HUMAN RELATIONS: THE NATIONAL CONFERENCE OF CHRISTIANS AND JEWS, INC.

The National Conference of Christians and Jews, Inc., is well known for its unstinting efforts in the area of human relations, exemplified particularly by its annual sponsorship of Brotherhood Week. National officers of the organization included Dwight D. Eisenhower, honorary chairman of Brotherhood Week campaign; Benjamin F. Fairless, Roger W. Straus, and James F. Twohy as co-chairmen of the Conference; and Everett R. Clinchy, president. World Brotherhood chairmen include Konrad Adenauer, Arthur H. Compton, and Carlos P. Romulo, among others. Some of the important concepts of The National Conference are explained in its various publications.

### WHAT IS THE NATIONAL CONFERENCE OF CHRISTIANS AND JEWS?

The National Conference of Christians and Jews is a civic organization of religiously motivated persons dedicated to building good will and understanding among Protestants, Catholics and Jews.

### WHEN WAS IT ESTABLISHED?

The NCCJ was founded in 1928 by Charles Evans Hughes, Newton D. Baker, S. Parkes Cadman, Roger W. Straus and Carlton J. H. Hayes. A quarter century ago the NCCJ operating organization consisted of two employees housed in one room. Today it is a network of 62 regional offices, each of which serves as a human relations center helping the residents of 3,000 villages, towns and cities in America to achieve the aims of brotherhood. Their goal: a single family of man under God.

## WHAT IS ITS PURPOSE?

". . . to promote justice, amity, understanding and cooperation among Protestants, Catholics and Jews, and to analyze, moderate and finally eliminate intergroup prejudices which disfigure and distort religious, business, social and political relations with a view to the establishment of a social order in which the religious ideals of brotherhood and justice shall become the standards of human relationships." (NCCJ By-Laws.)

## HOW IS ITS PROGRAM ORGANIZED?

To achieve its purpose, the NCCJ follows a program of *education for democracy*. It seeks to change undemocratic attitudes that conflict with American principles into attitudes that harmonize with our nation's moral and political ideals.

The NCCJ program is also designed to obtain double and triple values out of every dollar. Therefore it follows the advice of the social scientists and experts in the field of human relations who agree that the best results are obtained by working through the trunk lines of human conduct. Through these main channels of information and education the NCCJ is able to reach the whole people.

Accordingly, the NCCJ program has been organized on the basis of 5 National Commissions consisting of leading members of their professions operating in the fields of:

1. Educational Organizations
2. Religious Organizations
3. Community Organizations
4. Labor-Management Organizations
5. The Media of Mass Communications

Each of the 62 regional offices of the NCCJ carries on an extensive human relations program. The following are typical program activities conducted last year all through the country.

## IN THE FIELD OF EDUCATION

Through summer workshops, institutes and conferences, films, printed materials and the services of specialists, the National Conference of Christians and Jews assists public school systems, private and parochial schools and colleges to equip young people with knowledge and skills so they may live happily with those of other religious, racial and nationality backgrounds.

Thousands of teachers and millions of students are influenced each year by these activities.

## IN THE FIELD OF RELIGION

There are 300,000 churches and synagogues in the United States with a membership approaching 100,000,000. Without minimizing the differences or compromising beliefs NCCJ provides an instrument whereby ministers, priests, and rabbis—and their congregations—can join in the crusade for brotherhood.

To further this work, NCCJ created the Religious News Service to supply religious publications, newspapers, magazines and radio stations with news and pictures of religious groups.

## IN OUR COMMUNITY LIFE

Through 62 regional offices located in major cities, NCCJ serves as an agency of information and service to all local and national organizations concerned with promoting better intergroup relations and building brotherhood.

## IN BUSINESS AND INDUSTRY

The NCCJ program for business, industrial groups and labor unions includes speakers, film showings, panel discussions, program materials and a bulletin "Highlighting Human Relations in Business and Industry."

## TO REACH 165,000,000 AMERICANS

In a nationwide campaign against bigotry, NCCJ has enlisted the cooperation of newspapers, radio, television, motion pictures, advertising, magazines, books, pamphlets and speakers.

### Building for Brotherhood

NCCJ works with 2,500 women's organizations, 1,650 service clubs and a host of fraternal, veteran and farm organizations in carrying the message of good will to the people of our country. Two recent new developments: (1) a program of institutes on "Building a Better Community" in cooperation with local chapters of the Junior Chamber of Commerce; (2) a Rural Extension program of inter-cultural understanding in association with Federal, State and County agricultural extension services.

Through leadership training, clergy conferences, program services and Brotherhood Week materials, NCCJ reaches a major portion of the 300,000 churches and synagogues in the U.S.

## BUILDING FOR BROTHERHOOD—THROUGH MASS MEDIA

During Brotherhood Week, America's 12,000 daily and weekly newspapers, 3,000 radio stations, 450 TV outlets, 600 leading magazines and 6,000 outstanding industrial house organs use NCCJ materials prepared by outstanding media artists. As a result, Brotherhood Week has become a headlined event across the nation!

Last year NCCJ's constant day-by-day mass media campaign for better human relations resulted in:

—350 million home impressions from NCCJ radio and TV programs and spot announcements;

—180,000 showings of educational films reaching 70 million people;

—2.8 million pieces of literature distributed annually.

## BUILDING FOR BROTHERHOOD—THROUGH AN INTERNATIONAL RELIGIOUS NEWS SERVICE

Since 1934, NCCJ's Religious News Service has been offering a complete, objective and unbiased coverage of worldwide religious news to newspapers, news magazines, periodicals and radio stations.

Today 100 daily newspapers, 300 Christian and Jewish religious publications, and over 200 broadcasters make use of NCCJ's daily news dispatches, photo services, weekly newsfeatures, editorials and cartoons, and weekly radio and TV program "The Religious News Reporter."

Father John LaFarge, S. J., has said "The religious press is a powerful weapon in combating hatred and prejudice . . . and the Religious News Service has been doing an exceptional job."

## A TWENTY-EIGHT-YEAR RECORD OF ACHIEVEMENT

Twenty-eight years ago NCCJ began operations with a one-man office and an annual budget of $10,000. Today, it is a network of 62 regional offices serving more than 10,000 U.S. cities and villages.

NCCJ's first major program in the late twenties was a three-day conference at Columbia University which exposed the hate literature defaming Presidential candidate, Governor Alfred E. Smith, and the Catholic Church. In the thirties, NCCJ launched Brotherhood Week which has become a national institution, headed each year by the President of the United States.

In 1941, NCCJ began its summer workshop program for teachers. At the same time NCCJ sent speaker-teams to our Armed Forces in all parts of the U.S. and overseas. After the war, NCCJ's program was greatly expanded so that not only teachers but community leaders, police, businessmen, union leaders and youth groups were enlisted.

Thanks to a grant from Albert M. Greenfield, a Human Relations Center bearing his name was opened at the University of Pennsylvania. At the University of Miami a similar grant to NCCJ from Mr. and Mrs. Benjamin E. Bronston made possible the first Human Relations Department in an institution of higher learning.

In 1950, with the aid of NCCJ, World Brotherhood was organized in Paris. World leaders Carlos P. Romulo, Paul-Henri Spaak, Konrad Adenauer, Madame Vijaya Lakshmi Pandit and Arthur H. Compton are co-chairmen. Operating in 22 countries, it has held seminars and conferences in intergroup relations for educational, business and civic leaders in most of the major cities of Europe and in some parts of Asia.

## BUSINESS ETHICS: NATIONAL BETTER BUSINESS BUREAU

Although not, per se, a public relations organization, the National Better Business Bureau does operate in the broad area of public opinion, public relations, and the mass media. It was formed by business for the express purpose of elevating the standards of business practice and ethics, both from its own viewpoint as well as from that of the consumer. The following describes the structure, function, and objectives of the organization.

## Function of the Bureau

The National Better Business Bureau is a nonprofit organization which business established in 1912 to protect itself and its ultimate customer, the American public, from advertising or selling practices which are fraudulent, misleading or unfair where they exist on a national or regional scale.

Expressing the will of legitimate business to deal fairly with its customers, the Bureau thereby seeks to make friends for business.

It is impossible to make and retain friends for business without removing those things which cause public distrust of business. The chief objectives of the National Better Business Bureau have therefore been: (1) to discourage and eliminate from the buyer-seller relationship practices which cause legitimate consumer complaints; and (2) to strive for better consumer satisfaction by encouraging accurate representation of products, securities and services. In these endeavors, it cooperates with 108 autonomous local Better Business Bureaus throughout the United States and Canada.

## Publishing the Facts

We issued 251 bulletins during an average year—an average of better than one per working day, 23 of these releases went to the entire membership including 7 *News* bulletins containing 61 different articles. There were 100 bulletins sent to local Better Business Bureaus to assist them in their operations at the local level. Other bulletins were issued to special groups such as advertising media and advertising agencies, Chambers of Commerce and participants in group industry programs.

## COLLISION INSURANCE OVERCHARGES

Notable for its broad public interest was a bulletin entitled *Collision Insurance Overcharges Total Millions*. It reported how thousands of American motorists had paid millions of dollars in overcharges to a few insurance companies as a result of misclassifications of collision insurance on financed automobiles. The bulletin, which received widespread national publicity, also served the constructive purpose of telling automobile buyers how to protect themselves from excessive charges on time payment contracts.

Major articles entitled "The Abuse of Comparative Prices" and "Fictitious Comparatives Target of National Drive," appearing in NBBB *News* bulletins for March and November, respectively, helped to focus national attention on this serious problem. There was substantial distribution of both bulletins by interested national advertisers, local BBBs and Chambers of Commerce.

## PAINSTAKING RESEARCH REQUIRED

Weeks and even months of exhaustive research were required to develop the facts in many of the bulletins issued. Examples are: *Going Out of Business Sales*—a 20-page report of an NBBB survey of Better Business Bureau and Chamber of Commerce experience in this field and of existing laws regulating closing out sales.

*Buying a Family Coat of Arms*—authoritative facts to guide media and the public in considering advertising offering these symbols for sale.

*Alleged Weight Reducing Products Involving "Plans"*—recommended minimum standards for the advertising and sale of these products.

## DISTRIBUTION EXCEEDS ONE MILLION

Total annual distribution of bulletins and booklets by the National Better Business Bureau exceeded 1,000,000. The figure includes requests for many NBBB publications issued in previous years but having a continuing popularity such as those dealing with the practices of debt adjusters, vending machine promotions, room air-conditioners and television antenna systems. These and other NBBB releases provide a rich store of educational material designed to improve public understanding of business. The Bureau assisted in the preparation of revision of several titles in the *Fact* booklet series distributed by all BBBs to aid consumers in wise buying habits and in their everyday relations with business.

## Cooperation Secured—Advertising Corrected

Public resentment of objectionable advertising or selling practices is not limited to the guilty advertiser. It extends to the industry he represents and to advertising as a whole. Correction of such practices, where they exist on a national or regional scale, is a keystone to the success of the NBBB program of making friends for business.

In one year, we closed 376 major cases involving questioned advertising or selling practices—nearly two and one-half times as many as we were handling four years previously.

### 92 OUT OF 100 COOPERATE

In 39 cases, Bureau investigation failed to establish justification for the complaint.

There were 27 cases in which advertisers did not agree voluntarily to make indicated corrections. These cases were closed upon the issuance of NBBB bulletins and/or referral to the proper Government agency.

In the remaining 310 cases, the advertisers agreed voluntarily to correct the objectionable practices found to exist. Thus, cooperation where needed, was obtained from 92 out of every 100 advertisers approached.

### ROOM AIR-CONDITIONERS

Sometimes, the best results can be obtained by corrective action on an industry-wide basis. For example, following investigation of advertising which stated or implied that 7 amp. room air-conditioners could be installed without any electrical alterations, NBBB issued a research bulletin concluding that such claims required definite qualifications. Concomitantly, the Bureau sought and obtained assurance from seven manufacturers that their copy would be revised to embrace these recommendations.

At the same time, the markets were flooded with devices which were advertised as "air-conditioners" but did not perform the minimum functions of air-conditioning. Bulletins, casework and the cooperation of local BBBs combined virtually to eliminate this deceptive and unfair advertising.

In September, the Room Air-Conditioner Section of the Air-Conditioning and Refrigeration Institute (ARI) adopted a proposal to publish cooling capacity ratings in terms of Btus, based on standard test procedures. This climaxed a two-year program of NBBB-ARI cooperation to dispel public confusion resulting from the advertising of cooling capacities in terms of tons, horsepower or other measurements which were uninformative and often misleading.

## "FREE" OFFERS AND GUARANTEES

Most of the advertising problems which are brought to NBBB's doorstep are not confined to any one industry. Failure to disclose strings attached to "free" offers and guarantees provide a perennial example. Recently, agreement to make such disclosures (an FTC requirement) was obtained by NBBB from advertisers of *armature windings, automotive accessories, building materials, cosmetics, garden hose, gasoline, jewelry, laundry preparations, nursery stock, records, seat covers, tires* and *vitamins*. Four advertisers cooperated in the elimination of so-called *"lifetime" guarantees*, impractical of fulfillment.

Frankness makes friends for business by letting consumers know of any limitations on worthwhile offers before they purchase.

### Cooperation with Advertising Media

While the *correction* of objectionable advertising practices requires a major share of the Bureau's time, justified consumer complaints against business can be reduced more effectively by *preventing* such practices from occurring. The Bureau seeks to accomplish this objective through cooperation with advertising media.

Magazines, broadcasters and newspapers sought information from the Bureau on nearly 5,000 occasions during one year. The reliability of prospective advertisers of the validity of advertising claims was the basis of inquiry in most of these cases, and in most of them, the requests were made *before* the advertising was accepted.

The amount of objectionable national advertising *prevented* from appearing through this NBBB-media cooperation is incalculable. Friendships made or retained for business in the process are innumerable.

## BULLETIN SERVICE

Further to assist publishers and broadcasters in their copy acceptance problems, frequent bulletins, supplying up-to-date information on questionable advertisers and on good and bad advertising practices, are issued. During one year, seventy-two bulletins relating primarily to national advertising and advertisers were released to media. They discussed the advertising of air-conditioners, aluminum ware, arthritis "remedies," automobile accessories, battery additives, binoculars, books, bust developers, cold and cough preparations, comparative prices, cosmetics, depilatories, directories, display racks, dolls, fryer-cookers, homework schemes, hosiery, illuminated signs, lotteries, "lucky" stones, Meyer zoysia grass, nursery stock, obesity remedies, perfumes, photography, "rain-bullets," razor blades, real estate, reducing garments, seat covers, securities, stainless steel, storm windows, towels, used clothing, vending machines, wearing apparel and a variety of mail order and other propositions.

## MEDIA ACT IN PUBLIC INTEREST

Acting in the public interest, media decline millions of dollars in annual revenue by rejecting proffered advertising which does not meet their standards. Helping the national magazines to regulate their advertising columns has been a major NBBB activity since 1928. At that time, in trade practice conference, with the Federal Trade Commission, periodical publishers designated the Bureau as their agency of assistance in determining the acceptability of advertising copy. For many years, the major broadcasting networks have also participated in this activity and newspapers are making increasing use of the Bureau's services, reflecting a substantial rise in NBBB membership in this area.

Early in the year, the TV broadcasting industry was subjected to bitter attacks from various sources alleging that fraudulent advertising was rampant on the airways. Since these critics failed to distinguish between the continuity acceptance policies of the national networks and those of some independent stations, NBBB issued a bulletin clarifying the issue. Of its own experience, the Bureau reported that the TV networks, as is true of other national media, are scrupulous in denial of their facilities to fraudulent advertisers.

## ADVERTISERS SEEK COUNSEL

The problem of media is simplified when advertisers who are not sure of the accuracy or fairness of statements which they propose to make voluntarily seek NBBB's views on the claims before submittal. National advertisers, particularly in the mail order field, and their advertising agencies are following this procedure, which is entirely voluntary, in increasing numbers. Media, advertisers and agencies all benefit because the Bureau is able to respond promptly when questions are raised. The elimination of questionable claims before they appear serves the public interest and strengthens public friendship for the advertiser and for business generally.

### Making Friends for Direct Selling

Helping direct selling companies to conduct door-to-door sales in such manner as to justify consumer goodwill continues to be a major activity of the Bureau. Industry members cooperated to avoid justified public displeasure, whether this demanded corrective action in isolated instances or a complete revision of selling practices and methods of handling complaints.

## THE RIGHT OF FREE MEN TO ENGAGE IN LEGITIMATE BUSINESS

NBBB's capsule exposition of the direct selling industry, its origins, diversity and functions, was revised. Previous distribution of this bulletin has done much to create better public understanding of the industry and its importance in our economy.

## INDUSTRY-WIDE PROGRAMS CONTINUE

The Subscription Book Program completed its sixth year under the joint sponsorship of 52 publishers and distributors of encyclo-

pedias and other educational volumes in cooperation with Better
Business Bureaus and more than 600 Chambers of Commerce.
Criticisms of sales representatives reported by these local groups
were minimal in relation to the large volume of business involved,
convincing evidence of this industry's resolve to maintain high
selling standards through self-discipline.

The Central Registry Plan, undertaken to control door-to-door
selling of magazine subscriptions, completed its eighth year. Bureaus and Chambers in more than 750 cities participated in this program, made possible through the cooperation and financial support
of 36 leading magazine publishers and 57 magazine subscription
agencies. After making solid progress for several years, some serious
trouble spots developed in the program during a recent year. NBBB
and other participating groups have met the challenge by adopting
new methods which, it is hoped, will prevent or correct justified
consumer complaints in this field more effectively.

## EXPOSING THE SWINDLERS

In an effort to halt or impede the activities of swindlers operating
on the fringe of the legitimate direct selling industry, the activities
of more than 100 such transgressors were described in bulletins
sent to local Bureaus and Chambers during the year.

NBBB contributed much of the information used in preparing an
article on that nomadic band of confidence men and women, known
as the "Williamson Gang," which appeared in the *Saturday Evening
Post* and was later reprinted in *Readers Digest*.

## PERFUME "HOAX" CURBED

In previous years, door-to-door sales of supposedly nationally advertised perfume at spurious "bargain" prices has presented a serious
problem during each Christmas sales season. With the cooperation
of established perfume manufacturers, NBBB has waged a vigorous
campaign against this deception of the public with such success
that the "bargain" Christmas perfume hoax dwindled to insignificant
proportions.

## BOGUS RESEARCHERS

The Bureau enlisted the cooperation of distributors of silverware, books and various household goods in abandoning misleading "survey" approaches designed to obtain sales leads or entrance to a prospect's home. Further to combat this reprehensible direct-sales method, NBBB authorized the continued use by genuine researchers of our "Memo to the Public," a leaflet designed (1) to educate housewives on the fake pollster approach; and (2) to tell housewives how to distinguish between a true survey interviewer and the tricky salesman who merely poses as a researcher.

### The Community Protection Program

The Community Protection Program completed its twenty-second successful year with more than 800 Chambers of Commerce and similar organizations participating. These agencies of business were thereby enabled to furnish their members and communities with a measure of protection against frauds and other unfair practices. During the year, they asked for and received information and assistance in handling consumer and trade inquiries and complaints in more than 3,500 instances.

## BULLETINS AND PRESS RELEASES

The participating Chambers also received monthly service bulletins, each of which discussed a variety of propositions currently active on a national scale, and therefore likely to invade a given community at any time. The activities of 428 individuals and organizations were reported in these bulletins.

Special bulletins were also issued from time to time, a notable example being a report on *Chamber of Commerce Solicitations Control Program*. It summarized NBBB findings in a survey to determine what policies and procedures Chambers had adopted to protect their members from questionable requests for contributions and donations.

Further to spread the protective value of the service, the participating agencies were supplied with press releases on such newsworthy subjects as Bait Advertising, Chinchilla Farming, Comparative Price Abuses, Franchise Offers, Furnace Repair Gyps, Home Improvement Rackets, Homework Schemes, Moving and Storage Pitfalls, "Why People Complained about Business Transactions" and the "Williamson Gang."

## NATIONAL COVERAGE BROADENED

The Community Protection Program furthers NBBB's major purpose of protecting the public against fraud and unfair dealings to the end that public confidence in legitimate business may be maintained. Located in communities having no local Better Business Bureau, the participating organizations serve as 800 "listening posts" to keep the National Bureau informed of what is taking place in all sections of the country.

Subscribers to the Program are enabled to render more service to their members and, by being of greater value to the community, to make more friends for business.

### Youth Learns about Business

The Bureau's educational work continued in cooperation with the National Association of Secondary School Principals. This association's attention is being given to expanding and improving education about the American economy in all high schools.

Educators and businessmen have been concerned about the fact that young people are not being taught soundly why the American economy is superior to competing economies, a circumstance which presents several dangers. To cope with this grave problem, the Council for Advancement of Secondary Education was organized by the National Association of Secondary School Principals and the National Better Business Bureau. It is a nonprofit corporation governed by a board of 21 trustees composed of twelve educators and nine laymen, five of whom are nationally known business executives.

## FOUR-POINT PROGRAM

The Council for Advancement of Secondary Education has devoted its first three years exclusively to advancement of education about the American economy in high schools. The first task was to plan and outline a four-point program of action:

1. Research to determine what basic instruction about economics should be made available to our high schools;
2. Preparation of high school teaching materials suitable to accomplish the purpose;
3. Stimulation of public approval on the community level to obtain cooperation from local businesses and other local institutions in helping students observe economics in action in their own home towns:
4. Cooperation with teachers' colleges and other agencies in order that teachers may be trained to teach what the research has shown to be needed.

### PROGRESS REPORTED

The first phase of the program has been completed with a survey and study by the Council for Advancement of Secondary Education among more than 2,000 selected opinion leaders from business, education, labor and agriculture representing all parts of our country. It showed general agreement on the essentials of our economy which should be taught.

The council is now proceeding with the second phase of this important program. This is the preparation of teaching materials which will adapt themselves to the high school curriculum and enable a school to teach what it is agreed should be taught about the American economy.

### UNDERSTANDING BUILDS FRIENDSHIP

The extent of misinformation about economic subjects is astonishing. Public opinion surveys have shown that an alarmingly high percentage of high school seniors hold misconceptions about business of the most critical and derogatory nature. The cooperation of business and educators in seeking to dispel these misconceptions through the work of the Council for Advancement of Secondary Education is of vital importance to the national welfare.

Confidence and understanding are the twin pedestals upon which friendships can rest most securely. By contributing to a better public understanding of business through its educational work, the National Better Business Bureau performs one of the most important functions in its over-all program of *Making Friends for Business*.

# Selected Bibliography

## MASS COMMUNICATION

Barnouw, Eric, *Mass Communication*, New York, Rinehart & Company, Inc., 1957.

Bryson, Lyman (ed.), *The Communication of Ideas*, New York, Harper & Brothers, 1948.

Lazarsfeld, Paul F., and Stanton, Frank (eds.), *Communications Research, 1948–1949*, New York, Harper & Brothers, 1949.

Schramm, Wilbur (ed.), *Communications in Modern Society*, Urbana, University of Illinois Press, 1948.

Schramm, Wilbur (ed.), *Mass Communications*, Urbana, University of Illinois Press, 1950.

Seldes, Gilbert, *The Great Audience*, New York, The Viking Press, Inc., 1950.

## SEMANTICS

Chase, Stuart, *The Tyranny of Words*, New York, Harcourt, Brace & Co., 1938.

Flesch, Rudolf, *The Art of Readable Writing*, New York, Harper & Brothers, 1949.

Hayakawa, S. I., *Language in Thought and Action*, New York, Harcourt, Brace & Co., 1949.

Korzybski, Alfred, *Science and Sanity: An Introduction to Non-Aristotelian Systems and General Semantics*, Lancaster, Pa., Science Press, 1933.

Ogden, C. K., and Richards, I. A., *The Meaning of Meaning*, New York, Harcourt, Brace & Co., 3rd ed. rev., 1930.

## PUBLIC OPINION

Albig, William, *Public Opinion*, New York, McGraw-Hill Book Company, Inc., 1939.

Bernays, Edward L., *Crystallizing Public Opinion*, New York, Boni and Liveright, 1923.

Cantril, Hadley, *Gauging Public Opinion*, Princeton, Princeton University Press, 1944.

Childs, Harwood L., *An Introduction to Public Opinion*, New York, John Wiley & Sons, Inc., 1949.

Gallup, George, *Guide to Public Opinion Polls*, Princeton, Princeton University Press, 1944.

Gallup, George, *Public Opinion in a Democracy*, Princeton, Princeton University Press, 1939.

Lippmann, Walter, *Public Opinion*, New York, Harcourt, Brace & Co., 1922. (Reprinted in pocket-type editions.)

Powell, Norman John, *Anatomy of Public Opinion*, New York, Prentice-Hall, Inc., 1951.

Smith, George Horsley, *Motivation Research in Advertising and Marketing*, New York, McGraw-Hill Book Company, Inc., 1954.

## THE NEWSPAPER

Chenery, William L., *Freedom of the Press*, New York, Harcourt, Brace & Co., 1955.

Commission on Freedom of the Press, *A Free and Responsible Press*, Chicago, University of Chicago Press, 1947.

Gramling, Oliver, *AP: The Story of News*, New York, Farrar & Rinehart, 1940.

Hocking, William Ernest, *Freedom of the Press*, Chicago, University of Chicago Press, 1947.

Lee, Alfred McClung, *The Daily Newspaper in America*, New York, The Macmillan Company, 1937.

Mott, Frank Luther, *American Journalism: A History of Newspapers*, New York, The Macmillan Company, 1941.

## RADIO AND TELEVISION

Cantril, Hadley, and Allport, Gordon W., *The Psychology of Radio*, New York, Harper & Brothers, 1935.

Gross, Ben, *I Looked and I Listened*, New York, Random House, 1954.

Lazarsfeld, Paul F., *Radio and the Printed Page*, New York, Duell,

Sloan & Pearce, Inc., 1940.

Lazarsfeld, Paul F., and Kendall, Patricia R., *Radio Listening in America*, New York, Prentice-Hall, Inc., 1948.

Midgley, N., *The Advertising and Business Side of Radio*, New York, Prentice-Hall, Inc., 1948.

Siepmann, Charles A., *Radio, Television and Society*, New York, Oxford University Press, 1950.

## THE MOTION PICTURE

Gipson, Henry Clay, *Films in Business and Industry*, New York, McGraw-Hill Book Company, Inc., 1947.

Inglis, Ruth A., *Freedom for the Movies*, Chicago, University of Chicago Press, 1946.

Jacobs, Lewis, *The Rise of the American Film*, New York, Harcourt, Brace & Co., 1939.

Ramsaye, Terry, *A Million and One Nights*, New York, Simon and Schuster, Inc., 1926.

Rosten, Leo C., *Hollywood*, New York, Harcourt, Brace & Co., 1941.

## THE MAGAZINE

Wolseley, Roland E., *The Magazine World*, New York, Prentice-Hall, Inc., 1951.

## THE BOOK

McMurtrie, Douglas, *The Book: The Story of Printing and Bookmaking*, New York, Oxford University Press, rev. ed., 1942.

## INTERNATIONAL COMMUNICATIONS

Desmond, Robert W., *The Press and World Affairs*, New York, Appleton Century, 1937.

## PUBLIC RELATIONS

Baus, Herbert M., *Public Relations at Work*, New York, Harper & Brothers, 1948.

Burnett, Verne, *You and Your Public*, New York, Harper & Brothers, 1947.

Griswold, Glenn, and Griswold, Denny, *Your Public Relations—The Standard Public Relations Handbook,* New York, Funk & Wagnalls Co., 1948.

Harlow, Rex F., and Black, Marvin M., *Practical Public Relations,* New York, Harper & Brothers, 1946.

Lesly, Philip, *Public Relations Handbook,* New York, Prentice-Hall, Inc., 1950.

Lesly, Philip, *Public Relations in Action,* Chicago, Ziff-Davis Publishing Company, 1947.

Plackard, D. H., and Blackman, Clifton, *Blueprint for Public Relations,* New York, McGraw-Hill Book Company, Inc., 1949.

Sills, Theodore R., and Lesly, Philip, *Public Relations, Principles and Procedures,* Chicago, Richard D. Irwin Company, 1946.

## BUSINESS AND MANAGEMENT

Wright, J. Handy, and Christian, Byron H., *Public Relations in Management,* New York, McGraw-Hill Book Company, Inc., 1949.

## THE EMPLOYEE

Biklin, Paul F., and Breth, Robert D., *The Successful Employee Publication,* New York, McGraw-Hill Book Company, Inc., 1945.

Gardner, Burleigh G., *Human Relations in Industry,* Chicago, Richard D. Irwin, 1945.

Nyman, R. Carter, *Foundations for Constructive Industrial Relations,* New York, Funk & Wagnalls Co. in association with *Modern Industry Magazine,* 1949.

## THE COMMUNITY

Lundborg, Louis B., *Public Relations in the Local Community,* New York, Harper & Brothers, 1950.

## THE STOCKHOLDER

Sears, John H., *The New Place of the Stockholder,* New York, Harper & Brothers, 1939.

## THE GOVERNMENT

McCamy, James L., *Government Publicity*, Chicago, University of Chicago Press, 1939.

## EDUCATION

Fine, Benjamin, *Educational Publicity*, New York, Harper & Brothers, 1951.
*How Science Teachers Use Business-Sponsored Teaching Aids*, Washington, D.C., National Science Teachers Association, 1955.
Reck, W. Emerson, *College Publicity Manual*, New York, Harper & Brothers, 1948.

## ADVERTISING

Borden, Neil H., *Economic Effects of Advertising*, Chicago, Richard D. Irwin, 1942.
Hotchkiss, George B., *An Outline of Advertising*, New York, The Macmillan Company, 1940.
Kleppner, Otto, *Advertising Procedure*, New York, Prentice-Hall, Inc., 4th ed., 1950.

## THE PICTURE

Mich, Daniel, *Technique of the Picture Story*, New York, McGraw-Hill Book Company, Inc., 1946.

## PROMOTION AND PRODUCTION

Melcher, Daniel, and Larrick, Nancy, *Printing and Promotion Handbook* New York, McGraw-Hill Book Company, Inc., 1949.

## PROPAGANDA

Albig, William, *Public Opinion*, New York, McGraw-Hill Book Company, Inc., 1939.
Bernays, Edward L., *Propaganda*, New York, Liveright Publishing Corporation, 1928.

Doob, Leonard W., *Public Opinion and Propaganda,* New York, Henry Holt & Co., Inc., 1948.

Powell, Norman John, *Anatomy of Public Opinion,* New York, Prentice-Hall, Inc., 1951.

Smith, Bruce L.; Lasswell, Harold D.; and Casey, Ralph D., *Propaganda, Communication and Public Opinion: A Comprehensive Reference Guide,* Princeton, Princeton University Press, 1946.

## DIRECTORIES

*America's Educational Press,* Educational Press Association, Washington, D.C.

*American Educational Directory* (Patterson, Homer L.): American Education Company, Chicago (annually).

*Directory of Newspapers and Periodicals,* N. W. Ayer & Son, Philadelphia.

*Educational Directory,* Government Printing Office, Washington, D.C. (annual).

*Literary Market Place,* R. R. Bowker Company, New York.

*Trade and Professional Association of the United States,* U.S. Department of Commerce, Washington, D.C. (1949).

*Directory of House Organs,* Printers' Ink, New York.

*The Working Press of the Nation,* Farrell, New York.

## YEARBOOKS

*Directory of Newspapers and Periodicals,* N. W. Ayer & Son, Philadelphia.

*Broadcasting Annual,* Broadcasting Magazine, Washington, D.C.

*Editor & Publisher Yearbook,* Editor and Publisher, New York.

*Film Daily Yearbook,* Film Daily, New York.

*Printers' Ink Directory of House Organs,* Printers' Ink, New York.

*Radio Annual and Television Yearbook,* Radio and TV Daily, New York.

*Standard Rate and Data Service,* Chicago, New York, etc.

# Index